Sociology of Families

SAGE was founded in 1965 by Sara Miller McCune to support the dissemination of usable knowledge by publishing innovative and high-quality research and teaching content. Today, we publish over 900 journals, including those of more than 400 learned societies, more than 800 new books per year, and a growing range of library products including archives, data, case studies, reports, and video. SAGE remains majority-owned by our founder, and after Sara's lifetime will become owned by a charitable trust that secures our continued independence.

Los Angeles | London | New Delhi | Singapore | Washington DC | Melbourne

Sociology of Families

Change, Continuity, and Diversity

Teresa Ciabattari

Pacific Lutheran University

Los Angeles | London | New Delhi
Singapore | Washington DC | Melbourne

FOR INFORMATION:

SAGE Publications, Inc.
2455 Teller Road
Thousand Oaks, California 91320
E-mail: order@sagepub.com

SAGE Publications Ltd.
1 Oliver's Yard
55 City Road
London EC1Y 1SP
United Kingdom

SAGE Publications India Pvt. Ltd.
B 1/I 1 Mohan Cooperative Industrial Area
Mathura Road, New Delhi 110 044
India

SAGE Publications Asia-Pacific Pte. Ltd.
3 Church Street
#10-04 Samsung Hub
Singapore 049483

Publisher: Jeff Lasser
eLearning Editor: Gabrielle Piccininni
Editorial Assistant: Alexandra Croell
Production Editor: David C. Felts
Copy Editor: Sheree Van Vreede
Typesetter: C&M Digitals (P) Ltd.
Proofreader: Victoria Reed-Castro
Indexer: Teddy Diggs
Cover Designer: Anupama Krishnan
Marketing Manager: Kara Kindstrom

Printed in the United States of America

Library of Congress Cataloging-in-Publication Data

Names: Ciabattari, Teresa, author.

Title: Sociology of families : change, continuity, and diversity / Teresa Ciabattari, Pacific Lutheran University, United States.

Description: Los Angeles : SAGE, 2017. | Includes bibliographical references and index.

Identifiers: LCCN 2016010006 | ISBN 978-1-4833-7902-9 (pbk. : alk. paper)

Subjects: LCSH: Families.

Classification: LCC HQ519 .C53 2017 | DDC 306.85—dc23 LC record available at https://lccn.loc.gov/2016010006

This book is printed on acid-free paper.

SUSTAINABLE FORESTRY INITIATIVE
Certified Chain of Custody
Promoting Sustainable Forestry
www.sfiprogram.org
SFI-01268
SFI label applies to text stock

18 19 20 10 9 8 7 6 5 4 3 2

Brief Contents

Detailed Contents

About the Author

Teresa Ciabattari is an Associate Professor of Sociology at Pacific Lutheran University. After earning her undergraduate degree in sociology at Santa Clara University, she went on to earn a Ph.D. in Sociology at the University of Washington. As a scholar of family sociology, she has published articles on cohabitation, single mothers, and household labor. She is also a scholar of teaching and learning, publishing and presenting on topics including teaching writing to sociology majors, using quantitative data in the classroom, and assessment of student learning. She regularly teaches courses on the sociology of family, research methods, statistics, and gender.

Preface

I have been teaching courses on the sociology of American families for over 15 years. In that time, I have witnessed students' excitement in seeing their families represented in the scholarly literature; their discomfort in having their ideas about families challenged; their doubt when research findings are inconsistent with their own experience; and their growth as they developed a sociological imagination and applied it to the study of families. My goal was to write an accessible and engaging text to support students on this intellectual journey.

This text is unique in two ways. First, it considers not only how families in the United States have changed, but also how these changes reflect ideological continuities with longstanding trends in culture, law, and the economy. Change can feel threatening, but when we analyze these changes in their historical and social contexts, they often don't seem quite so radical. Second, this text is unique because it integrates family diversity into every chapter. Rather than having separate chapters on immigrant families, same-sex families or families of different racial-ethnic groups, the experiences of these families are discussed throughout the text. This reduces the tendency to "other" families that differ from an imagined norm. Instead, families of all kinds are visible in each chapter, emphasizing the growing diversity of families in the United States.

The first three chapters lay a sociological foundation for the rest of the book by introducing readers to the sociology of families, exploring a variety of ways to define family, and reviewing the theories and methods that sociologists use to study families. The remaining chapters focus on specific family experiences: the transition to adulthood, including discussion of dating and sexuality; marriage and cohabitation; divorce and relationship dissolution; parents and children; family work; and the family lives of older adults. In each of these chapters, patterns of change and continuity are explored, and family experiences based on race, class, gender, and sexuality are considered. The book ends with a discussion of family policy and how current family trends may shape American families in the future.

Acknowledgments

I offer deep gratitude to my students, past and present. They inspire me, challenge me, humble me, and help me grow as a teacher, scholar, and human being. I am especially grateful to the students in my Sociology of Families course in spring 2015 who did a test run of an earlier draft of this text. They read chapters, offered constructive feedback, and provided inspiration for the final stages of the book's development.

I am also grateful to my colleagues across the country who offered feedback at several stages of the book's development:

Cari Beecham-Bautista, College of DuPage

Linda Behrendt, Indiana State University

Alana M. Bibeau, University of Rhode Island

Michelle E. Deming, University of South Carolina

James J. Earhart, Columbia College

Marcie Hambrick, Georgia State University

Susan Holbrook, Southwestern Illinois College

Mary Ann Kanieski, Saint Mary's College

Mark Killian, Whitworth University

Liza L. Kuecker, Western New Mexico University

Tessa Le Roux, Lasell College

Roland Mitchell, Louisiana State University

Marla A. Perry, Nashville State Community College

Michael Polgar, Penn State University

Chris Wienke, Southern Illinois University Carbondale

Loreen Wolfer, University of Scranton

Introduction

Think of the word "family" and what comes to mind? Is it a husband and wife with a couple of children? Yes, that is one kind of family. But family structures in the United States go far beyond this one image. Consider the following:

- 42 percent of adult Americans have at least one steprelative, such as a stepparent, stepsibling, or stepchild (Pew Research Center, 2011).

- 16 percent of gay and lesbian couples are raising children (Vespa, Lewis, & Kreider, 2013).

- 24 percent of American children live in immigrant families (Kids Count, 2015), and tens of thousands of immigrants living in the United States are parenting children who still live in their country of origin.

- 3.7 million American **households** consist of families with three or more generations (Vespa et al., 2013).

- 26 percent of children live with a single parent (Livingstone, 2015).

Contemporary American families are certainly complex, but they have never been simple. In colonial families, because of high mortality rates, the average length of a marriage was less than 12 years, and stepfamilies were more common *then* than they are today (Coontz, 1992; 2005). Among American women born in the late 1920s, up to 15 percent were pregnant on their wedding day (England, Shafer, & Wu, 2012). Even in the 1950s, when the breadwinner–homemaker family was at its peak, **family diversity** was commonplace: More than one in four married women were employed (Cohany & Sok, 2007); half of children were living in something other than a traditional breadwinner–homemaker family (Livingstone, 2015); and one in three Americans older than 65 was poor, a rate that is three times higher than it is today (U.S. Census Bureau, 2014f).

Not only is diversity a long-standing feature of American families, so are concerns about family change. In 1642, the governors of the Massachusetts Bay colony decried the "great neglect in many parents and masters in training up their children in learning, and labor, and other employments" (Fass & Mason, 2000, p. 537). In 1905, Theodore

Roosevelt wrote a special letter to Congress saying, "There is a widespread conviction that the divorce laws are dangerously lax and indifferently administered . . . resulting in a diminishing regard for the sanctity of the marriage relation" (U.S. Census Bureau, 1909). Sociologists Talcott Parsons and Robert Bales (1955) wrote about the "profound process of change" that the American family had experienced in the early 20th century, including high rates of divorce and more lenient sexual morality.

Compared with today's patterns, the "lenient" sexual morality, "lax" divorce laws, and "indulgent" childrearing that these commentators were concerned with are anything but. Yet, these concerns, as well as the underlying changes that brought them about, can tell us a few things about American families. First, change is a fact of life, and that is no less true for the **institution** of the family than it is for anything else. Second, not everyone will be happy with those changes, and some level of public resistance will accompany almost every family change we observe. And, finally, idealized images of how families should be can make invisible the complex realities of how families actually are.

Family Change, Family Continuity

The family patterns we have seen in recent decades—**cohabitation**, divorce, nonmarital childbearing, same-sex marriage and childrearing—can seem

IPGGutenbergUKLtd/ iStock

Same-sex marriage is consistent with marital ideals that are more than 100 years old.

like radical changes from the past. At first glance, these patterns may challenge fundamental values, identities, and understandings. But when we look at these changes more closely, we can see that they are consistent with broader trends in culture, law, and the economy, many of which have been going on for centuries and around the world. Looking more closely helps us recognize not only change but also **family continuities** over time.

This consideration of both change *and* continuity in families is a major theme of this book. Family changes are evident to most of us. But family continuities, ideological and behavioral threads that link the family patterns of today to those in the past, are an important part of the story as well. For example, arguments for same-sex marriage are consistent with marital ideals that are more than 100 years old, ideals that emphasize marriage as a union based on romantic love, attraction, and partnership. Similarly, today's high rates of labor force participation among married White women are similar to patterns established by married middle-class Black women in the early 20th century (Landry, 2000). Another continuity is the practice of a wife taking her husband's last name, something that greater than 90 percent of American women still do (Gooding & Kreider, 2009) and that most Americans believe is best for families (Powell, Bolzendahl, Geist, & Steelman, 2010). This practice is rooted in the English common law principle of coverture, which stated that a husband and wife were a single legal entity; wives were subsumed under the personhood of their husbands as represented by her legal name as Mrs. John Doe. Although coverture no longer holds as a legal principle in the United States, its ideological foundation continues in marital naming practices. Examples like these demonstrate the ways that families have changed but also how today's patterns are rooted in past practices and meanings.

Family Diversity and Inequality

A second theme that is woven throughout the book is family diversity. The word *diversity* is often used to describe those who differ from some norm. This approach tends to center the experiences of the dominant group and to examine others as deviations from this norm. This book approaches diversity in a different way. I see diversity not as a characteristic of those who are different but as a way to describe variation—some families look like *X*, whereas other families look like *Y*. Some patterns may be more common than others, but all are families. For this reason, rather than having separate chapters on African American families or single-parent families or same-sex families, this text incorporates families of all types within each chapter. This is an intentional choice to emphasize the way that diversity describes variety among all families, not just those who differ from an ideological or statistical norm.

Family diversity exists because families, and individuals within them, have differential access to economic, legal, political, and cultural resources; thus, inequality is an important part of the conversation about families as well. Hierarchies of race (race-ethnicity), gender, sexual identity, and social class are especially influential for families. Each of these is a socially constructed system of stratification that divides people into groups and influences how resources are distributed in society. These inequalities shape family experiences and opportunities. For example, men and women and boys and girls experience families differently. Daughters in families are often given more chores to do than sons (Raley & Bianchi, 2006), and women's low pay relative to that of men increases the likelihood that single-mother families will live in poverty. Understanding these differences means looking beyond individual characteristics to see how structural inequality gives some groups more resources than others.

Extended families are central to family life for many Americans.

The sociological perspective accepts family diversity as a given. What sociologists investigate is why variation in family patterns exist and what consequences might emerge. For example, African Americans tend to have closer relationships with members of their extended families than do Whites (Sarkisian & Gerstel, 2012). There are more frequent calls and visits, more assistance with tasks such as childcare and transportation, and a more inclusive definition of who counts as part of the family. In investigating why, sociologists consider how **extended family** systems offer an adaptation to racial hierarchies. Extended family systems can provide a support system when other kinds of resources are lacking (Stack, 1974).

Family diversity results from the different **social locations** that families occupy. This applies to families who are disadvantaged by their social locations, as well as to those who are privileged. For example, higher education, an indicator of social class, has become one of the strongest predictors of marital and childbearing behaviors. Americans with a college degree tend to get married and then have children, whereas those without a college degree are more likely to have children without being married and may forego marriage all together. Both groups are influenced by their social location. Although we often pay more attention to those who are disadvantaged, occupying a privileged position on the top of a social hierarchy shapes family behaviors as much as a disadvantaged position on the bottom does. Understanding family diversity means looking at families in all social locations and at how inequality shapes those family experiences.

Sociological Perspective on Families

Sociologist Émile Durkheim, one of the founders of **sociology** in the 19th century, defined sociology as the scientific study of institutions. Sociologists use the **scientific method**—the careful collection and analysis of data to make appropriate theoretical and **empirical** generalizations—to ask and answer questions about families. This means that social scientists go beyond anecdote and their individual experiences to examine carefully collected data in a systematic way. For example, researchers who want to understand how couples divide the housework can't simply observe housework patterns in their households or the households of their friends and neighbors. Instead, they must carefully select a sample of couples to talk to and/or observe. And to understand the patterns they observe, they use social scientific theories, abstract statements that make sense of the empirical patterns. In Chapter 3, you will learn more about the theories and research methods that sociologists use to study families.

The second key concept in Durkheim's definition of sociology is *institution*. Sociology studies the family as a **social institution**, a cluster of patterned behaviors governed by social **norms** and enacted by individuals occupying social **roles**. We are so well socialized into institutions that we generally accept them "as the way things are" without much thought or protest. Sociologists work to identify the norms, roles, patterns, and social contexts that shape social institutions and to make them explicit.

Norms are social expectations that guide behavior. For example, one norm of the family institution in the United States is that parents financially support their children. This established behavioral norm is so taken for granted that most people don't even think about it—it is part of the parental role, especially for fathers. Parents who shirk this duty, such as nonresidential parents who do not pay child support, are sanctioned both informally (e.g., by being labeled a "dead beat parent") and formally (e.g., by wage garnishing or jail time). In fact, federal and state governments spend millions of dollars each year to enforce child support compliance. As an alternative, the government could spend those millions of dollars supporting the children directly, rather than using that money to compel parents to provide that support. But that would be inconsistent with the social norm that the financial support of children is the private responsibility of their parents.

As an institution, families are also made up of *roles*. A nonexhaustive list of family roles includes mother, father, son, daughter, sister, brother, cousin, mother-in-law, stepparent, grandparent, aunt, and uncle. Usually, one individual enacts multiple roles. For example, I am a daughter, sister, niece, wife, aunt, and granddaughter. Each of these roles has specific scripts, or rules governing behaviors and interactions, attached to it. The social rules about how to enact the mother role differ from the rules for the father role or the sibling role or the grandparent role. We don't expect mothers, fathers, siblings, and grandparents to behave in the same ways, but we do have fairly clear expectations for each of them.

Of course, role expectations are not static; they change over time, in new contexts, and among different social groups. But once they are entrenched, they can also be resistant to change. For example, in recent years, the expectations for the mother role have expanded to include economic provision, but mothers, even when they are employed, are still expected to be the primary caregivers for children. The contemporary motherhood role has changed to include economic provision even while it continues to emphasize caregiving.

In addition to norms and roles, a third feature of studying the family as an institution is the focus on **social patterns**. Rather than describing or predicting an individual's behavior, sociologists focus on patterns *across* individuals and families. Not all families will exhibit the pattern (in fact, there will usually be many individual exceptions), but the pattern is the focus of sociological analysis. Consider the relationship between age at marriage and divorce. Sociological research has consistently found a negative relationship between these two variables—those who marry at younger ages are more likely to divorce. This empirical pattern describes the relationship between the two variables (age at marriage and likelihood of divorce), but it cannot predict what will happen to any specific couple. In fact, you may be able to think of a couple who is an exception to this pattern, a couple who married young and stayed married for decades. These individual exceptions do not invalidate the pattern, and it is these patterns that are the focus of the sociological perspective.

In 1959, C. Wright Mills used the term **sociological imagination** to describe this focus on social patterns. He distinguished between "personal troubles" and "public issues." Personal troubles occur within an individual and his or her direct experience, whereas public issues transcend the individual to take place within social and structural context. Mills considered several examples. In the case of unemployment, if only one person is unemployed, one can look to the characteristics of that person to explain why he or she does not have a job. When millions are unemployed, the source of the problem lies in the economy, in the social and structural context that makes jobs scarce or otherwise difficult to find. Mills also considered divorce: "Inside a marriage a man and a woman may experience personal troubles, but when the divorce rate [is high], this is an indication of a structural issue having to do with the institutions of marriage and the family and other institutions that bear upon them" (Mills, 1959, p. 9). Sociologists turn our attention to these structural issues and the patterns of behavior they shape.

Finally, sociologists study institutions within their social contexts. Even though we think about families and households as the "private sphere," they are anything but private. Our family forms are rooted in historical, economic, political, social, and legal contexts. The characteristics of these contexts will shape the characteristics of families within them. For example, it is more common to see three-generation families living together in expensive cities than in cities with lower costs of living (Waters, Carr, & Kefalas, 2011). The high cost of housing combined with a family's economic constraints creates a social context in which shared households are more common.

Similarly, the legal context relating to marriage, childbearing, and inheritance defines who counts as a family and who does not. The social movement for the legal recognition of same-sex marriage emerged, in part, because same-sex couples were denied access to family rights including tax-free inheritance, medical decision making, and family reunification in immigration law. Stepfamilies are similarly undefined in the law. Unless a parent's new spouse legally adopts his or her child (which is rare because most children maintain legal ties with both biological parents and they can have only two legal parents in most states), stepparent–stepchild relationships are not legally recognized. Without this legal tie, stepparents and stepchildren have no formal rights or responsibilities in relationship to each other, which has implications for caregiving and decision making across the life course.

Applying the Sociological Perspective: The Standard North American Family and the Ideology of Separate Spheres

When asked to describe a traditional family, most Americans imagine a married heterosexual couple with children. The husband is employed, and his earnings are used to support the family. The wife's primary duty is caring for home, children, and husband, although she may also earn some income. Dorothy Smith (1993) used the term **Standard North American Family (SNAF)** to capture this image, one that is laden with ideological codes used to frame our family experiences. Even though most of us recognize that many families do not actually look like this, the image maintains powerful ideological sway.

By applying the lenses of change, continuity, diversity, and social context to this ideal, this section illustrates the major themes of the book.

The family ideals expressed in the SNAF image—breadwinning husband and homemaking wife—started to take hold in the United States in the 19th century. Before then, family codes looked different. Households were large, and they were highly integrated into and regulated by the small agrarian communities of which they were a part. As you will learn in later chapters, early American views on marriage and childrearing were much more utilitarian than they would become in the 19th and 20th centuries. All households members were household workers as the economic survival of the household required it. Women of all races devoted little of their energy to caring for children and instead, like men, were involved in the productive labor that households relied on to survive. Men planted crops and tended livestock; some men also worked in a trade such as blacksmithing. Women tended gardens, cared for smaller animals, worked in the fields, prepared meals, put up food for winter, and sewed and cared for clothing.

A NEW ENGLAND KITCHEN.
A HUNDRED YEARS AGO

Idealized image of a Colonial New England White family, as depicted in 1876.

Children were also put to work from a young age, starting to assist their parents with gender-specialized tasks by age seven or eight. It was also common, particularly among the Puritans, for parents to send their children to live with other families as servants for a period of time. This was intended to teach children industriousness and respect for authority, the most important childrearing values of the time. Households were legally and explicitly patriarchal, with the male head of household owning the labor of those within it. Few institutions outside of the family existed, so families were responsible for the education, health care, religious instruction, and vocational training of its members.

Over the course of the 19th century, American society experienced significant social change. Between 1810 and 1900, the share of the labor force working in manufacturing grew almost sevenfold, and the rural population declined from 93 to 60 percent of the total U.S. population. The end of slavery led to the dismantling of plantation agriculture, which gave way to sharecropping, and by the early decades of the 20th century, millions of African Americans abandoned the agricultural South to migrate to the industrial North. By 1920, more Americans lived in cities than in rural areas and more people worked in industry than in agriculture (U.S. Census Bureau, 1975). Fertility also declined dramatically during this period. Women born in the mid-1800s tended to give birth to more than five children. By the end of the 19th century, women were giving birth to just over three (Jones & Tertilt, 2006). In addition, families spread apart as young adults left the farms and moved to cities to find jobs in the growing manufacturing and trade sector. The expansion of public schooling in the early 20th century also helped to extend childhood and adolescence and to create a distinctive youth culture.

It is during this period of industrialization that our contemporary ideas about "traditional" American families emerged. Most significantly, this is when the **separate spheres ideology**, represented in the SNAF image, took hold. This ideology held that the public sphere of work and the private sphere of home were independent realms of existence, the former characterized by masculine ideals of competition and individualism and the latter by feminine ideals of nurturance and care. Men devoted their days to working in the market economy, and women spent theirs caring for children and the home. No longer seen as work, homemaking was redefined as an idealized expression of love.

Although this idealized division of labor was not the reality for most of the population, it was presented as universal. The experience of a small, privileged segment of the population was generalized to all, ignoring class, race, and regional differences in families. The reality is that many women continued to work in productive labor to support their families even in the 19th and early

Women working in a factory in 1895 Massachusetts. Working-class women were not able to live up to the separate spheres ideal.

20th centuries. This was true especially in rural areas and among unmarried working-class White women, married immigrant women, and women of color. In 1900, greater than 40 percent of African American women were employed as were 19 percent of Asian American women (Amott & Matthaei, 1996) and 44 percent of unmarried White women (U.S. Census Bureau, 2003).

Applying a class lens to the ideology of separate spheres is an important reminder that family diversity emerges because families are positioned in different social locations. The industrial economy developed in different parts of the United States at different times, and not everyone was granted the same access to this new sector. As a result, the family changes that accompanied industrialization also varied across class and racial-ethnic groups. Most African American families, for example, continued to live in the agricultural South throughout the early 20th century. As a result, their family patterns, including higher fertility and women's involvement in productive labor, reflected these agrarian conditions. The same was true for White rural families in the Midwest and Latino families in the Southwest.

The separate spheres ideology also ignores the reality of the many connections between the public and private spheres. Far from separate, they are highly integrated. Some men could devote their energies to breadwinning because they had a wife to take care of responsibilities at home. Some women could devote themselves to caregiving only because they were dependent on the wages of their husbands and the labor of other women to support their domesticity. Remember, separate spheres ideology emerged long before modern conveniences like off-the-rack clothing, washing machines, and refrigeration. Clothes had to be sewn and laundered by hand and food prepared from scratch. Middle-class women relied on the labor of working-class women, including European immigrants in the Northeast, Mexican Americans in the Southwest, and African Americans in the South, to get this work done. Much of the hard labor required to maintain the ideology of White feminine domesticity was made invisible.

The separation of work and home into two distinct spheres was an illusion in the 19th century when it first emerged, and it is an illusion that continues today. We can see this in the structure of the labor market, which assumes that workers do not have family responsibilities. A good worker is one who can be at work whenever a boss or client needs them. A good worker has no laundry to do, meals to prepare, or children to care for. A good worker puts work above all else. These expectations are fully rooted in the ideology of separate spheres as the only way these expectations can be met is if the worker has a full-time caregiver at home. The illusion of separate spheres is one reason why U.S. workers have no guarantee of paid family leave and why so many parents are struggling to balance their work and home responsibilities. The institution of work continues to be governed by the ideology of separate spheres and has not adjusted to contemporary family realities.

The example of separate spheres illustrates the major themes of this book. First, we can see change and continuity in how separate spheres ideals have changed over time and how this ideology continues to influence contemporary families. Second, we see the importance of family diversity and inequality, with families having differential access to the ideal depending on their social location. Finally, the example illustrates the sociological perspective by examining families in context, exploring how separate spheres ideology emerged in response to changing social and economic contexts.

Understanding Contemporary Families

The family changes that took place in the 19th century set the stage for what we are experiencing today. The shift to an industrial economy led to lower fertility rates and changing definitions of marriage. The romantic dyad became the core of the family, increasing expectations for intimacy and personal happiness. These high expectations, in turn, increased the risk of divorce and, more recently, the incidence of cohabitation. The redefinition of marriage as a relationship based on intimacy, attraction, and personal happiness also set the stage for legal recognition of same-sex couples.

At the same time that these interpersonal changes were taking place, changes in the economy also helped to change family life. The relative economic stability of the 1950s gave way to the instability of the 1970s and beyond. The disappearance of well-paid manufacturing jobs led to stagnation and decline in men's wages, and more women got jobs to support their families. This reduced women's dependence on men, helped to create more gender egalitarian relationships, and made it easier for women to support themselves without being married.

Expanding educational opportunities for young people—to high school in the early years of the 20th century and to college in the later years—has also changed family formation. The rise of the independent life stage, when young people live on their own, without parents or spouses, often hundreds of miles from where they grew up, has also helped to reduce parents' influence on the romantic behaviors and choices of their children (Rosenfeld, 2007). Young adults are left to date, mate, and marry whomever they choose, relatively free from the familial constraints faced by earlier generations of young people. This is not to say that parental influence has disappeared, nor that structural constraints no longer shape how we fall in love (which you will read about in Chapter 5), but compared with earlier generations, young people today have much more choice in their partnerships. As a result, untraditional matches, including interracial, interreligious, and same-sex relationships, are on the rise.

These are just a few examples of how today's family patterns and ideologies are linked to those of the past. They also show how family patterns result from what is going on in the broader context, although this context does not affect all families in the same ways. Studying families from a sociological perspective provides insights that historical, psychological, or theological perspectives cannot. Sociologists study families as an institution embedded in social context. Learning about the sociology of families will help you understand the variety of ideological, political, and economic forces that shape families and the opportunities available to them. Although sociologists focus on these social forces, we must keep in mind that these forces have real and direct influence on individual lives. By studying families from a sociological perspective, you will begin to recognize these interconnections between individual and society.

A Demographic Snapshot of the U.S. Population

Understanding American families means having an accurate picture of the American population more generally. Here, we will take a brief look at six population characteristics that have implications for families, which we will discuss in more detail in later chapters. First is the racial-ethnic makeup of the U.S. population (Figure 1.1). Race-ethnicity is a socially constructed classification system that divides people into groups based on phenotype and/or ancestry. Racial-ethnic classifications change over time and place. In the 19th century United States, for example, people from Ireland, Italy, and Greece were viewed as racially distinct from Anglo-Saxons. Over time, these distinct racial categories have merged, so that contemporary Americans consider anyone of European descent, including Irish, Italians, and Greeks, as White. Another example of the social construction of race can be seen in Brazil, where racial mixing has been the norm for centuries. There, an individual's race is based on his or her appearance, not on ancestry. Thus, one can have a different race than one's siblings or parents, depending on each individual's phenotype.

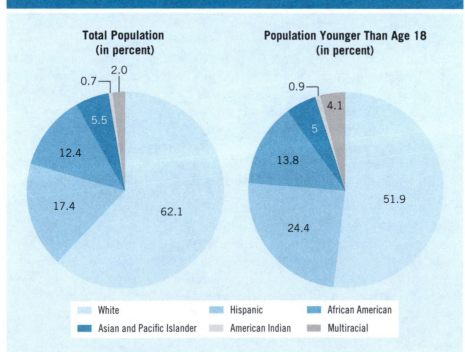

Figure 1.1   U.S. Population by Race and Ethnicity, 2014

Source: U.S. Census Bureau, 2014a.

A dark-skinned girl would be considered Black, whereas her lighter skinned sister would not be. Race in Brazil is an individual characteristic, not an indicator of group affiliation. These examples illustrate the idea that race-ethnicity is a social creation, not a natural one. In fact, there is more genetic variation within racial groups than between them (Tattersall & DeSalle, 2011).

The chart on the left of Figure 1.1 shows that approximately two out of three Americans are White and that Hispanics make up the largest minority group at 17 percent of the population. African Americans are 12 percent of the U.S. population, Asians and Pacific Islanders are slightly more than 5 percent, people who identify as multiracial are 2 percent, and Native Americans are less than 1 percent of the U.S. population. The chart on the right of Figure 1.1 shows the population younger than age 18. This younger generation of Americans is even more racially diverse. Whites make up slightly more than half of the population younger than age 18, with Hispanics accounting for 24 percent and African Americans 14 percent. Americans younger than age 18 are also twice as likely as the general population to be multiracial, although at 4 percent, they are still a relatively small group. That the youngest generation of Americans is more racially and ethnically diverse than older Americans gives us some idea of what the future will hold—an increasingly racially diverse population.

Growing diversity is also evident in patterns of immigration. In 2010, 13 percent of the population was foreign born, similar to the percentages at the turn of the 20th century. What has changed is the countries of origin for these immigrants. In 1900, 86 percent of the foreign born residing in the United States had been born in Europe, primarily eastern and southern Europe (Gibson & Lennon, 2011). In 2010, as shown in Figure 1.2, the largest groups of immigrants were from Mexico (29 percent) and countries throughout Asia (28 percent). Although the size of the immigrant population is large, the immigrant population is not spread evenly across the United States. More than a quarter of the foreign born live in a single state—California—and in 35 states, less than 10 percent of the population was born outside of the United States (Grieco et al., 2012).

Another demographic characteristic that influences families is the age structure of the population. In 2010, only 13 percent of the population was 65 years of age and older (Ortman, Velkoff, & Hogan, 2014), and the Census Bureau projects that by 2030, one in five Americans will be 65 or older. More Americans are also living to the oldest ages. This has implications for intergenerational caregiving, extended family relationships, health care, and government programs like Medicare and Social Security. Like the rest of the population, older Americans are becoming more racially diverse. Chapter 9 will focus on the implications of the aging population for families in more detail.

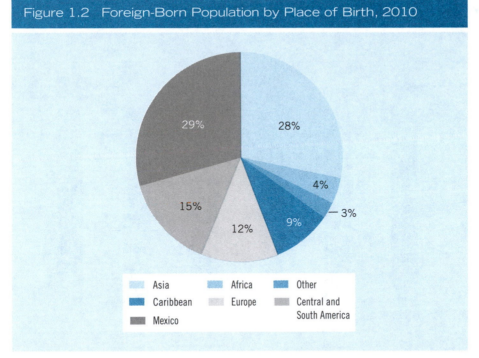

Figure 1.2 Foreign-Born Population by Place of Birth, 2010

29%

28%

4%

3%

15%

12%

9%

Asia

Caribbean

Mexico

Africa

Europe

Other

Central and
South America

Source: Greico et al., 2012.

Note: Other includes North America and Oceania.

The fourth population characteristic that has implications for families is income inequality, which has been increasing over the past several decades. Since 1967, household income inequality has increased 20 percent (U.S. Census Bureau, 2014e). Median income is lower today than it was in 1999 (adjusting for inflation), and only the top 20 percent of households has seen their share of total income increase; the other 80 percent are earning a lower percentage of aggregate U.S. income (U.S. Census Bureau, 2014d). You will see throughout this book that many family behaviors—such as marriage, childrearing, divorce, and cohabitation—are differentiated by social class. As inequality continues to increase, we will likely see growing differentiation in family patterns as well.

Figure 1.3 shows how household composition has changed since 1960. Married-couple households went from 74 to 49 percent of all households. Other family households, which includes mostly single-parent families, increased to 18 percent; households consisting of people living alone more than doubled to 28 percent; and other nonfamily households, which includes cohabiting couples without children and people living with roommates, grew to 6 percent. In these

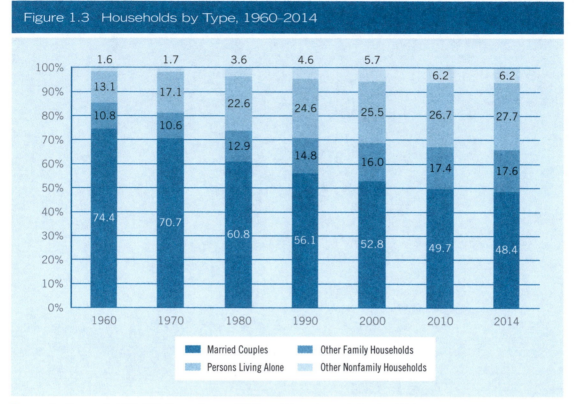

Figure 1.3   Households by Type, 1960–2014

Sources: Rawlings et al., 1979; U.S. Census Bureau, 2015b; and Vespa, Lewis, & Kreider, 2013.

changes, we can see the increasing diversity in living arrangements and family types even as marriage remains most common.

Finally, Figure 1.4 shows children's living arrangements. Most children (69 percent) live with two parents, and yet this is lower than it was in 1960 when 89 percent of children lived with two parents. Of the remaining children, 24 percent are currently living with their mother only, 4 percent with their father only, and 4 percent with neither parent. This latter category has remained consistent since 1960, and although the proportion of children living only with their fathers has quadrupled, it still represents a small minority of children. Most of the decline in children living with two parents can be explained by the increase in children living with their mothers. Figure 1.5 looks at the percentage of children living with only one parent by race-ethnicity. More than half of African American children are living with one parent, compared with one in three Hispanic children, one in five White children, and one in ten Asian American children.

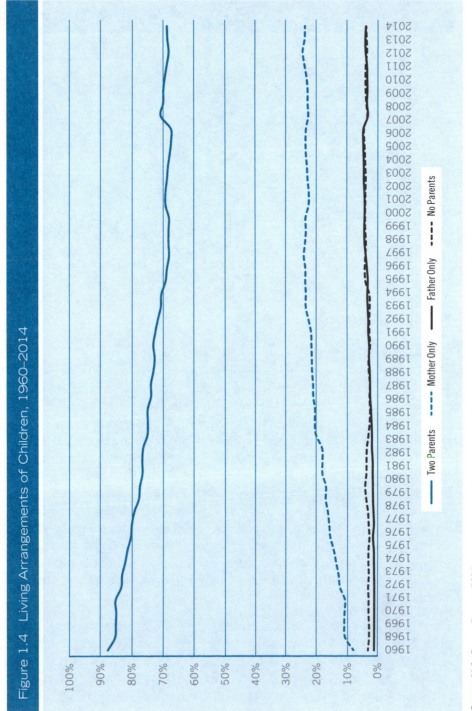

Figure 1.4 Living Arrangements of Children, 1960–2014

Two Parents ——— Mother Only - - - - - Father Only ——— No Parents - - - - -

Source: U.S. Census Bureau, 2015a.

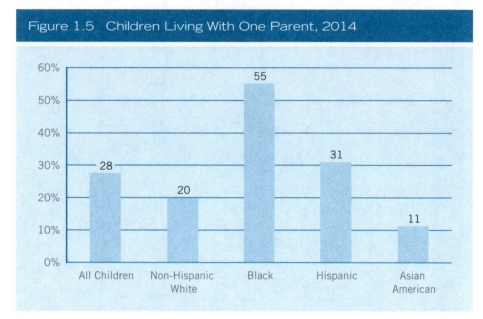

Figure 1.5 Children Living With One Parent, 2014

Source: U.S. Census Bureau, 2015b.

Looking Ahead

This text will introduce you to the sociological perspective on families with a focus on families in the United States. Three themes are integrated throughout. First, you will learn about the ways that families in the United States have changed, but you will also learn how current family patterns are rooted in the past. These continuities help us understand American families in their full complexity. Second, you will learn about the diversity of family structures and processes that exist in the United States. This text treats family diversity as a given and explores how a family's social location in race, class, gender, and sexual hierarchies shapes their opportunities and experiences. Finally, you will learn to apply your sociological imagination to the study of families. You will analyze families within their social contexts and understand how sociologists use social scientific methods and theories to understand the family as an institution.

Chapter 2 discusses how family is defined and the implications of these definitions. Chapter 3 provides an overview of the theories and methods that sociologists use to study families. Chapters 4 through 9 focus on specific areas of family life: the transition to adulthood; marriage and cohabitation; divorce and relationship dissolution; parents and children; work and family; and the family lives of older adults. Chapter 10 pulls together the major themes of the book and asks you to consider the future of families. By the time you finish this text, you will have a deeper understanding of contemporary U.S. families and how the sociological perspective can be used to understand them.

MAIN IDEAS

- Family change has always been a feature of U.S. families.

- Today's families are characterized by both change from and continuity with families in the past.

- Families in different social locations have differential access to resources, which creates family diversity and inequality.

- Sociology is the scientific study of institutions. Sociologists who study families consider norms, roles, patterns, and social context.

- The Standard North American Family (SNAF) and separate spheres ideology are historically specific ideals that continue to shape U.S. families. They also apply differently to families in different social locations.

- U.S. demographic patterns, including racial-ethnic structure, immigration, age structure, income inequality, and household composition, create the context for contemporary families.

CHAPTER 2

Defining Family

What is a family? This deceptively simple question lacks a simple answer. Does it mean a nuclear family—a married couple with children, all living in the same household? Does it include extended family members? And what about a couple without children—are they a family? Neither scholars nor the general public have expressed a clear consensus on who or what makes up a family. Although almost all Americans agree that the prototypical image of husband, wife, and children is a family (Powell, Bolzendahl, Geist, & Steelman, 2010; Weigel, 2008), many also agree that single parents and their children, gay and lesbian couples and their children, extended families, and married couples without children also count as family. In fact, most Americans agree that what is most important to families is loving and caring relationships, not any particular family form (Weigel, 2008).

Defining family is not simply an academic exercise as it has implications for custody, immigration, medical decision making, inheritance, and many other real-life concerns. For example, immigration policy prioritizes family reunification in assigning visas, and spouses and children are given priority over other family members. Legal spouses are exempt from paying estate taxes when a partner dies, but long-term cohabiting partners are not. A narrow focus on nuclear families—an adult couple and their children—also obscures much family life, particularly how it is experienced by people of color, gays and lesbians, and people living in poverty, all of whom have rich relationships in extended and nonkin family systems (Sarkisian & Gerstel, 2012).

This chapter begins with a discussion of four different approaches to defining family and then considers how our ideas about family shift when we move extended families to the center of analysis. Throughout, we will explore how family definitions are shaped by race, class, and sexuality. We will also consider how family definitions have changed over time and how they continue to prioritize marriage and children.

Defining Family: Four Approaches

Family can be defined in many ways, and sociologists have no agreement on the best way to do so. A useful starting point for our discussion is an influential definition of the family that was developed by sociologists Ernest W. Burgess and Harvey J. Locke in the mid-20th century, a time when the heterosexual breadwinner–homemaker family was at its peak:

> The family may now be defined as a group of persons united by ties of marriage, blood, or adoption; constituting a single household; interacting and communicating with each other in their respective social roles of husband and wife, mother and father, son and daughter, brother and sister; and creating and maintaining a common culture. (Burgess & Locke, 1945, p. 2)

Burgess and Locke's description includes four distinct approaches to defining family, each of which is still in use by sociologists today: (1) **structural**, (2) **household-based**, (3) **role-based**, and (4) **interactionist**. Let's explore each of these in turn.

1. Family as Structure

First, family is "a group of persons united by ties of marriage, blood, or adoption." This represents a *structural* approach to defining family, focusing on formal legal relationships between family members. This is the narrowest way to define families, and it is one that continues to have wide influence in the United States. Most research on families, including data collected by the U.S. Census Bureau, uses a structural definition, and legal and blood ties are the key to what many people consider "real" families. In addition, widespread benefits accrue to those who fall under this definition, from inheritance to immigration to insurance. A structural definition of family is exclusive in that it limits family members to those occupying those legal roles; a long-time cohabiting couple, for example, is not included, although a legally married same-sex couple is.

Both the symbolic and the practical influence of this structural definition of family is seen in the privileged place that marriage continues to hold in American families. Despite changing marriage patterns over the past few decades (which you will learn more about in Chapter 5), marriage continues to bestow legitimacy to relationships. Not only is "marital status a factor in determining or receiving benefits, rights, and privileges" in more than 1,100 federal laws (General Accounting Office, 2004), but marriage holds symbolic value as well. For example, gay and lesbian couples report that their co-workers and relatives finally recognize the legitimacy and seriousness of their relationships now that they are legally married (Kimport, 2014).

Marriage and family are so closely intertwined in our culture that it is difficult to be seen as a legitimate family without it. Some progressive activists, in fact, have

Most definitions of family rely on household-based definitions, which do not acknowledge family ties that cross households.

argued *against* same-sex marriage for exactly this reason, in that it continues to elevate marriage as the most legitimate family form. Instead of expanding marital privilege to include same-sex couples, they argue, we should dismantle marital privilege all together. In essence, these activists are arguing against a structural definition of family.

2. Family as Household

The second component of the Burgess and Locke (1945) definition of family is that family members "constitut[e] a single household." The terms *family* and *household* are often used interchangeably in the United States, but they are two distinct concepts. A household is a residential unit "within which . . . resources get distributed and connected" (Rapp, 1992, p. 51); it consists of everyone living under the same roof, whether that be a free-standing house or an apartment in a larger building. Households may consist of nuclear families, multigenerational families, cohabiting couples, friends living together as housemates, or some combination thereof. You will recall from Figure 1.3 in Chapter 1 that approximately one third of households are considered nonfamily households, as defined by the U.S. Census Bureau—consisting of a person living alone or living with other people to whom they are not related by marriage, blood, or adoption. In fact, the fastest growing household type in the United States is a person living alone. Extremely rare until the late 20th century—and illegal in some towns during the Colonial period—28 percent of households in 2014 consist of one person, more than double the rate in 1960.

Although the Burgess and Locke (1945) definition limits a family to a single household, families may in fact cross households. Consider a child whose parents are divorced. As joint custody has become more common (you will learn more about this in Chapter 6), children are likely to spend significant time in each parent's household. Yet, household-based definitions limit the child's family to just one. And what about a person living alone? Is this person without a family? Not at all—he or she is likely to have parents, siblings, extended family, and close friends considered to be family. Some even have long-term romantic partners from whom they have decided to live apart. Called **living apart together**, or LAT relationships for short, they have not been the focus of much research in the United States, reflecting a household bias in the definition of families. LATs do seem to be more common in Europe, where one third to one half of unmarried women are in LATs (Kiernan, 2000).

The common conflating of family and household in U.S. discourse reflects our bias toward the nuclear family. When we disentangle these two concepts, more complex family meanings emerge. For example, in her classic ethnographic study of African American families living in a poor Midwestern community that she called The Flats, Stack (1974) found that:

> [T]he "household" and its group composition was not a meaningful unit to isolate for analysis of family life in The Flats. A resident in The Flats who eats in one household may sleep in another, and contribute resources to yet another. He may consider himself a member of all three households. . . . The family network is diffused over several kin-based households, and fluctuations in household composition do not significantly affect cooperative familial arrangements. (p. 31)

Transnational families offer another example of a family type that transcends the household; in fact, these families transcend national borders. Whether it is due to legal restrictions, concern about the safety of the immigration crossing, or economic need, it is not uncommon for family members to be split across two countries (Foner & Dreby, 2011). This is certainly true for extended families, but it is also true for nuclear families. A husband may leave a spouse and children in his home country and migrate for work. A widowed or divorced mother may leave her children living with their grandmother for the same reason. Like other families who transcend households, transnational families highlight the limitations of a family definition that confines families to a single household.

3. Family Roles

The third part of the Burgess and Locke (1945) definition states that family members are "interacting and communicating with each other in their respective social roles of husband and wife, mother and father, son and daughter, brother and sister." As you learned in the previous chapter, family sociologists are interested in how individuals enact social roles and in the scripts associated with these roles. This third part of the definition acknowledges this sociological focus. How one behaves as a family member is not entirely up to the individual as each of us is strongly influenced by the

M_a_y_a/Istock

Interactionist definitions of family focus on the creation of family identity through shared activities, like holidays and other celebrations.

social roles we occupy. The scripts attached to these roles shape how family members behave and how they interact with each other.

A limitation in the way that Burgess and Locke (1945) describe these social roles is its focus on gender differentiation, heterosexuality, and the **nuclear family**. The husband role exists in opposition to the wifely role. The role of a son differs from that of a daughter. Although it is true that gendered expectations for spouses and for children are still strongly embedded in our families, which you will learn more about in later chapters, these specific family roles are not inherent to families, which the definition implies. One need not have a husband and a wife or a son and a daughter to have a family. And many families include roles beyond this limited list, such as extended family members and stepfamily members.

4. Family as Interaction: Doing Family

The final part of the definition states that through interaction and communication, family members are "creating and maintaining a common culture." This emphasizes the ways that families are actively created through interaction, what can be described as an interactionist approach to defining family. Sometimes called "doing family," this approach recognizes that families are a symbolic entity that gains meaning from shared activities and emotional attachment. As Christopher Carrington (1999) describes it, "what or who constitutes a family derives from whether the participants engage in a consistent and relatively reciprocal pattern of loving and caring activities and understand themselves to be bound to . . . other family members" (p. 5).

The interactionist approach to defining family argues that families are best understood as a pattern of shared activities and relationships rather than the fulfillment of structurally prescribed roles. It is in the process of sharing meals, celebrating holidays, and investing emotion, time, money, and other resources into a relationship that one becomes a family; it is not automatic, but it is created through these activities. Unlike definitions that focus on legal relationships, shared households, and family roles, interactionist definitions of family focus on the expressive (love and care) and instrumental (doing things for each other) activities that take place among groups of two or more people, even in the absence of formal family roles or legal ties.

Defining Family: A Summary

The Burgess and Locke (1945) definition of family, although limited when considered in full, effectively highlights four different ways to understand the family as a social institution:

1. *Structural definitions* focus on marriage, blood, and legally adoptive relationships

2. *Household-based definitions* consider family members living in a single household

3. *Role-based definitions* focus on family roles and their associated scripts

4. *Interactionist definitions* highlight the ways that families are actively created through interaction and relationship

The approach one takes to defining family will often depend on goals and circumstances. For a demographer at the U.S. Census Bureau who is interested in examining how family patterns have changed over time, a household-based structural definition might work best. If one is interested in the networks of care among extended families, then an interactionist definition would be more appropriate.

What this emphasizes is that the family is "as much idea as thing" (Gubrium & Holstein, 1990, p. 163). And how that idea gets expressed will shift over time, place, and situation, not only for different people but also for the same person in different circumstances. It is not uncommon, for example, for individuals to use structural or role-based definitions when defining family in the abstract and to use interactionist definitions when thinking about their own families (Powell et al., 2010). Similarly, in his research with gay and lesbian families, Carrington (1999) found that many of his respondents rejected narrow structural definitions of family and instead described family as a "way of behaving" (p. 5), which is a more interactionist understanding. At the same time, the same participants sometimes embraced structural definitions to advocate for gay and lesbian inclusion in them, such as with same-sex marriage. Like Carrington's respondents, I also define family differently in different circumstances. I am a family demographer, and my research uses structural and household-based definitions of family. Yet, when I teach about families and talk about families to a general audience, I tend to emphasize doing family, family as it is created through interaction, because it reflects the complexity of family life as it is actually lived by most Americans.

How Americans Define Family

It is clear to most observers that who counts as a family has changed over time. The narrow focus on a married heterosexual couple and their children has expanded to include other family types, including same-sex families, cohabiting

For people with exclusive definitions of family, only heterosexual married couples with children count as family.

couples, stepfamilies, and single parents and their children. The rhetoric around same-sex marriage has highlighted the competing definitions held by Americans, with some insisting that the only legitimate family is a married heterosexual couple and their children, whereas others insist that love makes a family, regardless of who is in it.

Sociologist Brian Powell and his colleagues wanted to answer the question "who counts as family?" and interviewed a nationally representative sample of Americans to find out how they define family, "who they believe fits under the abstract umbrella of 'family'" (Powell et al., 2010, p. 5). They found that Americans tend to fall into three categories—exclusionists, moderates, and inclusionists.

The exclusionists expressed the strictest definition of family, basing their ideas on structural and role-based understandings of family: "A family is a married couple with children" (Powell et al., 2010, p. 41), one respondent stated simply. This category of respondents identified heterosexual marriage and biological or adopted children as key features of a family; they were especially resistant to counting same-sex couples as a family. An analysis of their language use during the interviews found that they used role-based and gender-specific language like "husband" and "wife" much more frequently than other respondents. For exclusionists, marriage and family were one; as Powell and his colleagues write about their interviews with this group, "The transcripts of our interviews are replete with phrases such as 'the marriage vow,' 'the marriage covenant,' 'ceremonial arrangements,' 'legal marriage,' 'legal connection,' and 'legally binding'" (Powell et al., 2010, p. 38). Exclusionists made up approximately 45 percent of the sample in 2003, 38 percent in 2006, and 34 percent in 2010 (Powell, Bolzendahl, Geist, & Steelman, 2015).

Like the exclusionists, people in the moderate group also relied on structural definitions, but moderates incorporated more interactionist ideas about family as well. For most moderates, who made up approximately one third of the sample in all three study years, children make the family, regardless of the gender and marital status of their parents. Moderates said things like "I think you need children to be a real family" (Powell et al., 2010, p. 48) and "As soon as there are kids involved, then it's a family, whether they're both same sex or not" (p. 50).

Many moderates also "emphasized expressive qualities . . . such as love, caring, and emotional bonds, or instrumental qualities . . . such as taking care of each other, buying a house, and earning income" (Powell et al., 2010, p. 51), illustrating a more interactionist approach to defining family.

What was most unique about moderates was the ambivalence that was evident in their contradictory views. Their initial, unexamined views that marriage must be between a man and a woman often conflicted with their expressed ideas that a family is "just two people that love each other" (Powell et al., 2010, p. 52), which tended to emerge once they had time to think about their responses. Recognizing these contradictions, moderates became more inclusive in their definitions as they reflected on what makes a family.

An example of this shift comes from the parent of one of my former students. When I teach sociology of families, I ask students to replicate the Powell et al. (2010) study by asking their friends and family members to fill out the survey portion of the study, identifying which of 11 living arrangements count as family. Several years ago, one student's mother provided mostly exclusive definitions of family—she considered neither same-sex couples nor cohabiting couples with children real families. A few hours after filling out the survey, the mother called the student back, saying, "I want to change my answers." Upon reflection, she realized that she did believe that same-sex couples and cohabiting couples with children count as families. Like the moderates in Powell et al.'s (2010) study, her unexamined definitions of family became more inclusive after a bit of introspection. This isn't to say that this process happens for all moderates, but for those whose responses reflected a tension between structural and interactionist definitions, they tended to move toward inclusion (Powell et al., 2010).

The final category was the inclusionists, who tended to rely primarily on interactionist definitions of family. Respondents in this category were less concerned about roles and formal legal ties and more concerned with the love and commitment between family members. One respondent said, "A living arrangement doesn't make a family, period. How the people treat each other makes a family" (Powell et al., 2010, p. 55). Another said, "Two people living together who love each other. . . . It's got to have love in there to make a family" (p. 56), and "If you depend on each other to survive—well, if you're physically, mentally, or financially dependent on someone else—then I would consider them a family" (p. 58). Inclusionists frequently used words like "commitment," "responsibility," "love," and "emotional," which set them apart from other respondents. Over the seven years of the study, the proportion of the sample that was inclusive rose from 25 to 33 percent, with most of that change occurring between 2003 and 2006 (Powell et al., 2015).

The argument that "love is love" represents an inclusive definition of family.

Powell et al.'s (2010) study highlights the contradictory, complex, changing, and nuanced ways that Americans define the family. Some are firm in their beliefs, whereas others are more tenuous. Across all three categories, we see how Americans use structure, households, roles, and interactions to delineate who makes a family and who does not. We also see how definitions are shaped by social location as several factors emerged as important correlates of whether respondents were exclusive, moderate, or inclusive (Powell et al., 2010). One of these factors is gender, with men being more exclusive and women more inclusive. Another is age, with almost 80 percent of respondents younger than 30 years of age falling in the moderate or inclusive categories and almost 60 percent of those 65 or older being exclusive. We also see differences by level of education, with more than half of those with a high-school degree expressing exclusive definitions, whereas those with a college degree were about evenly split among the three categories. Few racial differences emerged, although there was a clear rural–urban divide, with rural residents being more exclusive. Finally, two thirds of religious fundamentalists were exclusive as were half of those who did not have any gays or lesbians in their social networks.

Extended Families

The nuclear family—parents and their children—is the prototypical family form in the United States (Weigel, 2008). Even as Americans are starting to expand their definitions of family, moving away from a narrow husband–wife–children definition, most of these expansions are variations on the nuclear family, such as a single parent and his or her children or a cohabiting couple with children. What tends to be obscured in these nuclear family ideologies are the complex networks of extended family members that are most resonant for many people. From childcare to economic support to social support, most Americans are deeply embedded in extended family networks. In fact, most of us couldn't get by without them.

For example, more than 40 percent of children in the United States younger than 5 years of age are regularly cared for by a relative, most often a grandparent, while their parents work (Laughlin, 2013). More than a quarter of respondents to a national survey reported that they had exchanged financial, housework, or transportation help with kin in the recent past (Sarkisian & Gerstel, 2004). In 2012, 3.7 million households were **multigenerational** (Vespa, Lewis, & Kreider, 2013). And older adults in need of assistance are most often cared for by family members. These examples illustrate the importance of extended families to family well-being even though much of this care is unseen and unacknowledged.

The term *extended family* generally applies to kin other than spouses and dependent children. It can include four types of relationships (Johnson, 2000), which are often referred to collectively as *kinship*. First are *lineal* relationships formed between direct descendants, such as grandparents, parents, and grandchildren. Second are *collateral* kin, to whom one is related by blood but not in a direct line, such as siblings, cousins, aunts, and uncles. Third are *in-law* relationships created through marriage. Finally, many people have family ties with those to whom they are not related by blood or marriage, what is variously called *fictive kin*, *chosen kin*, or *voluntary kin*. This would include godparents, informally adopted children, and long-time friends who are considered part of the family.

Several demographic changes are raising the visibility and importance of extended family relationships in the United States. First, longer life expectancies mean that three- and even four-generation families are not uncommon. Uhlenberg (1996) found that children born in the year 2000 are more likely to have a grandparent alive at age 20 than children born in the year 1900 were to have a mother alive at the same age. People are not only living longer but

Most Americans are deeply embedded in extended families.

Klaus Vedfelt/Getty Images

healthier as well, which increases their availability to be an active part of the lives of younger kin (you will read more about this in Chapter 9).

At the same time that longer life expectancies increase the availability of intergenerational ties, lower fertility results in fewer collateral relationships with similarly aged kin. In the early 20th century, the average woman had more than three children. That figure had been reduced to 1.9 by 2010. This not only means fewer siblings but fewer cousins, aunts, and uncles as well (although those aunts and uncles are also living to older ages). Demographers have come to describe the U.S. age structure as a **beanpole**—long and thin "with more family generations alive but with fewer members in each generation" (Bengston, 2001, p. 5).

Third, lower marriage rates and higher levels of relationship instability mean that extended family relationships may come to overshadow nuclear family ties for well-being and support over the life course (Bengston, 2001). **Multipartner fertility**, when an adult has children with more than one partner, also expands the pool of potential kin as shared children tend to create connections with each parent's family networks. However, more research is needed to know whether and how these relationships are activated and maintained over the long term (Furstenberg, 2014).

Finally, high rates of immigration from countries and regions that have more established traditions of extended family relations may also help to increase the role of extended families in the United States. *Compadrazgo* relationships among Latinos, filial piety among Asians, and West African kin patterns that place a high value on extended family relationships continue to influence the family experiences of people of color living in the United States, particularly among first and second generations. As immigrants from across the globe continue to migrate to the United States, more research will be needed on how their extended family traditions are integrated into, and adapted to, the U.S. context.

Scholars who study extended families have focused on two main areas: emotional ties between kin and the exchange of instrumental support. Overwhelmingly, most adult Americans report that they are emotionally close to their parents, to their adult children, and to their grandchildren (Swartz, 2009). Instrumental ties are also common. Extended family members exchange material support, such as monetary gifts, as well as practical support with things like housework, transportation, and caregiving. Most intergenerational assistance moves down the generations rather than up; it is only at the oldest and frailest ages that people receive more help than they give.

Racial-ethnic differences in extended family patterns have been well documented. One place that we see this is in multigenerational living: Three-generation households are far more common among people of color than among Whites (Lofquist, 2012). As shown in Figure 2.1, African American, Asian American, Hispanic, American Indian, and Native Hawaiian family households are more than twice as likely as White family households to be multigenerational. Multigenerational Latino and Asian households are especially likely to include at least one member who is foreign born (Vespa, Lewis, & Kreider, 2013). Sarkisian and Gerstel (2012) found that African Americans and Latinos were more likely than Whites to live not only with kin but also near kin and to exchange instrumental support with kin, such as helping with housework and providing transportation.

Although racial-ethnic differences in extended family relationships are evident, social class is an important part of the story as well. Compositional analysis of the differences between White and Mexican Americans in their levels of integration with kin, for example, found that culture explained little of the observed differences; most differences between these two racial-ethnic groups were explained by socioeconomic status (Sarkisian, Gerena, & Gerstel, 2007), with those of lower socioeconomic status reporting more interaction with kin that those with more resources.

Figure 2.1   Percentage of Multigenerational Family Households by Race, 2009–2011

- Non-Hispanic White: 3.7
- African American: 9.5
- Asian: 9.4
- Hispanic: 10.3
- American Indian: 10.7
- Native Hawaiians and Pacific Islanders: 13.0

Source: Lofquist, 2012.

Qualitative data show similar patterns. In their interviews with upper-class physicians and working-class nursing assistants, Sarkisian and Gerstel (2012) noted a marked difference in how their respondents talked about family. When the physicians were asked about their families, they talked about partners and children and, occasionally, their parents. When the nursing assistants spoke about their families, they included siblings, mothers, aunts, nieces, and nephews. One nursing assistant, a 20-year-old African American who lives with her partner and son, explained, "'I don't actually have family out here. My family's in Philly.' For her, family is not her partner and son; family is her relatives—her mother, cousins, and grandparents" (p. 33). As Sarkisian and Gerstel (2012) state, "Extended kin *are* family for these low wage nursing assistants" (p. 33, emphasis in original).

Extended families are also gendered, in that it is women who tend to do much of the **kinkeeping** that maintains relationships between extended family members. Women of all racial backgrounds organize family gatherings, cook holiday meals, and keep in touch with family members with phone calls and emails. Women also provide more practical help to family members than do men, including more childcare and elder care (Sarkisian & Gerstel, 2004, 2012).

Finally, extended families are also shaped by sexual identity. In her classic study of gays and lesbian families, Weston (1991) found that *chosen families*—families made up of partners, friends, and ex-partners—were common. Particularly for earlier generations of gays and lesbians for whom estrangement from families of origin was not uncommon, they were left to create families of their own, free from the constraints of nuclear family ideologies. Now that same-sex couples have access to legal marriage, additional research will be needed on how the changing legal context affects how gay men and lesbians define family.

Although the importance of extended family networks is well documented, the focus on nuclear families in family discourse obscures much of this family life. The myth of individualism masks the variety of ways that families rely on the people around them for support, sustenance, and care. Karen Hansen (2005) analyzed the "networks of care" for families in a range of social classes, and all of them, even the most privileged, relied on people outside of the nuclear family in their day-to-day lives. Yet this assistance was usually underplayed or even made invisible. Robert, one of her respondents, is adamant that he, alone, is the one who cares for his son when the son visits. Yet, when he tells his story in more detail, it is clear that he relies on his sister and her family, with whom he lives, and a best friend to assist with the tasks of caregiving. Like most parents, he is not doing it alone, but the American myth of individualism obscures many of these extended family exchanges.

What happens when researchers and policy makers assume that the only family that counts is nuclear families? The focus on marriage and childrearing as the defining features of family reinforces public concerns about family decline. However, families are "declining" only to the extent that marriage is becoming less common. Other types of family relationships, including relationships with extended kin, are as strong as they have ever been, if not stronger. For many, extended families have become more important as marriage has become less common. Without a lifelong partner, parents instead rely on extended family—their parents, siblings, and relatives—to help care for their children. So, rather than being an indicator of family decline, lower marriage rates may instead be an indicator of the growing importance of extended family relationships (Bengston, 2001).

Change, Continuity, and Diversity in Defining Families

Definitions of families have changed over time. Burgess and Locke's (1945) influential definition, which included structural, household-based, role-based, and interactionist components, assumed that a family should meet all four of these criteria. Today, more Americans are calling on only one or two of these criteria, rather than on all of them. In addition, many express conflicting views, sometimes relying on structural definitions and sometimes using more interactionist ideas. Powell et al.'s (2015) research demonstrates that Americans have become less exclusive in their definitions of family, primarily by becoming more accepting of gay and lesbian families.

What has remained consistent is the central role that marriage plays in defining family. Same-sex couples who legally marry gain legitimacy as a family that couples—gay or straight—who choose not to marry often lack. Similarly, children continue to be seen as a central definitional component of families. Even in the absence of marriage, the presence of children in a household makes it more likely to be perceived as a family, and couples without children are more often excluded.

That marriage and children remain central to family definitions shows how the nuclear family continues to dominate Americans' understandings about families. Family definitions have broadened in many ways, but variations of the nuclear family remain at the core. Extended families remain marginal in family research and discourse even though they are increasingly important in the lives of many.

MAIN IDEAS

- How one defines family has both symbolic and practical implications.

- Sociologists use four approaches to defining family: structural, household-based, role-based, and interactionist.

- Americans are becoming more inclusive in their definitions of family, integrating interactionist and structural definitions.

- Extended kin are becoming increasingly important in American families.

CHAPTER 3

Sociological Method and Theories in the Study of Families

To start our discussion of the scientific method, consider a recent article published by Elizabeth Aura McClintock (2014) in *American Sociological Review*, a leading journal that publishes sociological research studies. This study investigates the trophy wife stereotype in heterosexual relationships, the idea that attractive women marry rich men, which is a common image in popular culture. Exchange theory predicts that women exchange their most valued resource—their appearance—for men's most valued resource—status. McClintock argues, however, that this prediction does not take into account the fact that people tend to partner with others similar to themselves, what sociologists refer to as **homogamy**. Analyzing data from a nationally representative survey of young adults, McClintock finds no evidence that more attractive women partner with higher status men. In fact, she finds that higher status people, both men and women, are perceived to be more attractive. Thus, what appears to be an exchange of female beauty for male status disappears once female status and male attractiveness are included in the models. In other words, attractive, high-status women partner with attractive, high-status men. She concludes that homogamy is a better explanation than status exchange for patterns of heterosexual partnering.

This example illustrates several features of the scientific method: **theory**, empirical evidence, and systematic observation and analysis. It takes a common assumption rooted in casual observation, that rich men partner with attractive women, and turns it on its head. Yes, it is true that rich men partner with attractive women, but that is because the men are also attractive and the women are also rich. Instead of relying on casual and unsystematic observation of what is going on around us, on what everyone just knows to be true, McClintock uses the scientific method to test a **hypothesis** and draw empirical and theoretical conclusions. In this chapter, we will explore the scientific method in more detail as you learn about the variety of research methods and theoretical frameworks that sociologists use to study families.

Scientific Method

The term *scientific method* usually conjures up images of sterile laboratories filled with beakers, pipettes, and emergency eyewash stations. Although sociologists don't generally have much use for eyewash stations (except, perhaps, after being pepper sprayed while observing a political protest), the social sciences use the scientific method as well. What makes sociology a science is that it uses both theory and the systematic collection and analysis of data to understand the social world.

A theory offers an explanation for a phenomenon; this phenomenon could be in the natural world, like the evolution of species, or it could be in the social world, like inequality or social change. The key feature of a scientific theory is that it must be empirically testable, meaning that its propositions can be evaluated with observations. This feature is what differentiates scientific theory from other ways to understand the world, such as religion or philosophy. To test whether and in what circumstances a theory is accurate, scientists collect and analyze data.

Although the specific steps of the scientific method vary slightly depending on the discipline, Walter Wallace's (1971) description of how it is applied in sociology has been influential. Figure 3.1 shows two basic ways to approach scientific reasoning in sociology—**deductive** and **inductive**. Both incorporate theory and data analysis, but the starting point for each approach differs.

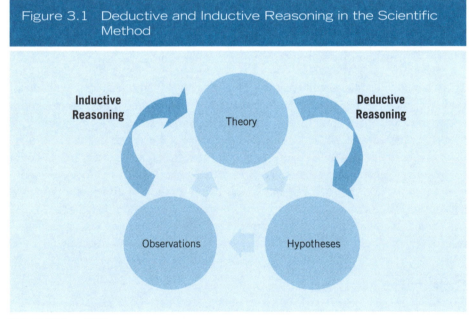

Figure 3.1   Deductive and Inductive Reasoning in the Scientific Method

Source: Wallace, 1971.

Deductive reasoning starts with theory. From this theory, a hypothesis or set of hypotheses is derived. Hypotheses—specific, testable statements—are then tested by collecting and analyzing empirical data. Based on these data, the hypotheses are supported or rejected, which in turn either supports or rejects the theory. For example, exchange theory explains inequality in romantic relationships by focusing on access to resources; the partner with more resources has more power. One hypothesis derived from exchange theory is that the higher earning partner in a relationship will spend less time on housework than the lower earning partner because the partner with higher earnings can use his or her power to get out of doing it. To test this hypothesis, researchers collect data on partners' earnings and on the time they spend on housework; analyze these data to see how these two variables are related; and, based on this analysis, draw conclusions about the accuracy of the hypothesis. If the hypothesis is confirmed, the theory is supported. If the hypothesis is not confirmed, neither is the theory, at least, not in that particular context.

The deductive approach to science moves from the general (e.g., abstract ideas expressed as a theory) to the specific (e.g., observations recorded as data). The inductive approach works in the opposite direction; it starts with specific observations, and from those observations, general theoretical ideas are developed. This process is depicted on the left side of Figure 3.1. Rather than testing hypotheses, inductive research instead is effective for identifying patterns and generating theoretical concepts. For example, a team of researchers interviews men and women about how they divide the housework with their heterosexual partners. Although the researchers have some ideas about what they might observe based on previous research, they are not testing a specific hypothesis. Rather, they are trying to find patterns or commonalities among their respondents to develop theoretical propositions. They might find that most women feel responsible for doing housework, no matter how much they earn, whereas many men don't think about housework much at all. From these observations, the researchers can develop theories about gender identity and housework performance, which can then be refined further with additional research.

You'll notice that both the deductive and inductive approaches to the scientific method are continuous and interrelated. The scientific method is depicted as a wheel because the process of discovery, theoretical refinement, and empirical analysis is ongoing. A theory may be well supported in one empirical context but not in another. Or relationships between variables may change over time, so a theory might become less useful in explaining a phenomenon as conditions change. This wheel of science emphasizes the ongoing nature of the scientific process.

Micro and Macro Approaches to Studying Families

The researchers in the earlier examples, who collected data on an individual's housework hours, earnings, and sense of responsibility for housework, were doing **micro-level research**, where the case being studied is the individual. Similarly, a researcher who wants to learn more about the people who use an Internet dating site is also doing micro-level research. She collects data on each user's gender, age, race, and relationship history, and then she uses these data to produce statistics, such as percentages or averages, that describe the characteristics of the users.

In contrast, **macro-level research** focuses on a larger social entity, such as a nation and, in so doing, highlights the ways that families are shaped by social and cultural contexts. For example, research that compares family policies in different countries is macro-level research. Becky Pettit and Jennifer Hook (2005) found that in countries with federally funded childcare, rates of maternal employment are higher. In this research, the variables describe a nation, not an individual. Each nation either funds childcare or not, and each nation has a specific rate of maternal employment. By focusing on a larger entity like a nation, Pettit and Hook were doing macro-level research.

Sometimes the unit of analysis is somewhere in between the micro and the macro. For example, Karen Hansen (2005) studied four families at different class levels and analyzed the networks they relied on to provide care to their families. She found that families in all social classes relied on caregivers outside of the immediate family to help provide care for their children. She also found that families with more financial resources were more likely to hire these caregivers than to rely on unpaid friends and family. All four families relied on the rhetoric of individualism that made much of this network support invisible. By focusing her analysis on social networks, Hansen highlighted the ways that families are embedded in networks of care that are invaluable for family life.

Research Methods

Family sociologists use a variety of methods to collect data, and these data can be quantitative or qualitative. **Quantitative data** are numbers, such as the percentage of families with children or the probability of divorce. Qualitative data are text or images, such as data collected through interviews or historical documents. Quantitative data do a good job describing the frequency of a phenomenon and determining causal relationships between variables; qualitative data are better for revealing commonalities, processes, and meaning.

For example, quantitative data on the transition to motherhood might measure how many women in the United States take paid parental leave; the length of that leave; and the number of hours per week mothers are employed when they do go back to work. Quantitative data could also analyze how these patterns vary by education level, race-ethnicity, or relationship status. On the other hand, qualitative data on the transition to motherhood could be collected from interviews with new mothers about their experiences, their employment plans, and the meaning that employment has for them now that they have taken on this new role as a parent.

Quantitative data are most often collected through surveys. Family sociologists frequently analyze data from nationally representative surveys like the Fragile Families and Child-Wellbeing Study, American Time Use Survey, and National Longitudinal Surveys. These data are collected by research centers or government organizations and then made available to scholars, and sometimes the general public, for analysis. Many of the research findings that you will read about in this text—such as the relationship between educational achievement and marriage patterns, the effects of divorce on children, or the number of hours that men and women spend on housework—are based on these kinds of data. For example, from the American Time Use Survey, we know that women spend approximately 60 percent more time on housework than men (Bianchi, Sayer, Milkie, & Robinson, 2012). From the Fragile Families and Child-Wellbeing Study, we know that the likelihood that unmarried parents will get married depends on the mother's education, the father's earnings, relationship quality, race, and whether the father has children with another woman (Carlson, McLanahan, & England, 2004). From the National Survey of Families and Households, we know that African Americans and Hispanics are more likely than Whites to express norms of filial responsibility, for example, that multiple generations should share households if needed (Burr & Mutchler, 1999). From the National Longitudinal Survey of Youth, we know that when men move in with a romantic partner, either through marriage or cohabitation, they reduce their participation in criminal acts, but marriage reduces criminality more than cohabitation does (Forrest, 2014). Nationally representative surveys like these provide invaluable data on the frequency of phenomena and on how variables are related to each other.

Researchers who are more interested in in-depth analysis of identity, meaning, and processes turn to qualitative methods, such as in-depth interviews and field research. Interviews allow respondents to tell their story in their own words, which helps researchers understand what is most important to them. In field research, which is also called ethnography or participant observation, researchers become immersed in a specific culture or setting, whether that be a neighborhood, community organization, or family. Field researchers combine direct observation and interviews to learn about the social organization of the setting, to identify patterns in people's behaviors and perceptions, and to highlight how the participants understand their experiences.

One well-known study based on qualitative interviews is *Making Ends Meet: How Single Mothers Survive Welfare and Low-Wage Work*, by Kathryn Edin and Laura Lein (1997). For this study, Edin and Lein conducted interviews with more than 400 low-income single mothers to understand how the mothers combined financial resources from work and welfare to support their families. The interviews gave the respondents the opportunity to explain the complex survival strategies that they pieced together to provide for their children's needs. Surveys would not have been able to capture these complexities.

More recently, Edin partnered with Timothy Nelson (2013) to use ethnographic methods to explore the lives of low-income unmarried fathers. They started by moving into the low-income neighborhood where they planned to do their research. By becoming part of the community, including raising their children there, the researchers were in a better position to understand the social context in which the men were living and parenting. Through this immersion, the researchers were able to build relationships and ultimately complete more than 100 interviews with fathers.

A strength of field research is the direct observation of people's behaviors because people don't always describe their behaviors accurately. For example, Christopher Carrington (1999) used ethnography to investigate how gays and lesbians divide the caregiving work in their families. Through interviews and direct observations of families in their homes, he observed a gap between what the respondents said about carework and what they actually did. Although most couples said during the interviews that they divided the carework equally, during the field work, he observed clear inequality. Other researchers have made similar observations among heterosexual couples (Hochschild, 1989). If researchers relied only on what respondents told them in surveys and interviews, we would have an inaccurate understanding of what the division of carework looks like. By combining direct observation with interviews, we not only gain a deeper insight into those behavioral patterns, but we also learn something about the importance couples place on appearing, to themselves and others, to have an equal division of labor even when they do not.

Qualitative methods are well suited to in-depth observation. Although these kinds of insights are useful for developing theoretical concepts and propositions, they are empirically limited in that they cannot be generalized and they cannot establish causal relationships between variables. Only nationally representative samples, like the surveys discussed earlier, can allow us to do this. Neither surveys nor qualitative research is inherently better than the other; they have complementary strengths and weaknesses.

Some researchers conduct **mixed methods**, research that combines both quantitative and qualitative data. Jennifer Lee and Frank Bean (2010), for example, investigated how racial and ethnic boundaries in the United States are changing because of increasing racial-ethnic intermarriage, increases in the number of Americans identifying as multiracial, and changing patterns of immigration. By analyzing quantitative data from the U.S. Census Bureau, they found that only 7 percent of marriages of native-born Whites include a spouse of a different race or ethnicity compared with 17 percent for African Americans, 73 percent for Asians and Pacific Islanders, and 53 percent for Latinos. They also found that structural factors like the level of racial-ethnic diversity in a community influenced rates of intermarriage and the likelihood of residents identifying as multiracial.

In addition to this "demographic-compositional" quantitative data from the U.S. Census Bureau, Lee and Bean (2010) also conducted in-depth interviews with interracial couples. These interviews provide "cultural-perceptual" information that "enables [the authors] to assess experiences with and subjective views about these phenomena" (p. 16). For example, they found in their interviews that for most Asian–White and Latino–White couples, race was a nonissue in their relationship; many did not even consider their partnerships interracial and were a little confused about being invited to participate in a study on interracial marriage. In contrast, Black–White couples were very aware of their racial differences, differences that were regularly commented on by friends, family members, and strangers.

By using mixed methods, Lee and Bean (2010) were able not only to identify the relative frequency of interracial marriages for different racial-ethnic groups in the United States but also to understand the different meanings that these partnerships have depending on the racial makeup of the couple. Alone, each of these methods tells a compelling, but incomplete, picture. Together, they offer a more comprehensive view of the complex relationships among race, marriage, and identity.

Theoretical Frameworks in the Sociology of Families

As you learned at the beginning of this chapter, theory is a central part of the scientific process. Social scientists want to do more than simply describe family patterns; they also want to understand how and why these family patterns exist and how and why they might change over time. The theoretical frameworks discussed in this section represent the main schools of thought in the sociology of families. Each framework approaches the study of families from different sets of assumptions about families and society. Is power and inequality inherent to families? Are families formed through a rational exchange of resources? Is the overall well-being of society improved if families look and behave a particular way?

Structural-Functionalism

The theoretical framework referred to as **structural-functionalism** goes back to sociology's origins in the 19th century and was influential in family sociology throughout much of the 20th century. Although few contemporary sociologists identify themselves as structural-functionalists, this theoretical perspective continues to influence both popular and scholarly thinking about families.

The structural-functionalist framework likens society to an organism, made up of many parts, all of which are important to the overall functioning of the being. For the organism to survive, its various body parts must be functioning optimally and in sync with each other. Social institutions, such as the family, are society's body parts, and, according to structural-functionalism, they ensure society's survival by fulfilling specific functions (Kingsbury & Scanzoni, 1993). In 1949, George Murdock identified four basic functions that families serve for society: sexual regulation; reproduction; socialization; and distribution of resources. According to structural-functionalism, when families adequately fulfill these functions, then society as a whole can thrive. When families fail to fulfill these functions, the broader society suffers.

The most well-known family sociologist in the structural-functionalist tradition is Talcott Parsons. Parsons and his colleague Robert Bales (1955) argued that families function most effectively when they exhibit role complementarity, with one partner taking on an instrumental role and the other partner taking on an expressive role. The instrumental role, occupied by the husband-father, includes task-oriented behaviors like economic provision and leadership. The expressive role, occupied by the wife-mother, is concerned with socioemotional support and relationship building. You'll notice that Parsons and Bales are relying on structural and role-based definitions of family that you learned about in the previous chapter, assuming that all families, or at least the well-functioning ones, are heterosexual and have a breadwinner husband and homemaking wife.

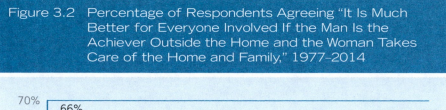

Figure 3.2　Percentage of Respondents Agreeing "It Is Much Better for Everyone Involved If the Man Is the Achiever Outside the Home and the Woman Takes Care of the Home and Family," 1977–2014

Source: Smith, Marsden, & Hout, 2015.

Although the structural-functionalist framework is no longer used frequently in sociological research, its assumptions continue to influence contemporary thinking about families. In 2014, almost one third of Americans agreed that families work best when husbands work and wives take care of the home (Figure 3.2). This is much less than the two thirds who agreed in 1977, but the fact that one in three Americans continues to believe that the instrumental-masculine/expressive-feminine divide is most functional for families reflects the continued influence of Parsons' and Bales' ideas.

The logic of structural-functionalism is also embedded in U.S. laws. The text of the Personal Responsibility and Work Opportunity Reconciliation Act (PRWORA), which created current welfare programs in 1996, states that "Marriage is the foundation of a successful society." More recently, the majority Supreme Court opinion in *Obergefell v. Hodges* (2015), which found that gay marriage bans are unconstitutional, states that "marriage is a keystone of the Nation's social order." These legal and policy statements explicitly state that marriage is necessary to maintain social order and to have a successful society, ideas that are firmly rooted in structural-functionalist assumptions about how social organization works.

Conflict Theory

Like structural-functionalism, **conflict theory** is also a foundational framework in sociology, but its focus is different. Instead of viewing society as an organism with its parts working together to improve functioning, conflict theory emphasizes unequal power relationships and competition for scarce resources. If we extend the organism metaphor, it would be as if your heart and liver were constantly fighting each other for adequate oxygen all the while that your spleen is hoarding it for its own use. This framework recognizes conflict as a basic part of social organization. Social order is not natural; it is achieved through a continual process of conflict, negotiation, and reconciliation. Although this focus on inequality and competition challenges the common view of families as a place of harmony and love, conflict theorists argue that they are regular parts of family life on both the macro- and micro-levels.

Sociologists who apply the conflict framework to families emphasize social inequality and the differential opportunities that result. Conflict theorists focus on how hierarchies based on gender, race, class, age, sexuality, and immigrant status structure experiences within and between families. As Suzanne Smith, Raeann Hamon, Bron Ingoldsby, and Elizabeth Miller (2009) state:

> [C]onflict theorists look at issues of conflict between classes of people who have privilege or dominance and those who are disadvantaged—the "haves" versus the "have-nots"—(e.g. men versus women, rich versus poor, Whites versus Blacks, those with access to health care versus those without, employed versus unemployed, heterosexuals versus gays and lesbians, adults versus children, married versus single, married versus divorced). (p. 165)

For example, conflict theorists might consider age hierarchies, analyzing how children are subject to the authority of their parents. Even adolescents cannot engage in certain behaviors, such as employment or participating in school athletics, without their parents' permission. In some cultures, where norms of filial piety are stronger than they are in the more individualistic United States, this parental authority continues into adulthood.

Another example of how conflict theory can be applied to families is by looking at wealth inequality between families. White households in the United States have 13 times more wealth than Black households and 10 times more wealth than Hispanic households (Pew Research Center, 2014). Melvin Oliver

Conflict theory focuses on inequalities among families.

and Thomas Shapiro (2006) argue that one of the primary reasons for this discrepancy between Whites and Blacks is the "racialization of state policy," a concept that considers "how state policy has impaired the ability of many black Americans to accumulate wealth—and discouraged them from doing so—from the beginning of slavery throughout American history" (p. 4). Because much wealth accumulation occurs intergenerationally, any policy in American history that helped some families accumulate wealth and prevented others from doing so has a direct effect on today's families. The most obvious example of this is slavery, but policies that seem on their surface to be race neutral, like homesteading laws, home mortgage rules, and qualification for unemployment benefits, have also contributed to the creation and perpetuation of this inequality. Conflict theorists emphasize how state policies tend to benefit the haves over the have-nots, creating opportunities for the former and limiting opportunities for the latter.

Conflict theorists also consider how inequalities are shaped by ideology: "[C]onflict theorists help to deconstruct and analyze the ways in which our society ascribes values and how this leads to inequality in the family" (Smith et al., 2009, pp. 165–166). For example, Annette Lareau's (2000, 2003) research on the interconnections between families and social institutions has highlighted the way that institutions, like schools and health care, operate by using a middle-class logic that privileges middle- and upper-class families and disadvantages working-class and lower-class families who are less adept at negotiating these assumptions. The unspoken ideologies in social institutions reinforce inequalities between families.

Symbolic Interactionism

Symbolic interactionism understands social life as a system of meanings created through interaction. Herbert Blumer (1969), who coined the term symbolic interactionism, identified three premises on which this framework rests. First, he wrote that "human beings act toward things on the basis of the meanings that the things have for them" (p. 2). This means that our reactions to objects, persons, and events are not about those things but about the meanings we attach to those things. For example, contemporary Americans attach meaning to a ring worn on the fourth finger of the left hand. We interpret a ring worn on that finger as a symbol of marriage and then interact with the person wearing that ring on that basis.

The second premise of symbolic interactionism is that "the meaning of such things is derived from, or arises out of, the social interaction that one has with one's fellows" (p. 2). Let's go back to the wedding ring: There is no inherent, objective meaning in a ring worn on the fourth finger of the left hand. It's just a piece of jewelry. We learn that a ring worn on this finger is a symbol of marriage through our interactions with others. For example, it is common for wedding photographers to take photos of a couple's hands to display their rings. These

mikhail choumiatsky/Istock

Wedding rings are symbols that we learn to interpret.

photos communicate that these rings are important in some way—why else would you pay a professional photographer to take a photograph of your hands? It is through photographs like these, as well as through advertisements for wedding rings, friends squealing with delight at the sight of a new engagement ring, and countless movies and television shows portraying the exchange of rings at a wedding ceremony, that we learn the meaning of these rings. Without these social interactions, the meaning would be absent.

Finally, Blumer (1969) wrote that the third premise of symbolic interactionism is that "these meanings are handled in, and modified through, an interpretative process used by the person in dealing with the things [one] encounters" (p. 2). In other words, we must *interpret* the things that we see to attach meaning to them. When we see a gold band or diamond ring worn on the left hand, this interpretive process is quick and unconscious (once we have learned to assign meaning to these rings). But when the ring doesn't look like a traditional ring—when it is a different kind of stone or an unusual material or shape—we become more conscious of the interpretive process. We might think to ourselves, "hmmm. She is wearing the ring on her left hand, but it doesn't really look like a wedding ring. I wonder if she is married or if she just likes to wear rings on that finger?" This third premise of symbolic interactionism emphasizes that symbols must always be understood in context and that we attach meaning to symbols by interpreting them.

Symbolic interactionism is a micro-level perspective. Instead of examining broader social institutions and structures, like the structural functionalism and conflict frameworks do, symbolic interactionism focuses on interactions within and between individuals. In the context of families, researchers have used this framework to understand the meanings that particular types of behaviors have for family members. For example, in her research on feeding work—the work women do to prepare food for their families—Marjorie DeVault (1991) discovered that feeding work is not simply about meeting family member's nutritional needs, but it is also a symbol of caring, nurturing, and family identity.

Other researchers have focused on rituals as a process of creating family meaning (Lewin, 1998). For example, before gays and lesbians were allowed to marry legally, many had commitment ceremonies. These ceremonies were a public statement of love and commitment, made in front of family and friends, and often accompanied by a reception. Although not legally binding, these ceremonies became a symbol of a couple's commitment and love, not only for the couple but also for the people around them. The ritual of a wedding has a shared cultural meaning; gay men and lesbians tapped into this meaning structure in celebrating their own wedding rituals even without the legal contract.

Feminist Theories

Feminist theories analyze gender inequalities and how these inequalities frame women's and men's family experiences. Although feminism exists in many variations, Linda Gordon (1979) offers a succinct definition that captures this variety: "an analysis of women's subordination for the purpose of figuring out how to change it" (p. 107). Applying feminist theories to the sociological study of families involves analyzing the family as a gendered institution.

Feminist family sociology arose in the 1960s and 1970s, in part, as a response to the problematic gender assumptions of structural-functionalism, which were dominant in family sociology at the time. Structural-functionalist arguments about instrumental and expressive role complementarity were inadequate to explain both the power imbalances between women and men within families and the diversity of family experiences. In 1972, Jessie Bernard used the terms *his marriage* and *her marriage* to emphasize how marriage was experienced differently by men and by women; married men were privileged with power, authority, and enhanced well-being, whereas married women experienced dependency and diminished well-being. The gendered power structures in marriage lead to different family experiences for husbands and wives.

Later feminist theorists argued that focusing on gender is not enough; families should be understood through an **intersectional** lens, one that investigates how gender, race, class, and sexuality intersect and interact to shape family experiences. For example, Patricia Hill Collins (1994) argued that early feminist theorizing about motherhood that focused on women's struggle for autonomy in the patriarchal private sphere did not represent the mothering experiences of women of color. Centering women of color in feminist theories leads to different kinds of theories about mothering, ones that emphasize how mothers provide for the survival of their children and communities and how mothers seek empowerment in and protection from racial and economic hierarchies that harm both them and their children.

Katie Acosta's recent book (2013) on how lesbian, bisexual, and queer (LBQ) Latinas negotiate their family behaviors and identities is another good example of sociological feminist theorizing. Through interviews and field research, she found that LBQ Latinas felt a strong attachment both to their families of origin and to the families they created in adulthood, and they worked hard to integrate these disparate family identities into a coherent whole. By applying an intersectional, feminist lens, Acosta highlights "how family is done across race, sexuality, and gender lines" (p. 133).

Social Exchange Theory

Social exchange theory emerged in the mid-20th century to explain how relationships are built through an exchange of resources. This framework considers how individuals act in self-interested ways to seek rewards and avoid costs and how relationships are "formed, maintained, and dissolved" (Smith et al., 2009, p. 203) through resource exchange. Power and dependency are key concepts in the application of exchange theory to families. In short, the more resources partner A has relative to partner B, the less dependent A is on B and the more power A has in the exchange.

One application of social exchange theory in family sociology is how it explains marital dissolution. Essentially, spouses compare the relative costs and benefits of remaining in the marriage to the costs and benefits of ending it. When a spouse feels that the alternatives to the marriage—either a new partner or living alone—offer a more promising reward–cost ratio than staying in the marriage, then divorce is likely. For example, a wife who is economically dependent on her spouse will face higher costs of relationship dissolution than a wife who has her own earnings, so a dependent wife would be less likely to seek a divorce. Even in the case of domestic violence, where the rewards of leaving the relationship are high, financial resources matter. Derek Kreager, Richard Felson, Cody Warner, and Marin Wenger (2013) found that for a woman in an abusive relationship, the more income and educational resources she has, the more likely she is to leave. Her economic and educational resources reduce her dependency and increase the likelihood of divorce.

Another common application of exchange theory in families is to explain the division of household labor. Exchange theory predicts that if partner A has higher earnings than partner B, then A will do less housework than B. Empirical tests of this hypothesis in same-sex couples show some support, especially for gay men (Peplau & Fingerhut, 2007). Applying this theory to heterosexual couples is a bit more complicated because of the confounding effects of gender; social exchanges are not gender neutral. Research shows that although wives do more housework than husbands regardless of their relative incomes, the division of housework becomes more equal as her earnings approach his.

Exchange theory can help explain the gendered division of household labor.

This holds until she starts to earn more than him, when inequality in housework again grows (you will read more about this dynamic in Chapter 8). This suggests that financial resources, although important, are not the only source of power in relationships. In the case of housework in heterosexual relationships, gender resources count as well.

This points to another feature of exchange: Nonmaterial resources and rewards like approval, prestige, or status can be just as important to exchanges as economic resources and rewards (Sabatelli & Shehan, 1993). Thus, a higher status partner will have more power in an exchange than a lower status partner. Returning to the example of housework in heterosexual marriages, patriarchal tradition and history give husbands a higher status than wives; as a result, even when a wife has more financial resources than her husband, he can use his higher cultural resources to avoid doing household labor.

Life Course Theory

The passage of time is a central component of **life course theory**. This framework explores how an individual's family experiences change over the course of one's life, and how transitions and pathways are shaped by both aging and historical context.

A central theme in the life course framework is the link between age and historical period. As Glen Elder (1994) explains, "Especially in rapidly changing societies, differences in birth year expose individuals to differences in historical worlds, with their constraints and options" (p. 5). A child born in 1900 faced a very different life than a child born in 2000. Life expectancy for a child born in the United States in 1900 was 47 years (Caplow, Hicks, & Wattenberg, 2000), only 51 percent of White children and 28 percent of Black children were enrolled in school (Snyder, 1993), and one's parents were likely to work in farming, manufacturing, or a trade (Caplow et al., 2000). For a child born 100 years later, life expectancy was 77 years (Arias, 2002), greater than 90 percent of children were enrolled in school (Day & Jamieson, 2003), and one's parents were likely to be working in professional or service occupations (Caplow et al., 2000). The life course perspective emphasizes the importance of understanding families within their historical worlds.

Another idea that is central to the life course perspective is the timing of life events: "[T]he same events or experiences may affect individuals in different ways depending on when they occur in the life course" (Elder, Johnson, & Crosnoe, 2003, p. 12). In other words, how one experiences family and life transitions will depend on one's age. For example, the transition to parenthood will be experienced differently by someone who is a first-time parent at age 40 than someone who is a first-time parent at age 20. Similarly, consider how the transition to retirement might be different for someone who retires at 55 versus 75 or if one divorces at 28 versus 58. In each case, even though the person is experiencing a similar transition, the resources and background that one brings to the transition will be shaped by one's age. Of course, other characteristics will shape these transitions too, but the life course perspective brings attention to time as a central part of the story.

The life course perspective also considers the ways that our life paths intersect with the life paths of significant others. As Elder (1985) explains:

> Failed marriages and careers frequently lead adult sons and daughters back to the parental household and have profound implications for the parents' life plans on their later years. Conversely, economic setbacks and divorce among the parents of adolescents may impede their transition to adulthood by postponing leaving home, undertaking higher education or employment and marriage. Each generation is bound to fateful decisions and events in the other's life course. (p. 40)

No one's life course is uninfluenced by others. These effects can be negative, or they can be positive (or, most frequently, they can be a bit of both), but the effects are there regardless. A child's serious illness redirects the life trajectories of parents, siblings, and grandparents. A parent's divorce affects the children. A spouse's new job that relocates a couple to a new city shapes the life course of both members of the partnership.

The life course perspective on families is unique in that it understands life as a dynamic trajectory, a "sequence of roles and experiences" (Elder et al., 2003, p. 8). As Kathleen Gerson (2011) puts it, "family life is a film, not a snapshot" (p. 9). In her analysis of family trajectories, Gerson found that family processes were more important than family structure in shaping child well-being. Whether one grew up with a single parent or married parents, for example, was less important than a family's ability to respond with flexibility and creativity to the inevitable challenges of family life. For families who had that ability, their trajectories were stable or improving. For families without that ability, the trajectory was less positive. The life course perspective emphasizes that, "Families are not a stable set of relationships frozen in time but a dynamic process that changes daily, monthly, and yearly as children grow" (Gerson, 2011, p. 9).

Change, Continuity, and Diversity in Family Methods and Theories

Since its founding in the 19th century, sociology has been a social science, incorporating both theoretical and empirical elements. This is a big part of what differentiated sociology from the philosophical and religious perspectives that dominated at the time. Émile Durkheim's famous study of suicide in 1897 is a perfect example of what made sociology unique; rather than just making an argument that more socially integrated communities would have lower rates of suicide, as a philosopher or theologian may have done, he analyzed quantitative data collected by governments to assess the accuracy of this idea.

As depicted in the wheel of science in Figure 3.1, the process of creating, testing, and refining theories is an ongoing one. No study will ever provide the final answer to a social question. And no single theory can provide a complete explanation for the complexities of social life. Instead, theories and research methods are in conversation with each other. New theoretical ideas emerge out of older ones. Critiques of an existing theoretical framework inspire a new one. New concepts generated from a qualitative study are tested with a follow-up study that uses nationally representative quantitative data. Ultimately, social scientists are in conversation with each other to make sense of the social world.

MAIN IDEAS

- Sociology is a social science that uses theory and empirical evidence to understand the social world.

- Scientific reasoning can be deductive or inductive.

- Sociologists engage in both macro- and micro-level research, and they use both quantitative and qualitative methods.

- Quantitative methods like surveys are useful for describing the frequency of phenomena and the relationships between variables, and qualitative methods like interviews and field research are useful for analysis of identity, meaning, and processes.

- The primary theoretical perspectives used in the sociology of families include structural-functionalism; conflict; symbolic interactionism; feminist; social exchange; and life course.

Young Adults and the Transition to Adulthood

Tom was born and raised in a small town in Iowa. He married his high-school girlfriend at age 22 after they had been together five years. When asked why they decided to marry at that time, Tom said, "I was finishing school and had a job" (Carr & Kefalas, 2011, p. 52). In Minnesota, Jake followed a different pathway. Jake's parents financed his prestigious undergraduate and law school educations. Now 29 and an attorney in a corporate law firm, he is looking to get married, although he is "in no rush to get married to the wrong person" (Swartz, Hartmann, & Mortimer, 2011, p. 88). And in New York, Francisco joined the U.S. Navy after high school in the hopes of getting his education paid for, but health problems prevented him from serving. Later he enrolled in a vocational program, but he did not finish because he had to work full time to support himself and pay his tuition, which left no time to study. Now 27, he is working as a truck driver. He wants to go back to school, but he has a family and "could not see his way to going back" (Holdaway, 2011, p. 110).

These three young men followed three different pathways to adulthood. Tom took a traditional route—early marriage to a high-school sweetheart. Although this has become less common than it was in the 1950s, it is not an unusual path in the rural Midwest and South, even today (Furstenberg, 2010). The low cost of living means that financial independence can be achieved relatively easily, and young people who stay in their hometowns settle down with marriage and childbearing in their early 20s. Young adults like Jake, whose parents provide significant financial and social support in the transition to adulthood, enter adulthood with a solid economic foundation and have a leg up on their less privileged peers. Like Tom, Jake followed a linear path, although Jake spent his 20s focusing on education and career and waited until he approached 30 to start thinking about marriage and children. For young people like Francisco, living in expensive urban areas and lacking family financial means, the pathway to adulthood was less predictable:

> [T]hey worked while in high school and sometimes also cared
> for children, alone or with the help of parents or partners.
> In their late teens and early 20s some mixed work with

schooling, or went back and forth between the two. Others did not get to college until their late 20s and early 30s, after working or raising children. Many continued to live at home until well into their 20s, and some stayed even after having their own children. (Holdaway, 2011, pp. 110–111)

As these examples illustrate, the pathway to adulthood looks different for young people in different social locations. Race and class hierarchies shape the kinds of resources young people have access to during this transition, and these inequalities reverberate throughout the life course. Although this has always been the case, the complexity and unpredictability of the transition has increased in recent years, and the gap between the advantaged and the disadvantaged is larger than it was for much of the 20th century. Economic uncertainty and the costs of higher education mean that many young adults are dependent on their parents well into their 20s. For more privileged young adults, this time offers a chance to go to college and explore careers, sexuality, and relationships with the strong scaffolding of family support around them. Those who are less privileged face more uncertainty, limiting their options and increasing their economic vulnerability. Changing expectations for higher education, marriage, and childbearing, along with the intergenerational transmission of privilege, creates the context for the transition to adulthood in the early 21st century.

Defining the Transition to Adulthood

Adulthood is not simply a matter of chronological age. Even in the legal realm, the age of adulthood varies. At age 18, one can vote, serve on juries, and serve in the armed forces. But it is not until reaching 21 years of age that one can legally purchase and consume alcohol. You have to be 25 years old to rent a car; yet teens as young as 13 can be tried as an adult in some states. Sociologists consider adulthood not a marker of chronological age but an achieved status, one that is reached only after certain milestones have been met. Traditionally, researchers have focused on the Big 5 indicators of adulthood (Settersten, 2012): finishing school, getting a full-time job, moving out of the parental home, getting married, and having children (Figure 4.1). Most Americans believe that completing one's education, being employed full time, and being financially independent are the most important markers of being an adult (Smith, 2004). Less important is being married or having a child, with almost half of Americans stating that these transitions are "not at all important" or "not too important" for achieving adulthood. Young people tend to say the same thing—they felt like an adult once they became financially independent. For example, one young woman said,

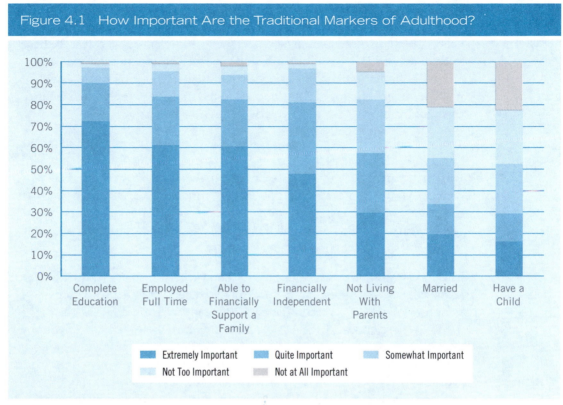

Figure 4.1 How Important Are the Traditional Markers of Adulthood?

Legend: Extremely Important | Quite Important | Somewhat Important | Not Too Important | Not at All Important

Source: Smith, 2004.

"I began to think of myself as an adult, probably at 21. . . . I finished school. Finally working. Taking care of myself. And no longer dependent on my parents" (Settersten, 2011, p. 170).

On average, Americans say that by age 21, young adults should be financially independent, living away from parents, and working full time; they should be done with their education by 22, ready to support a family by age 24 to 25, and married with children by age 26 (Smith, 2004). This represents a five-year transition period, starting with financial independence at 21 and ending with marriage and childbearing at 26. These age norms, however, vary by social class. In general, more educated and higher income Americans report that the transitions should happen later than less educated and lower income Americans find ideal.

These different age norms reflect the diverse experiences of Americans in different social locations. Young people who grow up in more financially privileged families tend to experience a more prolonged and less uncertain transition. Most will graduate from high school, attend a four-year college, perhaps attend graduate school, and get settled into a career in the mid-to-late 20s. They may cohabit with a partner or two, but few will marry or have children until getting established in their career. Their parents will make significant financial contributions to the transition, including paying for their education.

Young people from less advantaged families experience the transition differently. Some will attend college, but they will do so while working full time and living with their parents. Many will have children in their early 20s. The competing demands on their time and energy—school, work, and parenting—means that many will not finish college or will cycle in and out of school and work over several years. Those who can will live with their parents to save up money and to try to achieve some level of economic stability.

The variability in the transition to adulthood—both between and within social classes—suggests that the pathway is uncertain. In some periods, like the post–World War II era in the mid-20th century United States, the Big 5 adult milestones were met easily and in quick succession by most young people. This was facilitated by a healthy economy and government supports for higher education and home ownership for young men who had served in World War II. In other periods, achieving adulthood has been more difficult. In fact, today's prolonged period of uncertainty and semidependence in young adulthood has some commonalities with what was typical in the 18th and 19th centuries, reflecting the relative social and economic uncertainty of both eras.

Transition to Adulthood in Historical Context

The transition to adulthood in the pre-industrial United States was "a long and difficult process. . . . Adulthood was not a status that was routine and automatic. It was one that had to be achieved, sometimes at a great personal cost" (Farrell, 1999, p. 68). In an agrarian economy, economic independence required access to land. Young White men often had to wait until their mid-to-late 20s to inherit land, marry, and set up their household. In 1890, the median age at marriage for men was 26. Women tended to marry at younger ages—the median age for women in 1890 was 22—although even here there are variations. For example, youngest daughters were often expected to remain at home to care for their parents as they aged (Farrell, 1999). A woman in this position postponed marriage until her parents died or did not marry at all. This meant that many

In the 1920s, adolescence was redefined as a time for carefree fun.

© Kirn Vintage Stock/Corbis

women also postponed childbearing: In Massachusetts, 30 percent of married women born between 1856 and 1865 were childless in their 20s, and in several New York counties in 1865, almost one in three married women in their early 20s had never had children (Carter et al., 2006).

Although achieving full adult status did not occur until one's 20s, the transition to adulthood tended to start much earlier than it does today, creating a prolonged period of semidependence between young adults and their parents. Once children were old enough to contribute to the family economy, they were expected to do so. Few young people were enrolled in school. Even as late as 1900, a 16-year-old White male was as likely to be in the labor force as he was to be in school and a 16-year-old Black male was twice as likely to be working than in school (Fussell & Furstenberg, 2005). This semidependent relationship between young adults and their parents could last a decade or more (Farrell, 1999), starting in the early teens and lasting into the 20s.

In the early decades of the 20th century, the relationship between children and parents during the teen years became more dependent than semidependent. Increasingly, middle-class young people were expected to be in school rather than to work, and the dependency of childhood was extended into the adolescent years. The expansion of public high schools meant that more teens were staying in school for longer periods, and the percentage of the population with a high-school degree increased (Figure 4.2), starting with the middle class and eventually spreading throughout the population. By the 1940s, wider access to schooling and a growing youth-oriented consumer culture changed the way that adolescence was understood; it came to be seen as a unique and universal life stage characterized by the physical and emotional challenges of puberty rather than as simply a younger version of adulthood. An adolescent identity, distinct from both childhood and adulthood, was created. The creation of adolescence as a unique stage of life delayed the beginning of the transition to adulthood by several years as those aged 12 to 18 became fully dependent on their parents and were not expected to begin the transition to adulthood until graduating high school around age 18.

Because of the economic stability of the postwar years, the transition to adulthood in the middle of the 20th century was "more orderly, predictable, and condensed" (Farrell, 1999, p. 68) than it was in prior years. In 1960, most young people were done with school, living on their own, married, and raising children by the time they were 25 years old (Fussell & Furstenberg, 2005), a stark difference from the patterns 100 years earlier *and* the patterns today. When we use the mid-20th century as our point of comparison, today's patterns seem

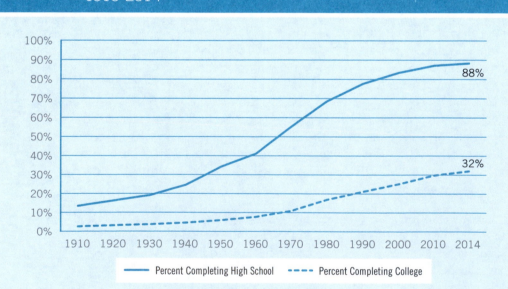

Figure 4.2   Educational Attainment for the Population Aged 25 and Older, 1910–2014

Source: National Center for Education Statistics, 2015.

Figure 4.3	Adolescence and Young Adulthood in Historical Context		
	18th and 19th Centuries	**20th Century**	**21st Century**
Childhood (birth to age 12)	Dependent	Dependent	Dependent
Adolescence (age 12 to 18)	Semidependent	Dependent	Dependent
Young Adulthood (age 18 to 24)	Semidependent	Independent	Semidependent

unusual (and, to some, problematic). But, as you will see, today's young adult is not so different from the young adults of the pre-industrial era—remaining semidependent on one's parents for several years as one builds a stable enough financial foundation to go out on one's own. Figure 4.3 summarizes these historical shifts.

Transition to Adulthood in the Early 21st Century

In the 1990s and 2000s, scholars and journalists started to notice that young people were not settling down into steady jobs, marriage, childrearing, and home ownership the way their parents and grandparents had. These changes were met with some dismay and were referred to with phrases like "prolonged adolescence," "delayed adulthood," and "failure to launch." In Japan, the less-than-flattering term to describe young adults who continue to live with their parents is "parasite singles."

The negative connotations of these phrases suggest that the lengthening of the transition to adulthood has not been viewed favorably. This disfavor, however, misses two important facts. First, although the transition to adulthood today is different from the patterns of the mid-20th century, they are not nearly so unusual when viewed from a broader historical viewpoint. As you learned earlier, until the 1940s and 1950s, it was not uncommon for young adults to remain semidependent on parents well into their 20s. Thus, it was the mid-20th century that was unusual, not what is going on today. Second, concern about the lengthening transition tends to individualize the young adults' behaviors as "the personal decisions of each adolescent" rather than viewing them as "the collective consequences of family and community demands" (Farrell, 1999, p. 68).

That these patterns are happening throughout much of the industrialized world also suggests that a broader perspective is warranted. To use the language of sociologist C. Wright Mills (1959) that we discussed in Chapter 1, rather than being a private trouble reflecting an individual's laziness, lack of ambition, or immaturity, the expansion of young adulthood is a public issue that results from a changing economy, changing family patterns of family formation, and changing relationships between parents and children.

Economic Uncertainty and Higher Education

Today's young adults face very different economic prospects than their parents and grandparents did. High rates of unemployment for workers in their 20s, the shrinking middle class, and stagnant wages for all but the most privileged mean that economic uncertainty is high. Only about half of Americans believe that today's youth are likely to have a better life than their parents, the lowest proportion in more than 15 years (Saad, 2013). This uncharacteristic pessimism reflects public fear about the changes they see going on around them. The American dream ideology that was epitomized in the 1950s, which included idealized images of family stability, certain economic prospects, and homeownership, is increasingly out of reach. Most of today's young people want

More young people than ever before are attending college.

the stable families and financial well-being of earlier generations. Structural shifts, however, mean this stability is not as easy to achieve.

Young people have gotten the message that the main way to secure a well-paying job is to get a college degree. And they have responded by attending college at unprecedented rates. The percentage of Americans with a college degree has tripled since 1970, reaching 30 percent in 2014 (Figure 4.2). When we look specifically at younger Americans aged 25 to 29, 34 percent had a college degree in 2014. The rate is highest among Asians and Pacific Islanders, followed by Whites and people who identify as multiracial, and lowest for African Americans, Hispanics, and American Indians (Figure 4.4). As you will learn in later chapters, this racial disparity in education has important implications for family patterns.

Although these figures show an impressive growth in college completion, they mask another trend: the number of people who attend college but do not finish. Forty percent of first-year students at four-year colleges do not earn a degree

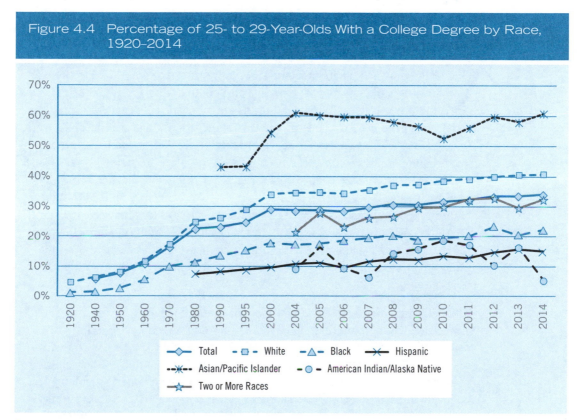

Figure 4.4   Percentage of 25- to 29-Year-Olds With a College Degree by Race, 1920–2014

Source: National Center for Education Statistics, 2015.

within six years (National Center for Education Statistics, 2014a). Graduation rates at community and vocational colleges are even lower. Young people who take on educational debt to attend college for a year or two but do not earn a degree are especially economically vulnerable. They have taken on the costs of higher education without receiving the financial benefits.

And the financial benefits of a college degree are clear. On average, college graduates earn twice as much as high-school graduates (Leonhardt, 2014), a difference that adds up to more than $1 million over a lifetime (Carnevale, Rose, & Cheah, 2014c). But even college graduates can have a hard time achieving financial stability (Settersten, 2012), especially those who graduated in the middle of the 2007–2009 Great Recession. A tough labor market, stagnant wages, and college loan debt mean that it can take several years after finishing college to feel economically secure. Things are even more insecure for the two thirds of young people who do not graduate from college. Almost one in five high-school graduates in their early 20s is unemployed. The rate is almost one in three for African Americans and Native Americans (National Center for Education Statistics, 2014b).

Changing Patterns of Family Formation

One of the most talked about features of the transition to adulthood in the 21st century is the low rates of marriage and childbearing among 20-somethings. Only about one in ten 20- to 24-year-olds are married (U.S. Census Bureau, 2014c), and the median age at marriage is higher than it has ever been—29 for men and 27 for women. However, although only half of young people are marrying by their late 20s, this does not mean that they are staying single. Most young people have cohabited with a romantic partner, and they tend to do so at relatively young ages—22 for women and 23.5 for men. In fact, Wendy Manning, Susan Brown, and Krista Payne (2014) found that between 1984 and 2010, the age at first union—whether marriage or cohabitation—remained steady at 22 to 23 years old. Thus, young people are partnering at about the same time that their parents did; they are just doing it as cohabitors rather than as spouses.

The delay in marriage has also meant a delay in childbearing for most, but not all, young people. Three in ten 20- to 24-year-old women have children; this rises to about half for 25- to 29-year-olds (Monte & Ellis, 2014). As you will read about in the next chapter, rates of marital and nonmarital childbearing vary significantly by education level. Most young women who go to a four-year college will postpone childbearing until they are done with their education. Young women who do not attend college are more likely to have a child in their early 20s; 80 percent of these young women are single or cohabiting rather than married (Monte & Ellis, 2013).

Changing Relationships With Parents

Parents play an important role in young people's transition to adulthood. Young people who have healthy relationships with parents and who have access to parental resources benefit from this interpersonal and financial support. Parents are involved in their young adult children's lives in many ways, and for most, these involvements "foster (rather than hinder) a successful transition into adulthood" (Fingerman, Cheng, Tighe, Birditt, & Zarit, 2012, p. 79).

Because of low wages, the uncertain economy, and the expansion of higher education, many young people remain financially dependent on their parents into their 20s. Robert Schoeni and Karen Ross (2005) estimate that "on average parents provide roughly $38,000 in material assistance—housing, food, educational expenses, or direct cash assistance—through the transition to adulthood" (p. 414). This is a significant amount, but there is "substantial variation among youth in the amount of assistance they receive, with some youth receiving many tens of thousands of dollars, while others receive very little or no support" (p. 414). One place where we see this gap in family assistance is in paying for college. On average, parents contributed about $7,700 in 2014–2015 to their children's undergraduate education, not counting parent borrowing (Sallie Mae, 2015). However, this varies widely by socioeconomic status: Low-income parents contribute approximately $4,300, middle-income parents contribute $6,000, and high-income parents contribute more than $15,000. This discrepancy gives children from wealthier families a significant advantage over their peers; they can transition into adulthood with lower debt and a more stable economic foundation for work and family that will reverberate throughout their lives (Shapiro, 2004).

In addition to helping pay for college, parents also support their young adult children by allowing them to live in the parents' home while paying little or no rent. Figure 4.5 shows young adults' living arrangements in 2012. Most 18- to 24-year-old men and women are living with a parent (this includes students who are living at a residential college). These patterns have been fairly consistent over the past 25 years with a slight increase of young people living with parents during the recent economic downturn (Fingerman et al., 2012).

When we look at slightly older adults, aged 25 to 34, we can see that their living arrangements are different than those of their younger peers. Most are living with a spouse or romantic partner, and only 10 percent of women and 16 percent of men are living with parents. Although significantly lower than

Figure 4.5 Living Arrangements of Young Adults, 2012

	Men Age 18 to 24	Women Age 18 to 24	Men Age 25 to 34	Women Age 25 to 34
Other Living Arrangement	22.6	21.8	17.9	19.6
Living With Parent	59.4	50.9	15.9	9.7
Living With Spouse			14.6	13.8
Living With an Unmarried Partner	7.6	11.8	40.3	48.4
Living Alone	6.1	10.6	11.4	8.5
	4.3	4.8		

Legend:
- Living Alone
- Living With an Unmarried Partner
- Other Living Arrangement
- Living With Spouse
- Living With Parent

Source: Vespa, Lewis, & Kreider, 2013.

the rates for younger adults, some critics find these rates alarmingly high, particularly in comparison with the mid-20th century. But if we look at them in historical context, these 21st century patterns are not that unique. In 1900, 32 percent of 25-year-old White men and 14 percent of 30-year-old White men were unmarried, childless, and living with their parents (Fussell & Furstenberg, 2005), not too different from the patterns today.

Notions of American individualism and the idealization of 1950s family patterns reinforce the idea that shared living between young adults and their parents is a problematic indicator of young adults' ongoing dependence on their parents. Yet other interpretations are possible. For example, more than one third of single mothers live with their parents at some point after the birth of their child (Bumpass & Raley, 1995), and in 2011, 17 percent of children living with a single parent also lived with a grandparent (Williams, 2014). This co-residence can provide important financial, familial, and social stability for unmarried mothers and their young children, which has a positive effect on family well-being. Parents can also serve as a safety net to counter the uncertainty in other aspects of young adults' lives. For example, many of the 30-something adults who are living with parents have not been doing so continuously. More likely, they lived independently for a while and returned to the parental home due to job loss, returning to school, or the breakup of a romantic relationship; Katherine Newman (2012) refers to these as "boomerang kids." In addition, adult children who live with their parents contribute economically and instrumentally to the household and value being able to care for parents as they age (Foner & Dreby, 2011), which we will discuss in more detail in Chapter 9. Thus, far from a "prolonged adolescence" or "failure to launch," let alone Japan's "parasites," co-residence between young adults and their parents can be understood as a positive sign of family solidarity and support, which is a healthy interdependence between the generations.

Norms about the appropriateness of young adults living with their parents also vary across social groups. In some **immigrant families** living in the United States, adult children are expected to live with parents until, and sometimes even after, marriage. Eduardo is a U.S.-born son of Columbian parents. He is a 33-year-old college-educated professional who, along with his spouse and child, live with his parents. He contrasts Columbian cultural expectations with the typical American ones: "A lot of South American families live together until whenever you decide to leave—it's not like here in America. In America, when you're 18, get out. Get out, you know what I mean?" (Holdaway, 2011, p. 117). Similarly, a 28-year-old West Indian women lived with her daughter, her mother, and her sister. She said, "It's not . . . in my culture to push, to get away from my mother and push her away for my own life and my own family. I think that you can maintain both" (Holdaway, 2011, p. 116).

Young Adult Sexuality and Romantic Partnerships

The relationship between young adults and their families has moved from semidependence in the 18th and 19th centuries to independence in the 20th century and back to semidependence today (Figure 4.3). Yet, even as young people remain economically and educationally semidependent on their parents into their 20s, they have also become increasingly independent in the realm of sexuality and romantic relationships (Rosenfeld, 2007). Although most young people delay marriage, cohabitation, and childbearing until their 20s, they begin to explore romantic and sexual relationships far earlier. A decade-long gap between first sexual experiences in the teen years and first cohabitation and marriage experiences in the 20s (Finer & Philbin, 2014) creates a context for both exploration and ambiguity, and unlike in earlier generations, most American young people navigate these experiences with minimal input from parents.

Dating in Historical Context

As historian Beth Bailey (1988) describes in her book *From Front Porch to Back Seat*, the decades immediately before and after the turn of the 20th century saw rapid change in how young people experienced their romantic and sexual lives. The processes of urbanization and industrialization moved many Americans from farms to cities and changed how young people socialized. Middle-class teens and young adults had disposable income, which they spent in the urban environments of dance halls, movies, clubs, and amusement parks. The anonymity of the city protected young people from the watchful eyes of community mores that characterized small rural towns. It became common and accepted for young people to spend time together in mixed-gender pairs or groups without chaperones. The parent-controlled system of **calling**, in which a young man was invited to call on a woman in her home to visit with both the young woman and her mother, transitioned to dating, which was entirely in the hands of young people.

© Bettmann/CORBIS

The 1920s were a time of sexual exploration.

Dating emerged first among youth in the lower classes, from which it spread to young people in other class locations. Unlike more privileged young women who entertained male suitors in the family home, young women who lived with large families in small apartments did not have the luxury to invite men to visit. There just wasn't the room. So, instead, they went out on dates, seeking entertainment not in the privacy of home but in the dance halls and movie theaters in the public sphere. What was a necessity for poor and working-class youth was viewed with envy by youth in the upper classes as dating gave young people much more independence than the calling system allowed. By providing young people more freedom, dating shifted the balance of power in courtship from parents to youth. Young people were less dependent on parental approval of their dates and were able to spend time with each other away from parental control.

Dating represented not only a generational shift in who controlled the process but a gender shift as well. Calling was firmly the purview of women: Calling took place in the domestic sphere—women's realm of influence—and men could not show up at a woman's home without an invitation. This gave women the initiative to decide whom to invite and when to invite him. Dating changed all this. Because dating took place in the public sphere, men were in charge. A man who invited women on dates was taking them into the masculine sphere, where he planned and paid for their activities. In essence, under the calling system, women were the hosts. With dating, that role shifted to men.

Dating emerged in a broader social context of growing sexual freedoms. The turn of the 20th century saw a retreat from Victorian ideals emphasizing sexual control and regulation to an "emphasis on using sex to achieve personal satisfaction, self-expression, and erotic pleasure" (Farrell, 1999, p. 71). Margaret Sanger and other activists crusaded for women's sexual autonomy by making contraception more readily available. Gay subcultures formed in urban centers, allowing gay men and lesbians a place to explore this emerging identity. Hollywood films and popular books and magazines portrayed sex and sexuality as a natural and healthy component of romantic attraction. Although the term *sexual revolution* is usually applied to the youth culture of the 1960s, the 1920s were equally revolutionary:

> By the 1920s, Americans were clearly entering a new sexual era . . . The new positive value attributed to the erotic, the growing autonomy of youth, the association of sex with commercialized leisure and self-expression, the pursuit of love, the visibility of the erotic in popular culture, the social interaction of men and women in public, the legitimation of female interest in the sexual: all of these were to be seen in America in the twenties. (D'Emilio & Freedman, 1988, p. 233)

© Camerique/ClassicStock/Corbis

By the 1950s, the most popular youth were those who had a steady boyfriend or girlfriend.

Although these trends were not as pervasive nor as explicit as they would become 40 years later (D'Emilio & Freedman, 1988), the seeds of sexual liberation were planted in the 1920s. This was the context in which dating emerged.

Dating was a perfect fit for the newly emerging focus on commercialized leisure in early 20th-century America. Leisure became an arena for carefree fun, self-expression, and freedom from work and family responsibilities. Dating, with its focus on commercialized fun and consumption in the public sphere, was a natural part of this new leisure environment. As Bailey (1988) explains, "All the polls and columns and books on dating . . . made abundantly clear that American youth did not consider spending time with a member of the opposite sex the same as dating. In almost all instances, a date centered around an act of consumption" (p. 58).

Dating's consumerist orientation also encouraged peer competition. Popularity for young people was measured by the number and variety of dates they had. The most popular men were those with material resources that they could use to date several different women. The most popular women were those who dated several popular men. As a result, men cultivated the appearance of affluence, and women cultivated an appearance of having a busy schedule of dates, to increase their popularity relative to their peers. Willard Waller's 1937 article in *American Sociological Review* describes this competitive process on a college campus as the **rating and dating complex**:

> [C]ompetition for dates among both men and women is extremely keen. . . . In order to have [a high] rating [young men] must belong to one of the better fraternities, be prominent in activities, have a copious supply of spending money, be well-dressed, "smooth" in manners and appearance, have a "good line," dance well, and have access to an automobile. . . . The factors which appear to be important for girls are good clothes, a smooth line, ability to dance well, and popularity as a date. The most important of these factors is the last, for the girl's prestige depends upon dating more than anything else; here as nowhere else nothing succeeds

like success. Therefore the clever coed contrives to give the impression of being much sought after even if she is not. It has been reported by many observers that a girl who is called to the telephone in the dormitories will often allow herself to be called several times, in order to give all the other girls ample opportunity to hear her paged. Coeds who wish campus prestige must never be available for last minute dates; they must avoid being seen too often with the same boy, in order that others may not be frightened away or discouraged; they must be seen when they go out, and therefore must go to the popular (and expensive) meeting places; they must have many partners at the dances. (p. 730)

One consequence of this competitive rating and dating complex was the way it enforced conformity to peer norms. Dating may have freed adolescents and young adults from parental control, but that parental control was quickly replaced by pressures to conform to peer expectations for popularity and status.

Popularity in the 1920s was based on how many different people one dated. By the 1940s, however, the criteria for popularity had shifted. With so many young men in the armed forces during World War II, eligible men were a scarce commodity. The dating economy had shifted so that the most popular women were now those who could secure one of those available men as a "steady." Instead of cultivating an active social life with a variety of dates, the young people who had a steady boyfriend or girlfriend were the most popular with their peers. This was a far cry from the situation 20 years earlier when going steady was stigmatized as it implied that you weren't good enough to attract attention from more than one person.

Decline of Dating and the Rise of Hookup Culture

The dating scripts that were dominant in the 20th century have given way to new forms of romantic and sexual behaviors for teens and young adults. The traditional heterosexual date, where a boy asks a girl out, picks her up, treats her to a movie or dinner, and takes her home at the end of the evening is no longer common. When these kinds of exchanges do occur, it is usually in the context of an already established romantic relationship rather than something you do to get to know someone new. Romantic relationships among teens and young adults often start more casually—hanging out, **hooking up**, and then sometimes becoming a couple. Although described as dating, it looks different from a 20th century date.

One of the defining features of contemporary romantic and sexual relationships for young adults is their ambiguity, which makes them difficult for social scientists to study. Some datasets have defined the relationships broadly (e.g., "when you like a guy [girl] and he [she] like you back") and others have defined them more narrowly (e.g., whether one currently has a special romantic relationship; Giordano, Manning, & Longmore, 2006). Giordano et al. (2006) argue that a broader definition is most useful because it captures the full range of both informal and formal romantic experiences that are meaningful for young people; the downside of this inclusivity is that it also means combining a variety of different experiences into a single category. When using a broad definition of romantic involvement, Giordano et al. found that 32 percent of 7th graders, 41 percent of 9th graders, and 59 percent of 11th graders in their sample were currently romantically involved. In comparison, the proportions of those who have a "special romantic relationship" are 17 percent, 32 percent, and 44 percent, respectively; these lower numbers reflect a narrower definition of romantic involvement. By the time they are 18 years old, almost 70 percent of boys and 76 percent of girls have had a recent romantic relationship (Carver, Joyner, & Udry, 2003).

Most young Americans have romantic and sexual relationships in high school. This can be more complicated, however, for young adults in immigrant families, particularly those whose parents are from cultures that do not practice dating. These youth often experience a clash between the American culture in which they were raised and the culture of origin for their families. These young adults report that their parents discourage or forbid dating, particularly outside of their ethnic or religious groups, and especially for daughters. Sons are given a bit more freedom as are younger siblings who come of age after parents have had more time to assimilate to American culture (Nesteruk & Gramescu, 2012). Yuying Tong (2013) found that more assimilated Asian American teens, as measured by household language use and generation status, were more likely to be sexually active than those who are less assimilated to American culture.

Sexual Debut Romantic relationships provide the context for most teens' first sexual experiences, which researchers refer to as **sexual debut**. About half of teenagers have sex during the high-school years (the median age for first intercourse is 18), and 75 percent of these teens have sex for the first time in the context of a dating relationship (Guttmacher Institute, 2014; Manning et al., 2006). Compared with teens in the 1990s, more of today's teens are older when they have sex for the first time; fewer have sex before age 15; more use contraception; and fewer teen girls become pregnant. Although the teen pregnancy rate is half of what it was at its peak in 1990, the United States still has one of the highest teen pregnancy rates in the developed world.

These data focus on sexual intercourse, but sexual activity can be defined more broadly. A significant proportion of teens have engaged in genital touching and/or oral sex with a partner (Rapsey & Murachver, 2006). For some teens, these activities are a substitute for vaginal intercourse; for most, it is a precursor or complement to intercourse. Although many youth are engaging in these sexual behaviors, they don't necessarily define them as having sex. In one survey of college students, more than 90 percent report having given or received oral sex, but only about one in five defined this behavior as having sex, about half as many young people who classified this as sex in 1991 (Hans, Gillen, & Akande, 2010).

The visibility of gay and lesbian relationships is increasing for youth as well as for adults.

Researchers are also starting to learn more about same-sex attraction and gay, lesbian, bisexual, and transgendered (**GLBT**) identities among adolescents. One challenge in studying these groups in the teen years is the fluidity of early sexual development. Some youth identify as GLBT from a young age, but for others, it is an identity that emerges later; evidence from one survey shows that the median age that GLBT adults first thought they were something other than straight is 12 years old (Pew Research Center, 2013b). There is also the question of how to define sexual minority status—should it be based on attraction, identity, and/or behavior? Youth may experience same-sex attraction or engage in sexual behavior with someone of the same sex but not identify as GLBT. Others may experience same-sex attraction or identify as GLBT but not have same-sex sexual experience. Because teens are still developing sexually, the lines between attraction, identity, and behavior are not always clear. Research has shown that most youth who identify as GLBT have experienced sexual activity with someone of the same sex; yet most, especially boys, also report sexual activity with members of the other sex (Collins, Welsh, & Furman, 2009).

Some evidence also suggests that gays and lesbians are **coming out**—being open about their sexual identity with family and friends—at younger ages than in the past. In a national survey of gay and lesbian adults, 43 percent were age 20 or older when they first came out, but for the adults younger than 30, two thirds had shared their sexual orientation before they were 20 years old (Pew Research Center, 2013b). Savin-Williams and Diamond (2000) found that, on average, young people came out around 18 years old. Although same-sex attraction and identity is becoming more visible in American culture, not all GLBT youth are safe or welcomed in their families and communities. For example, same-sex dating during adolescence is less common in areas where fewer gay, lesbian, and bisexual youth are out (Collins et al., 2009). In addition, sexual minority youth are at risk of bullying, harassment, and violence (Biblarz & Savci, 2010), and 40 percent of homeless youth identify as gay, lesbian, bisexual, or transgendered, far higher than their proportion in the general population (Durso & Gates, 2012).

Hooking Up Although most teens' first sexual encounters take place in the context of a romantic relationship, it is also true that three out of five teens who are sexually active have also had sex with partners whom they are not dating (Manning et al., 2006). This is common in college, too, with 71 percent of men and 70 percent of college women reporting that they have hooked up at least once by their senior year (Ford, England, & Bearak, 2015).

The term *hooking up* refers to sexual encounters that take place outside of, and with no expectation for, an exclusive or committed relationship. The phrase captures a range of sexual behaviors, from kissing to oral sex to intercourse. The ambiguity of the phrase is part of the appeal as it allows young people to share their experiences with friends without being too explicit (Bogle, 2008). The ambiguity is also a useful gender strategy to deal with the sexual double standard. Men can use the phrase to imply that they have had sex with their hookup partner, enhancing their reputation, whereas women can use the phrase to protect their sexual reputation as it could mean that she simply kissed her partner and did nothing more. In his survey of college students on two campuses, Jesse Owen, Galena Rhoades, Scott Stanley, and Frank Fincham (2010) found that hooking up was more common among White students, students who drink, and students who are from families with higher incomes, suggesting that hooking up is more common among more privileged students.

Most hookups, for both teens and young adults, take place with a friend, a former girlfriend or boyfriend, or someone they know pretty well, not with someone they have just met. Almost half of Manning et al.'s (2006) high-school sample hooked up with a friend, and another 14 percent hooked up with an ex-romantic partner. Less than a third hooked up with an acquaintance or someone they didn't know. Similarly, the Online College Social Life Survey (OCSLS) found that 46 percent of college students knew their most recent hookup partner moderately or very well and only 13 percent reported not knowing their partner at all (Ford et al., 2015).

The OCSLS, collected by sociologist Paula England and her colleagues, is a rich source of data on the sexual experiences of college students. England et al. collected data from more than 20,000 students at 21 colleges and universities to learn more about their sexual and romantic histories. These data show that even though hooking up is widespread, so are committed relationships: 66 percent of men and 74 percent of women have had a romantic relationship lasting at least six months by their senior year of college. In addition, most men and women are interested in pursuing a romantic relationship with their most recent hookup partner, although women are more likely than men to express this interest. Men, however, are more likely to initiate the DTR—the conversation to "define the relationship" and to transition to an exclusive dating partnership.

Despite fears to the contrary, hookup culture has not displaced dating. Most young people experience both.

Hookup culture is gendered in another way. Heterosexual hookups tend to be more focused on men's sexual pleasure than on women's: Men are almost three times as likely as women to have an orgasm in a hookup with a new partner (Armstrong, England, & Fogarty, 2012). In contrast, sex that takes place in the context of a heterosexual romantic relationship tends to include a wider variety of sexual behaviors, and as a result, women are more likely to have an orgasm in relationship sex than they are in hookups. Same-sex hookups, for both men and women, are the most reciprocal with both partners equally likely to have an orgasm (Ford et al., 2015).

Hookup culture is not only gendered, but it is shaped by social class as well. Laura Hamilton and Elizabeth Armstrong (2009) applied a class lens to the study of women's sexuality on college campuses. They found that women from privileged backgrounds were more interested in and involved with hookup culture, whereas women from working-class backgrounds were uninterested and excluded. By using what Hamilton and Armstrong describe as a "self-development logic," privileged women saw college as a time to focus on themselves—to meet new people, focus on their studies and career goals, and have fun. Romantic relationships were viewed as greedy—demanding a lot of time and energy—and were thus incompatible with this focus on self. Hooking up allowed women to enjoy sexual activity without the burdens of a romantic relationship.

Working-class students, in contrast, did not see romantic relationships and self-development as incompatible. Many expressed interest in marrying and having children during or immediately after college. The college years were a time to grow up and settle down, not to postpone the responsibilities of adulthood by "sleeping around," as one respondent put it (Hamilton & Armstrong, 2009, p. 607). Because "college culture reflects the beliefs of the more privileged classes" (p. 606), working-class students were alienated from the self-development logic and hookup culture that surrounded them. Instead, they were pulled toward high-school friends and boyfriends, who were ready to settle down, and pulled away from college life. Less privileged women in Hamilton and Armstrong's sample were eight times more likely than more privileged women to drop out of college, and the mismatch between their own sexual and romantic goals and that of the college culture was one influential factor in their decision to leave.

Change, Continuity, and Diversity in the Transition to Adulthood

Like other family patterns, today's transition to adulthood is characterized by many changes. But there are also linkages between today's patterns and those of the past. For example, the semidependent economic relationship between young adults and parents during the transition is similar to what was common prior to the 20th century. Although the transition today starts later than it did then, for example, after one graduates from high school rather than in the early teens, its length and purpose (to gain financial stability) would have been familiar to those living more than 100 years ago. One contextual factor that shapes this continuity is the expansion of education. In the 1900s, adolescents started to become more dependent on parents because more of them attended high school. Similarly, today's 18- to 22-year-olds are more dependent on parents because more of them attend college. And early marriage and childrearing has not completely disappeared; in some rural towns, this is still the most typical transition to adulthood. This emphasizes the fact that young adults in different social locations experience the transition differently.

Where we see the biggest change is in youth's growing sexual and romantic independence. Parents in nonimmigrant families have little explicit influence on who young people date or become romantically involved with. As the stigma around nonmarital sexual activity has declined, youth have more sexual experience and are more likely to cohabit than marry when they are ready to form a co-residential union. More privileged youth start thinking about marriage and childbearing in the late 20s after they have gotten established in their careers. Less privileged youth are more likely to have children with their cohabiting partners in their early 20s. The next chapter explores these patterns in more detail.

MAIN IDEAS

- The transition to adulthood is a prolonged and uncertain time of life and varies by young people's social location.

- Before the 20th century, the transition to adulthood started in the early teens and lasted up to 10 years. In the 20th century, adolescents became dependent on their parents, and the transition to adulthood did not begin until one graduated from high school and tended to last only a few years.

- Today, the transition to adulthood is shaped by economic uncertainty; expansion of higher education; delayed marriage; and semidependent relationships with parents into the mid-20s.

- Young adults are increasingly independent in their sexual and romantic relationships, starting with the shift from calling to dating and continuing today with hookup culture.

CHAPTER

5

Marriage and Cohabitation

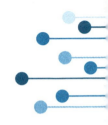

In 2010, *TIME* magazine asked, "Who Needs Marriage?" (Luscombe, 2010). Around the same time, research reports described the "Decline in Marriage" (Pew Research Center, 2010) and what happens "When Marriage Disappears" (The National Marriage Project, 2010). These headlines reflect public concern about changing marriage patterns. In 2014, the median age of marriage was at a historical high of 29 for men and 27 for women. More than forty percent of births are to unmarried mothers. Many couples—almost 8 million in 2014— are living together without being married, and the United States has one of the highest divorce rates in the world.

But I can point to other patterns to demonstrate the continuing importance of marriage in U.S. culture. Only 8 percent of American woman older than age 45 have never been married. Most Americans believe marriage is the ideal place to raise children. Even people who have divorced remain committed to marriage, with the majority remarrying within a few years. And activists fought for more than 20 years to legalize same-sex marriage. If marriage were no longer important, there would be no reason for this fight.

In his book *The Marriage-Go-Round* (2009), sociologist Andrew Cherlin argues that America is unique in that we embrace two competing cultural models: a **culture of marriage** and a **culture of individualism**. The culture of marriage valorizes marriage as the ideal way to live one's life, sees divorce as a last resort, and thinks that marriage is best for everyone—men, women, and children. Many cultures share these values, but what makes the United States unique is that we simultaneously celebrate a culture of individualism. This individualism celebrates independence, autonomy, being true to oneself, and standing on one's own two feet, values that can undermine marital stability. As a result of these two cultural models, the United States has among the highest marriage rates and the highest divorce rates in the industrialized world.

We live in a paradoxical time. As the practical significance of marriage has declined, its symbolic importance has increased. No longer taken for granted as the only way to achieve adult status or to have a family, marriage has become the ultimate status symbol, a marker of relationship and personal success. It is a capstone rather than a cornerstone (Cherlin, 2004). Instead of a way to begin one's adult life, it is something we enter into only after reaching other milestones, such as finishing our education, getting established in jobs or careers, and paying off debt. Unfortunately, these milestones have become increasingly difficult for Americans with fewer resources to attain, particularly those who lack a college education and who work low-paying jobs. Although marriage is highly valued by all segments of the population, economic instability frequently gets in the way of its achievement.

This chapter focuses on marriage and cohabitation. But you will notice that divorce comes up quite a bit as well. Many people think that marriage and divorce are opposing forces, one working against the other. But we can also look at marriage and divorce as two sides of the same coin. It is our high expectations about marriage and about what it means to live happily ever after that contribute to our high rates of divorce. And fear of divorce contributes to delaying marriage or avoiding marriage all together. To understand why our divorce rates are so high—and why so many couples are living together and having children without getting married—we must understand the interrelationships among marriage, cohabitation, and divorce. Thus, this chapter will make connections when appropriate, and divorce and relationship dissolution will be explored in more detail in the next chapter.

Marriage and Divorce in Historical Context

Marriage exists in a social context. As the conditions of that context change, so does marriage. Far from a constant, the meaning and role of marriage has shifted throughout history. Early Christian theologians saw marriage as a necessary evil, to be entered into only by men who lacked the fortitude to remain celibate. In colonial America, many marriages were informal, lacking the blessing of church or government: "In 1786, an Anglican minister, Rev. Henry Addison, stated, 'If the rule was Established here that no marriage should be deemed valid that had not been registered in the Parish Book it would I am persuaded bastardize nine tenths of the People in the Country'" (Walsh, 1979, p. 130). Today, we would refer to these "unregistered marriages" as cohabitation.

Scholars who study the history of marriage in the United States have identified three types of marriage, each of which arose in a specific economic, demographic, and cultural context. It is useful to use theorist Max Weber's **ideal type** framework to understand these three categories. An ideal type is a way to describe characteristics of a construct or phenomenon. Weber uses the word "ideal" not to mean perfect or best but in the sense of ideas, constructs, abstract ways of thinking about a phenomenon. We can use this ideal type framework to classify three broad types of marriage, each of which existed in different historical periods. No marriage comprises every one of the characteristics, but these general characteristics typify the construct of marriage in these three eras.

Institutional Marriage

Institutional marriage characterized American marriages before industrialization and was built on economic necessity, familial and community obligation, and social regulations. Nineteenth-century marriage manuals described a sound marriage as one "based on being religious, industrious, and healthy, and sex is for the purpose of procreation only. Women are advised to seek a husband who values home life and has good morals and then to obey him and be hardworking and good tempered" (Cancian, 1987, p. 29). Although spouses often felt affection and care for each other, romantic love as we know it was not central to the decision of who to marry; love was more of a by-product of a happy marriage than a foundation for it. And, even then, it was a love based on familial duty more than on romantic intimacy (Cancian, 1987). In fact, some argued that romantic love was a threat to successful marriage; following your heart instead of your head could lead you to choose a mate that lacked the thrift and industriousness that were the most valued characteristics in a spouse. One's spouse was expected to be a helpmate, not a soul mate. Divorce during this era was highly restricted and rare. The colonies allowed divorce in the cases of adultery and desertion primarily as a way to reestablish community order and allow the aggrieved party to remarry since unmarried households were discouraged. In the rare cases of divorce, custody of children was awarded to the father.

Unlike many other cultures in which arranged marriages were (and are) common, young people of European descent in the colonies and young republic chose their mates from a limited pool of potential partners of similar age and social status in their own or nearby communities. They were not free to choose whomever they wanted, however, as parents were also involved in finding suitable matches. Young people were dependent on parental approval to secure the economic foundation they needed to form their own household, a level of parental involvement much higher than what would be acceptable to most Americans today.

The legal rights of women in institutional marriage were nonexistent. As you learned in the first chapter, marriages were based on the legal doctrine of coverture, in which "the very being or legal existence of the woman is suspended during the marriage, or at least is incorporated and consolidated into that of the husband" (Blackstone, 1765/1979, p. 430). Women could not own property, could not sign contracts, and were required to live with their husbands (Coltrane, 1998). Husbands were allowed to discipline their wives physically to encourage obedience and subordination. Women's sexuality was considered the property of their husbands, and husbands had the right to have sex with them whenever they desired it. Feminist activists in the 19th century challenged coverture laws, arguing that for women to be recognized as equal citizens, they needed to be able to retain rights over their personhood, physical bodies, and property. Over the next century, these laws were repealed, although as you learned in Chapter 1, their ideology lives on in marital naming practices.

Companionate Marriage

As the United States industrialized and urbanized over the course of the 19th century, marriage became more companionate. **Companionate marriage** was based on the emotional ties between wife and husband—"their companionship, friendship, romantic love, and sex life" (Cherlin, 2009, p. 68). Instead of being viewed as a threat to, or by-product of, marriage, romantic love became its foundation. Couples expected to find happiness in their marriages by

© Camerique/ClassicStock/Corbis

Companionate marriage reached its peak in the mid-20th century.

building an emotionally meaningful partnership with each other and by fulfilling their distinct roles as husbands and wives. A husband's breadwinning role was seen as a complement to his wife's role as caregiver. Although both husband and wife were expected to provide emotional support to and understanding for each other, women were considered the experts on love. They were responsible for creating successful marriages by making themselves attractive, interesting, and pleasant partners (Cancian, 1987).

What brought about this shift? The 19th and early 20th centuries were turbulent times in the United States. The economy was shifting from an agricultural to an industrial base. People were leaving farms and moving to growing cities. Immigration rates were high, and immigrants were arriving from a host of new countries, including Italy, China, and Russia. Internal migration was also high with millions of African Americans leaving the South and settling throughout the country. All of this movement not only brought greater numbers to American cities, it also diversified them.

By the 1920s, increased economic security, expansion of consumer culture, and the increasingly visible youth culture based in public high schools, which you learned about in the previous chapter, had set the stage for the growing importance of romantic love. Young people became more independent in their romantic lives, and courtship moved "from front porch to back seat" (Bailey, 1988). By spending time alone, couples were able to evaluate their romantic compatibility and consider marriage only *after* they had fallen in love. Romantic love had become a prerequisite for marriage.

One consequence of these changing ideas about marriage was an increase in the divorce rate. As we'll discuss more in the next chapter, divorce rates in the United States started rising in the late 19th century just as romantic love became the foundation for marriage. It turns out that critics of love-based marriage were right to warn against the dangers of love. For as satisfying as love can be, it is also a less stable foundation for marriage than are economic necessity and familial and social obligation. Love and passion can fade. And when they do, in a social context where they are seen as necessary to a successful marriage, divorce becomes a logical outcome.

Individualized Marriage

Companionate marriage thrived until the final decades of the 20th century when **individualized marriage** started to grow. Now, we judge the success of our marriages by how happy and fulfilled we are as individuals within them. Of course, this does not mean that romantic love and family responsibility are no longer important. But it does mean that those things matter only to the extent that we feel personally fulfilled by them. We have high expectations for our marriages, expecting our spouse to be "the one"—the one person in the world who can meet our emotional, social, sexual, financial, spiritual, and interpersonal needs.

Here's how historian Stephanie Coontz (2005) describes contemporary marriage:

> First, [spouses] must love each other deeply and choose each other unswayed by outside pressure. From then on, each must make the partner the top priority in life, putting that relationship above any and all competing ties. A husband and wife, we believe, owe their highest obligations and deepest loyalties to each other and the marriage. Married couples should be best friends, sharing their most intimate feelings and secrets. They should express affection openly but also talk candidly about problems. And of course they should be sexually faithful to each other. (p. 20)

These expectations create a high bar for marital success, and they contribute to both the delay in marriage (young people are waiting to find "the one") and the divorce rate because when these expectations are not met, we are encouraged to find a new partner who will meet them.

Ray Laskowitz/Getty Images

Today's couples are searching for a soul mate, a much higher standard for a spouse than in earlier generations.

Contemporary Coupling

As marriages became more companionate in the 19th century, no one would have predicted that it would set the stage for individuals to seek emotional and sexual satisfaction outside of the marital bond. But, by the end of the 20th century, this is exactly what happened. The seeds that were planted in companionate marriage, celebrating love, passion, and romance, soon spread beyond marital confines. Nonmarital sexual activity increased as sex was redefined, culturally and legally, as a private matter between consenting adults. Court cases removed legal proscriptions against contraception for married couples in 1965 and for all couples in 1972; these cases argued that the government had no right to interfere in the private lives of citizens. *Roe v. Wade*, the Supreme Court case that legalized abortion in 1973, is based on this same legal argument: Sexual and reproductive decision making lies in the hands of individuals, not communities nor the state. This legal logic was further extended to same-sex couples in 2003 when the Supreme Court ruled in *Lawrence v. Texas* that anti-sodomy laws were unconstitutional. Thus, by the early 21st century, the privatization of sexual activity that began 100 years earlier had become codified.

It is in this changing context of privacy and individual choice that the links between marriage, sex, and reproduction were weakened, leading to three major family changes that took hold in the late 20th century and continue today: (1) increases in nonmarital cohabitation; (2) rising nonmarital fertility; and (3) the legal recognition and growing acceptance of same-sex marriage.

Cohabitation

The rise in nonmarital cohabitation has been one of the most dramatic and unexpected family changes we have seen in the last 40 years. It went from rare to commonplace in a generation. There were about 1.5 million heterosexual cohabiting households in 1980, which increased to about 4.0 million households in 2000 and to 7.9 million in 2014. Cohabitation has become the normative way to begin a co-residential union. For every couple that married between 1997 and 2001, two moved in together without getting married, and 62 percent of women 19 to 44 years of age cohabited before their first marriage (Kennedy & Fitch, 2012). Between 2006 and 2010, more than three quarters of new unions were cohabiting relationships, not marriage (Manning, Brown, & Payne, 2014).

Although cohabitation has become commonplace, not everyone approves of it. Figure 5.1 shows the percentage of Americans who agree that it is okay for couples to live together without intending to get married. In 1994, more than half of people younger than age 50 thought this was okay, but approval

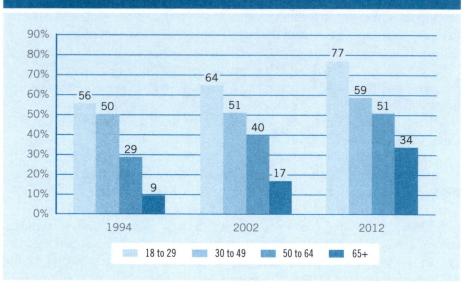

Figure 5.1   Approval of Cohabitation

90%
80%   77
70%   64
60%   56   59
50%   50   51   51
40%   40
30%   29   34
20%   17
10%   9
0%
        1994   2002   2012

        ▢ 18 to 29   ▢ 30 to 49   ▢ 50 to 64   ▢ 65+

Source: Smith, Marsden, & Hout, 2015.

was much lower among those aged 50 and older. In more recent years, these age differences have persisted even as the overall approval of cohabitation has increased for all age groups. Yet, even in 2012, almost one in four adults younger than age 30 do not think it is okay for couples to live together if they do not intend to get married. These young people are more likely to describe themselves as very religious and to live in the South.

As cohabitation has become more common, researchers have spent a lot of time trying to figure out what it means for families. High-quality data on cohabitation became available only in the late 1980s, and patterns of cohabitation have continued to change rapidly since then. In fact, researchers are still trying to figure out how to measure this phenomenon appropriately. Researchers have discovered that surveys that ask people if they are living with an unmarried partner, a typical way to ask about cohabitation, tend to miss a lot of cohabiting couples (Manning & Smock, 2005). Many respondents don't use that language to apply to their relationship. They are living with a boyfriend or girlfriend or fiancé(e), not with an unmarried partner. Similarly, many of the national level datasets that measure cohabitation only recently started counting unmarried couples who are living with other adults, such as parents or housemates, as cohabitors (Kennedy & Fitch, 2012), suggesting that earlier figures may underestimate the frequency of cohabitation.

Making sense of cohabitation is like taking aim at a moving target. But even with that caveat, we can identify four trends in cohabitation that help us understand its role in contemporary families. First, although cohabitation has increased among all segments of the population, it is more common with some than others. Women with less education and lower income are more likely to cohabit than are more educated and higher income women (Manning, 2013). Those who are more religious and have more traditional ideas about gender and family are less likely to cohabit (Lehrer, 2004; Smock, 2000). Younger generations are more likely than older generations to have cohabitation experience, but the rate of cohabitation is increasing fastest among the oldest Americans (Manning, 2013).

Second, couples choose to live together for a variety of reasons. For some, it is a stage in the dating process. For others, it is a step toward marriage. For a small minority, it is a long-term alternative to marriage. Understanding why couples cohabit is more complex than it appears at first blush. The term itself encompasses a diversity of couples, from young college students sharing a room in a parental home to a widow living with, but not marrying, her partner so as to avoid losing her late husband's pension. Some couples move in together relatively quickly as one partner's lease is up early in a new relationship, and others take their time, sharing a household only after a long-term commitment has been made.

Another challenge is that many couples don't make an explicit decision to live together. Instead, it happens gradually, sometimes imperceptibly, what Wendy Manning and Pamela Smock (2005) call a "slide" into cohabitation. For example, one of their respondents described the beginning of her cohabiting relationship like this: "[H]e had come over, . . . he had spent the night and then from then on he had stayed the night, so basically he ended up staying there, he just never went home, he just honestly never went home" (p. 134). Another respondent said, "She stayed at my house more and more from spending the night once to not going home to her parents' house for a week at a time and then you know . . . so there was no official starting date. I did take note when the frilly fufu soaps showed up in my bathroom that she'd probably moved in at that point" (p. 135).

When asked, couples report both emotional and financial reasons for living together. Emotionally, it is a way to spend more time together and to move a dating relationship to a more serious stage. Financially, cohabitation offers a way to share household expenses. Partners don't necessarily have a common understanding of why they are living together and what the future of the relationship might be. Penelope Huang, Pamela Smock, Wendy Manning, and Cara Bergstrom-Lynch (2011) found that women were more likely to view cohabitation as a step toward marriage or at least as a way of testing compatibility for marriage, whereas men were more likely to report on the financial and sexual benefits of cohabitation.

A third trend in cohabitation is that the outcomes of cohabiting relationships—to break up, marry, or continue cohabiting—have changed over time. The link between cohabitation and marriage has weakened in that fewer couples transition to marriage than in the past. In fact, it is now more common for cohabiting couples to break up than to marry (Lichter, Qian, & Mellott, 2006). Few couples cohabit for more than a few years, although long-term cohabitation is more common among poor women than it is for women with more financial resources. The declining link between cohabitation and marriage has led to an increase in **serial cohabitation** when people cohabit with a series of partners in relatively short-term and unstable unions. Although serial cohabitation is on the rise, a minority of cohabiting women (25 percent) experience it, and they are concentrated among women who are the most economically disadvantaged (Lichter, Turner, & Sassler, 2010).

Finally, the relationship between cohabitation and divorce has also changed over time. The first waves of research on cohabitation in the 1980s and early 1990s found, counter-intuitively, that couples who lived together before marrying had a higher risk of divorce. How could this be? If cohabitation provided an arena to test marital compatibility, wouldn't cohabitation make divorce *less* likely? This surprising finding has been explained in two ways. One focuses on the *experience* of cohabitation as a risk factor for divorce. This argument suggests that cohabitation undermines marital stability by changing people's attitudes about the permanence of relationships (Axinn & Thornton, 1992). It reinforces individualism and makes breaking up a more acceptable option for an unhappy relationship. A second explanation focuses on *selection*—compared with couples who got married without cohabiting, couples who lived together first were less committed, had lower relationship quality, and had sociodemographic characteristics that increased the likelihood of divorce, such as lower levels of income and education. In addition, the most traditional couples, who are less likely to divorce, were more likely to marry without cohabiting first. Thus, the selection argument says that it is not cohabitation that raised the risk of divorce, but the characteristics of individuals who cohabited that created the effect.

More recent research on this question has challenged this link between cohabitation and divorce. Now that cohabitation has become normative, its effects on marital stability are limited. Women who have cohabited only with their future spouse and not with other partners are at no higher risk of divorce

(Teachman, 2003). In addition, Kuperberg (2014) finds that the link between cohabitation and divorce can be explained by the relatively young age at which cohabitors move in together. Couples who began living together at older ages have dissolution rates similar to those of couples who did not cohabit.

Nonmarital Fertility

Like sharing a household with a romantic partner, reproduction is also no longer confined to marriage. More than 43 percent of births between 2005 and 2010 were to unmarried mothers (Payne, Manning, & Brown, 2012). Although often referred to as single, most of these unmarried women—57 percent—are living in cohabiting relationships at the time of birth (Payne et al., 2012). Figure 5.2 shows how nonmarital childbearing varies by education level. More than half of women with a high-school degree or less are unmarried when they have their children, compared with only nine percent of those with a college degree.

Forty percent of cohabiting couples have children in their households (Kennedy & Fitch, 2012), and about half of those households include biological children of both partners. In 2013, seven percent of children were currently living with cohabiting parents (Payne, 2013), although it is estimated that many more than this will live with cohabiting parents at some point during their childhoods. Children living with cohabiting parents are at higher risk of experiencing negative outcomes, including lower academic achievement and behavioral

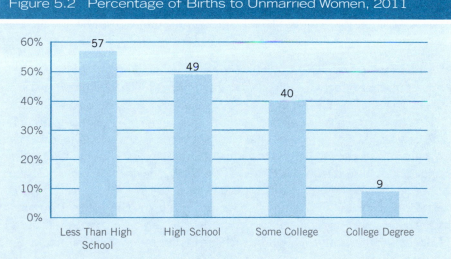

Figure 5.2 Percentage of Births to Unmarried Women, 2011

Source: Shattuck & Kreider, 2013.

challenges (Rose-Greenland & Smock, 2013). This is largely explained by the lower socioeconomic status of these families, as well as by their relative instability (Brown, 2004). By age 10, more than 60 percent of children born into cohabiting relationships will experience parental relationship disruption, compared with less than 30 percent for children born into marriage (Manning, Smock, & Majumdar, 2004).

More recent research (Musick & Michelmore, 2015) has found that relationship instability is especially high for cohabiting couples with children who never marry. Couples with no cohabitation history who had their first child when married; couples who cohabited and then had their first birth in marriage; and couples who had their first birth during cohabitation and later married all had similarly low rates of relationship dissolution. It was the cohabiting couples who had children and never married that were the most unstable. Thus, the children in these relationships are the ones most at risk of negative outcomes, which you will learn more about in the next chapter.

Why are these parents choosing not to get married? Economic uncertainty is a big part of the story. As one of Pamela Smock, Wendy Manning, and Meredith Porter's (2005) respondents put it, "Everything's there except money" (p. 687). Unmarried parents hope and plan to marry, but they also want to be financially stable before taking on the long-term commitment that marriage requires. Changes in the economy, including stagnant wages and the disappearance of manufacturing jobs, mean that financial stability is increasingly difficult for workers without a college degree to achieve. Kristen Harknett and Arielle Kuperberg (2011) estimate that if less educated parents had the same favorable labor market conditions as more educated parents, they would marry at similar rates.

In her interviews with almost 300 low-income single mothers of various racial-ethnic backgrounds, researcher Kathryn Edin (2000) identifies five reasons why they are choosing not to get married. The first one is affordability. Low-income women have children with low-income men. When the men cannot bring in a steady income, women are reluctant to marry them as it increases their financial burden to have to take care of him as well as the children. As one respondent said, "I can do bad by myself" (p. 119), she doesn't need a husband in an equally precarious economic situation. By not marrying, she leaves open the possibility of finding a partner who is more economically stable. A second reason single mothers don't get married is the high value they place on marriage. This seems counterintuitive, but the high expectations they have for marriage— the personal, interpersonal, and financial prerequisites for marriage—are difficult for low-income couples to achieve. They believe that marriage is a sacred

Legal arguments for same-sex marriage emphasized the role of love in contemporary marriages.

commitment that should last forever; if they are not 100 percent sure that they will be able to make a lifelong commitment, they won't marry. Why get married just to get divorced, they asked.

Third, many women that Edin (2000) interviewed were afraid that becoming a wife would require deference to their husband, a deference they were unwilling to provide. They were justifiably proud of their hard work in financially supporting and raising their children, and they were afraid that a husband would get in the way of this independence. Fourth, high levels of infidelity and mistrust between mothers and their partners means they are wary about making a lifelong commitment. Finally, interpersonal violence was also common, and women would not marry someone who was abusive. As much as the women in Edin's study hoped and planned for marriage, their uncertain life circumstances put this goal out of reach. Instead, they focused their family lives on their children, rather than on a romantic partner.

Same-Sex Marriage

In 1970, Richard Baker and James Michael McConnell were denied a marriage license by a county clerk in Minnesota. The courts upheld that denial. Twenty-three years later, the issue of same-sex marriage returned to national consciousness when the Hawaiian Supreme Court ruled that denying same-sex couples the right to marry violated the Equal Protection Clause of the Hawaii Constitution. For the first time in history, legally recognized same-sex marriage in a U.S. state became a real possibility. In response, Congress passed and President Bill Clinton signed the 1996 Defense of Marriage Act (DOMA). This law defined marriage as a union between one man and one woman and did not require states to recognize same-sex marriages enacted in other jurisdictions. No same-sex marriages were ever enacted in Hawaii as Hawaiian voters amended their constitution to forbid it. Many other states followed suit. Same-sex couples continued to challenge these bans, and in 2004, Massachusetts became the first U.S. state to allow same-sex marriage. It had been legal in the Netherlands, the first nation to legalize same-sex marriage, since 2000.

By the time that the U.S. Supreme Court struck down DOMA in June 2013, 12 states and the District of Columbia had already begun licensing same-sex marriages. In deciding that DOMA was unconstitutional, the Court paved the way for federal recognition of same-sex marriages. This meant that same-sex couples could now file their federal taxes together, receive Social Security and military survivorship benefits, and apply for a green card. Two years later, the Supreme Court heard another set of cases to decide whether state-level bans on same-sex marriage were also unconstitutional. In June 2015, they ruled 5–4 that

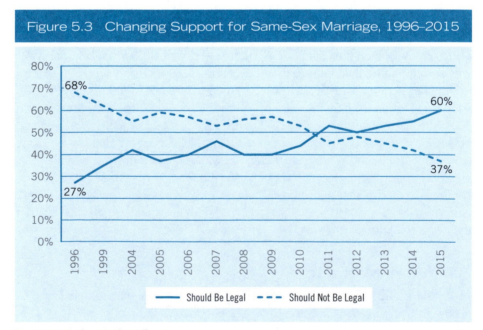

Figure 5.3 Changing Support for Same-Sex Marriage, 1996–2015

Source: McCarthy, 2015b. Gallup, Inc.

the bans were unconstitutional and that all states must perform and recognize same-sex marriages.

The pace of change in the public's approval for same-sex marriage has been extraordinary (Figure 5.3). In 1996, when DOMA was passed, only 27 percent of Americans thought that same-sex marriage should be legal. Less than 20 years later in 2015, that percentage more than doubled to 60 percent. This change can be explained in two ways. One is an attitude change on the individual level; for example, an individual who disapproved of same-sex marriage in 1996 now approves of it in 2015. The other way attitudinal change takes place is with **cohort or generational replacement**. This process describes a shift in the overall population—as older people with more conservative ideas die, they are replaced in the adult population by younger, less conservative people. On this issue especially, age is very important (Figure 5.4). In 2015, 76 percent of Americans younger than age 30 supported same-sex marriage, which is significantly more than any other age group. Even in 1996, the youngest Americans were more likely to approve.

The growing acceptance of same-sex marriage is consistent with our individualized ideas about marriage and romantic relationships. If marriage is about personal commitment and love, as most Americans believe, then two adults who feel this

Figure 5.4 Support for Same-Sex Marriage, by Age

Source: Jones, 2013; McCarthy, 2015b. Gallup, Inc.

commitment and love should be able to marry, regardless of gender. As California Chief Justice Ronald M. George wrote in his decision to strike down the state's Proposition 8 banning same-sex marriage, "The right to marry represents the *right of an individual* to establish a legally recognized family *with a person of one's choice* and, as such, is of fundamental significance both to society and to the individual" (Liptak, 2013, emphases added). Although some have argued that same-sex marriage is a dramatic turn away from traditional ideas about marriage, it is much less dramatic when we consider it in context: Same-sex marriage is perfectly consistent with contemporary ideas about the role of love and marriage in individual lives, ideas that have been part of American culture for more than 100 years.

Marriage Markets

Although we tend to think about falling in love as an individual and a personal thing—which, of course, it is—there are also clear structural patterns in whom we partner with and marry. On the most basic level, we cannot begin a relationship with someone we have never met, so to the extent that our social circles are limited by geography, education, age, and race, our pool of potential romantic partners will be limited as well. This is a major reason why homogamy—partnering with others with characteristics similar to ourselves—is so common.

Social scientists use the term **marriage market** to understand the structural patterns that shape our romantic choices (and although the term focuses on marriage, it can be used to understand other kinds of romantic partnerships as well). The marriage market analogy likens the search for a romantic partner to the search for a job in the labor market. The market has a pool of available jobs (partners) of varying levels of desirability to which one can apply (meet or date). One's success in finding a good fit depends on the number of jobs (partners) available, the kinds of jobs (partners) available, and the resources (desirable characteristics) that one brings to the search. Just as a job seeker with resources such as a college degree and relevant work experience is more desirable to employers, someone with desirable romantic characteristics like good looks, steady income, and emotional intelligence will be a more sought-after romantic partner. It also means that no matter how desirable one may be, if the pool of available partners is limited, one will have a harder time finding a mate, just as a well-qualified person has a harder time finding a job in a tight economy. This is referred to as a **marriage squeeze**.

Although marriage markets have always been present, the analogy has become more explicit in recent years with online dating and dating apps. Here, the dating sites are the marketplace in which individuals exchange their resources for their preferred characteristics in a partner. The main benefit of online dating sites is that they extend the pool of potential partners beyond those you would run into in your regular social circles. In theory, online dating should reduce homogamy because it makes it easier to search for partners whose characteristics differ from one's own, people you would be unlikely to cross paths with in offline life. Some research (Rosenfeld & Thomas, 2012) has shown that interreligious couples are more likely than same-religion couples to have met online, reinforcing the idea that online dating may reduce homogamy. However, other research on online dating has shown that most people end up messaging and meeting partners who are pretty similar to themselves in terms of race, education level, and religion (Hitsch, Hortaçsu, & Ariely, 2010). Groups that do seem to benefit from the expanded pool offered by online dating are those who are in a thin market (Rosenfeld & Thomas, 2012), meaning that few potential partners are available. This is the case for middle-aged heterosexuals, most of whom are already partnered and thus unavailable for new relationships, and gays and lesbians, who make up a small minority of the population. For these groups, the expansion of the dating and marriage market provided by dating sites and apps minimizes the marriage squeeze and increases their likelihood of finding a partner.

Marriage, Cohabitation, and Education

It has always been the case that individuals marry others who are similar to themselves in terms of race and ethnicity, religion, education, and social background. Over time, however, certain characteristics have become less important in how we find a mate and others have become more important. Racial homogamy continues to be the norm in the United States, although racial intermarriage is becoming more common. Religious homogamy has declined as fewer Americans affiliate with a specific religious denomination throughout their adult lives. Educational homogamy, however, is on the upswing. Since 1960, spouses have become more educationally similar, from 45 percent of marriages in 1960 to 55 percent in 2003 (Schwartz & Mare, 2005). In addition, fewer couples today cross more than one educational category, such as a college graduate marrying someone with only a high-school degree.

Figure 5.5 shows the percentage of Americans who are currently married by educational attainment. There are several trends to note. First, between 1960 and 2008, the percentage married in all education categories declined. Second,

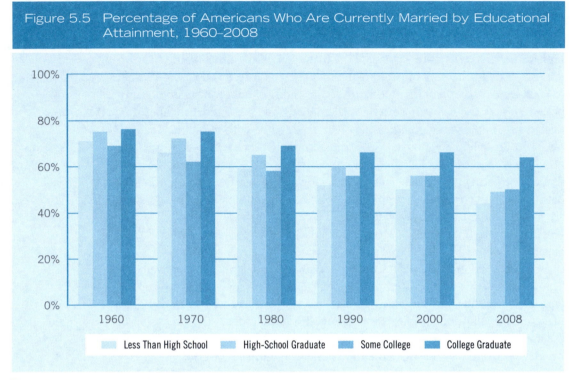

Figure 5.5 Percentage of Americans Who Are Currently Married by Educational Attainment, 1960–2008

Less Than High School   High-School Graduate   Some College   College Graduate

Source: Pew Research Center, 2010.

in all years, college graduates are more likely to be married than those with less education. However, we can also see that the gap between the education groups has grown larger between 1960 and 2008. In 1960, there was only a seven percentage point gap between the highest and lowest education levels. In 2008, the gap was 20 percentage points. Finally, we can also see that the decline in the share married is less steep for college graduates than for everyone else.

We see similar patterns in the relationship between education and divorce. Figure 5.6 shows the percentage of women divorced before their 10th anniversary (the period in which most divorces take place) by education and marriage cohort (marriage cohort refers to the time period in which the women got married; for example, the 1960–1964 marriage cohort is made up of women who got married between 1960 and 1964). We see that across cohorts, women without a college degree have become more likely to divorce today than they were in the past. However, for women with a college degree, the percentage who divorce has *declined* since 1975–1979. For the 1975–1979

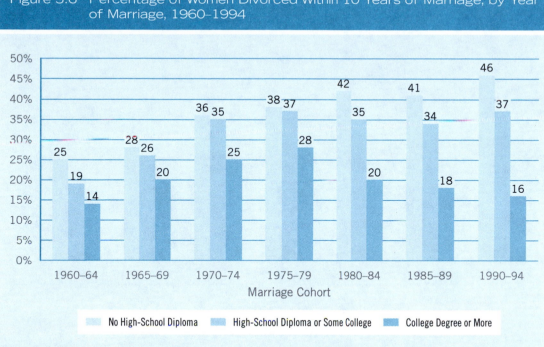

Figure 5.6 Percentage of Women Divorced Within 10 Years of Marriage, by Year of Marriage, 1960–1994

Marriage Cohort

■ No High-School Diploma   ■ High-School Diploma or Some College   ■ College Degree or More

Source: Martin, 2006.

marriage cohort, 28 percent of those with a college degree divorced within 10 years; by the 1990–1994 cohort, only 16 percent divorced within 10 years. That is 65 percent fewer than those without a high-school diploma, and only two points higher than for those married in 1960 to 1964.

Trends in nonmarital cohabitation by education level show similar patterns: less education, more cohabitation. Figure 5.7 shows the percentage of women aged 19–44 who have ever cohabited, from 1987 to 2009–2010. In all years, less educated women are more likely to have cohabitation experience. In addition, although cohabitation has become more common for women in all educational groups, the increase is larger for women without a college degree. More educated cohabiters are also more likely to marry their partners. The probability that a first cohabitation will transition to marriage within three years is highest for women with a Bachelor's degree (64%) and lowest for women without a high-school diploma or GED (37%). Similarly, less educated women have a higher probability that their cohabitation will remain intact for three years or more (Goodwin, Mosher, & Chandra, 2010).

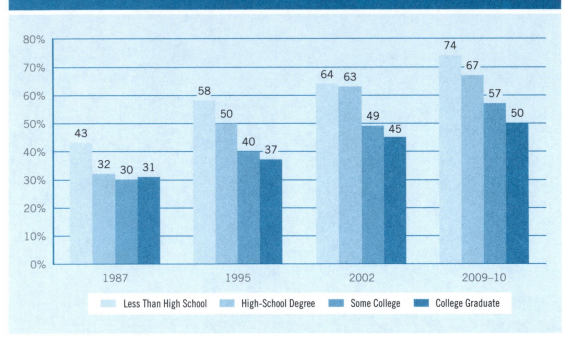

Figure 5.7   Percentage of Women Aged 18–44 Who Have Ever Cohabited, 1987–2010

1987: 43, 32, 30, 31
1995: 58, 50, 40, 37
2002: 64, 63, 49, 45
2009–10: 74, 67, 57, 50

Legend: Less Than High School · High-School Degree · Some College · College Graduate

Source: Manning, 2013.

Marriage, Cohabitation, and Race-Ethnicity

Because race and ethnicity are linked so closely with other important social characteristics, including education level, social class, and neighborhood, they also shape how we form romantic relationships and with whom. Consider marriage rates; in 2013, 30 percent of African Americans were currently married, compared with 43 percent of Latinos, 54 percent of Whites, and 57 percent of Asian Americans (U.S. Census Bureau, 2014c). Sociologists try to understand these differences by looking at social structure—how do these different marriage patterns reflect the different social locations that racial-ethnic groups occupy in American society?

Consider Asian Americans, for example. One reason that a higher proportion of Asian Americans are married is because they are more likely than other Americans to have a college degree. In addition, compared with Whites and African Americans, a higher proportion of Asian Americans are foreign born or second generation, which means they are influenced by the practices of their families' countries of origin, which have higher expectations for marriage than in the United States. In fact, when broken down by nativity, 67% of foreign-born Asian Americans are married, compared with only 35% of native-born Asian Americans. Age is part of the story as well, as the native-born Asian American population is younger than that of the foreign-born population, which means that marital differences between these groups partly reflect delayed rather than foregone marriage; many of these younger people will eventually marry (Pew Research Center, 2013a).

Age, nativity, education: As you can see, the simple question of marriage rates by race quickly gets complicated by the intersection of race with other sociodemographic characteristics. Oversimplified explanations for racial differences in marriage often look to cultural values without considering the role of structure. For example, some critics decry the low rates of marriage among African Americans as a cultural defect—African Americans do not value marriage. Instead, we can see how structural conditions shape marriage patterns among African Americans, just as they do among other racial-ethnic groups.

You have already learned that patterns of marriage and divorce are stratified by education. Thus, one reason why African Americans have lower marriage rates and higher divorce rates than other groups is because fewer African Americans have college degrees. Economic inequalities that make African Americans less financially secure than other groups also reduce marriage rates and increase the risk of divorce. The marriage gap between Whites and African Americans has actually grown in recent decades as "economic factors have become increasingly important for marriage formation and stability, and blacks continue to face economic disadvantage" (Raley, Sweeney, & Wondra, 2015, p. 104). A third reason that African Americans have lower marriage rates than other groups can be understood by going back to the marriage market analogy. High rates of unemployment and incarceration of young Black men in poor communities limit the supply of eligible spouses for heterosexual Black women in those communities (who have low rates of intermarriage with men of other racial-ethnic groups). Men without a steady job or with a criminal history lack the resources to be successful in the marriage market, limiting the pool of "marriageable" men (Wilson, 1987) and leaving some Black women less able to find a suitable long-term partner.

Interracial marriages are more common among new cohorts of newlyweds.

The marriage market can also help explain increasing rates of racial intermarriage. In 2010, 15 percent of new marriages were between partners of different races, more than double the rate in 1980 (Pew Research Center, 2012). Asians and Hispanics have the highest rates of intermarriage, and African Americans, particularly women, have the lowest. In 2010, 43 percent of new interracial marriages were White–Hispanic couples and 14 percent were White–Asian couples. White–Black couples were 12 percent, and the remaining 30 percent were other mixed marriages. We can also look at patterns within racial-ethnic groups. For example, South Asian and East Asian immigrants are less likely to marry a U.S.-born White spouse than are immigrants from Southeast Asia (Bohra-Mishra & Massey, 2015).

As the social distance between racial groups breaks down, people of different races interact more frequently with each other (Gordon, 1964). They live near each other, go to school with each other, and work with each other. These structural shifts not only widen the pool of potential romantic partners, but they also increase the social acceptance of interracial and interethnic unions. This is exactly what happened in the early 20th century among European immigrants to the United States. Although initially part of unique subcultures based on country-of-origin, language, religion, occupation, and residence, these differences were minimized after a generation or two and ethnic Europeans started marrying each other at much higher rates. Now, of course, we would hardly consider a marriage between an American of Irish descent and an American of Italian descent an intermarriage, but 100 years ago, it certainly would have been. Similarly, even a generation or two ago, a marriage between a Japanese American and a Chinese American would have been considered a mixed marriage, often met with disapproval from parents and family members (Tuan, 1998).

Contemporary patterns of immigration and intermarriage are a bit more complex than they were in the early 20th century. In 1921, immigration from Europe was essentially cut off (Qian & Lichter, 2011), so ties to home countries weakened, facilitating assimilation and integration. Today, ties to countries of origin remain stronger, even among the second and third generations. Not only does ongoing immigration keep language and culture alive in the United States, but international travel and communication are also much cheaper and easier than they were 100 years ago. This ongoing influx of immigrants has widened the pool of same-race partners available to U.S.-born minorities, and as a result, marriage rates between U.S.-born and foreign-born ethnic minorities has increased. For example, in 1980, only about 4 percent of U.S.-born women of Asian descent were married to foreign-born Asian men; this increased to more than 20 percent in 2008 (Qian & Lichter, 2011).

Public approval of interracial marriage is at an all-time high. Sixty-three percent of Americans said they would be fine with a family member being married to someone of a different race or ethnicity (Pew Research Center, 2012). Of course, this also means that 37 percent—a significant minority—would not be fine with it. Approval rates are highest among African Americans, younger people, the college educated, liberals, and people living in the West.

Change, Continuity, and Diversity in Marriage and Cohabitation

This chapter discussed changes and continuities in how Americans form romantic partnerships. We are marrying later and cohabiting more, but most people still get married and those who aren't married hope and plan to marry in the future. Our romantic choices continue to be shaped by structural conditions, and even the rise of Internet dating has not dramatically changed the characteristics we are looking for in a spouse; essentially, we are looking for someone pretty similar to ourselves. Interracial relationships are on the rise, but most people still partner with someone in their racial-ethnic group. Same-sex marriage is becoming more accepted and has been legally recognized; the fight for same-sex marriage emphasizes the central place that marriage continues to hold in American family life.

The most significant change around marriage and cohabitation that we have seen is the diverging patterns in how we form our families by social class. Those who have a four-year degree tend to follow a more marriage-centered path. They go to college and marry in their late 20s or early 30s after cohabiting with their future spouse and maybe one other partner. After they get married, they have children. Only one in five will get divorced, and those who do are likely to remarry within a couple of years. The trajectory is different for those who do not have a college degree. Like their college-educated counterparts, they will cohabit with a partner or two in their 20s. But they are far more likely to have a child with that partner, and most cohabiting relationships break up within a few years. When they do marry, people without a college degree are more likely to get divorced—60 percent within 20 years.

Thus, when we talk about changes in marriage, we are really talking about two different patterns of change. Marriage patterns for the college educated do not look that different from marriage in earlier generations; they just start them a few years later than their parents and grandparents did. For those who are less educated, however, the changes in marriage are more stark.

MAIN IDEAS

- American marriage patterns are shaped in contradictory ways by a culture of marriage and a culture of individualism.

- The history of marriage includes three ideal types of marriage: institutional, companionate, and individualized. Institutional marriage emphasized community and familial obligations; companionate marriage prioritized the romantic dyad and fulfillment of gender-specific roles; and today's individualized marriage is focused on self-fulfillment and personal growth.

- Cohabitation is becoming an increasingly common family form, especially among Americans with lower levels of education.

- Nonmarital fertility is also rising, which creates instability in the family lives of children.

- The legalization of same-sex marriage is consistent with the romantic and individualistic focus of contemporary marriages.

- Marriage markets are shaped by homogamy—we tend to marry others similar to ourselves.

- Marriage patterns are closely tied to education level.

- Racial differences in marriage can largely be explained by social class and immigration.

CHAPTER 6

Divorce and Relationship Dissolution

> *I had really wanted out of the relationship for ten years. It was all I had thought about. When he left, I did not once regret it or miss him. Yet when I read the separation agreement and saw his name and my name, the date and place of our marriage, the names and birthdates of our children, I was overwhelmed. Twenty years of a life were ending and reduced to a few pieces of paper.*
>
> (Vaughan, 1986, p. 173)

> *At that time I was thinking that I didn't know if I loved her. I had lived with this so long. I didn't know what real love was.*
>
> (Kayser & Rao, 2006, p. 210)

> *We won't get to be Ozzie and Harriet.*
>
> (Kayser & Rao, 2006, p. 213)

These are the words of people who have experienced the breakup of a marriage or cohabiting relationship. In the first quote, Diane Vaughn's respondent voices the grief that people go through when a marriage ends, even when they are glad that it did. The second quotation is from a young man who had fallen out of love with his partner, leading to the end of their relationship; few Americans would question his decision to leave given the absence of romantic love. The reference to the 1950s sitcom *Ozzie and Harriet* in the third quotation suggests that these family ideals from the postwar era continue to be a yardstick by which we judge our own relationships, no matter how unrealistic they may be.

And what about children whose parents divorced? Two of Kathleen Gerson's (2011) respondents provide insight on their experiences:

> My mother ended up going on welfare. We went from a nice place to living in a really cruddy building. And she's still in the same apartment. To this day, my sister will not speak to my father because of what he's done to us. (p. 88)

> You miss your parents being together, but some people are better off being friends. . . . After they broke up, they had a good relationship with each other and with me. That's why I think I'm well adjusted. (p. 32)

In the first quotation, we can see the negative outcomes for which children are at higher risk when their parents' relationship dissolves, including economic vulnerability, residential instability, and estranged relationships with one or both parents. But in the second quotation, the respondent reminds us that divorce can also be a positive change for all members of the family.

Marriage and divorce are two sides of the same coin. On the one side, we have a culture of marriage that values marriage as the pinnacle of emotional and familial success, and on the other side, we have the consequences of these high expectations, a culture of individualism that values the pursuit of happiness as a birthright. Divorce may represent a breakdown of a single marriage, but it does not represent the breakdown of marriage as an institution. On the contrary, divorce is a natural consequence of a marriage system built on norms of romantic love, companionship, and individual happiness. The culture of marriage and the culture of individualism, which you learned about in the previous chapter, work together to reinforce the prevalence of both marriage and divorce in American culture. These tensions between marriage and individualism have become more complex in recent years as cohabitation, which has an even higher rate of dissolution than marriage, has become more common.

This chapter builds on the previous one to delve more deeply into divorce and relationship dissolution—historical patterns, who is most at risk, the multifaceted process of **uncoupling**, the consequences of divorce and relationship dissolution for children, and the dynamics of remarriage and stepfamilies. Although the rapid rise in divorce in the 1970s was a dramatic shift from previous decades, the long-term trend illustrates important continuities with the past.

Rising—and Declining—Divorce

Figure 6.1 shows the U.S. divorce rate from 1867 to 2014. Divorce rates started rising in the late 19th century with an incline commensurate with the rise of companionate marriage and growing individualism in U.S. culture. When the general public refers to the rise in divorce, they are usually not referring to this long-term trend. Rather, it is the sharp rise in divorce in the 1970s that caused the widespread cultural concern that continues today. The economic changes that took place in the 1970s, which you will learn more about in Chapter 8, weakened men's earning power and pushed more women into the labor force. Both of these trends increased the risk of divorce—men's economic losses put added financial burdens on families and women's employment made them less economically dependent on their husbands. Social and cultural attitudes toward divorce also changed during this period—divorce no longer carried the same stigma it used to. In a 1962 survey of mothers, about half approved of parents divorcing if they didn't get along. Fifteen years later, in 1977, that number jumped to 80 percent of

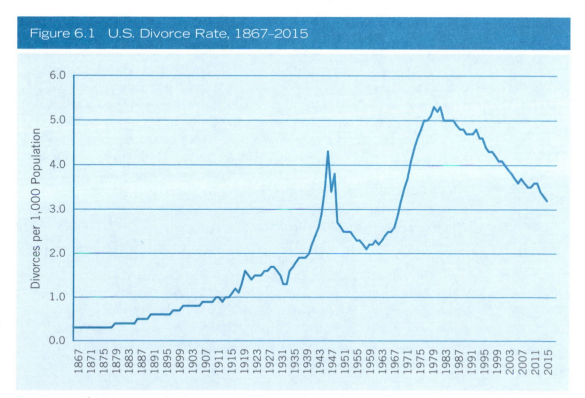

Figure 6.1   U.S. Divorce Rate, 1867–2015

Source: Centers for Disease Control and Prevention, 2015; National Center for Health Statistics, 1973; U.S. Census Bureau, 1975; U.S. Census Bureau, 2003b.

this same group of mothers (Thornton, 1989). This period also saw legal changes that made divorce less onerous to obtain, although most scholars now agree that the legal changes were a consequence, not a cause, of changing divorce attitudes and behaviors (we'll discuss these laws in more detail in this chapter).

The divorce rate peaked in 1981 and has been declining since then. That's right—divorce has been declining for the past 30 years. This is not to say that our divorce rate is low; far from it, as it remains one of the highest in the world. But it is significantly lower than it was at its peak. One major reason why divorce rates have declined is because of changes in who gets married. As we will discuss, the risk of divorce varies widely across the population. Since the 1980s and 1990s, population groups who are most at risk of divorce—those with lower income, less education, and early age at relationship formation—are choosing to cohabit instead of getting married. If they aren't married, they can't get divorced. Thus, divorce rates are lower because the current pool of people at risk for divorce—married couples—comprises couples whose characteristics make them less likely to split up.

Demography of Divorce

You may have heard the statistic that about half of marriages end in divorce. Measuring divorce, however, is more difficult than it seems. This 50 percent statistic is based on a ratio of divorces to marriages in a given year. Each year in the United States, about half as many couples get divorced as get married; dividing the number of divorces by the number of marriages gives you 50 percent. This measure is limited, however, because the people getting divorced in a given year probably got married years earlier. It tells us the relative number of new divorces and new marriages for each year, but it doesn't tell us anything about the likelihood that a marriage will end. In recent years, this ratio has become even more problematic as several states no longer report their marriage and divorce data to the federal government.

Instead of the ratio of divorces to marriages, what most people are interested in is the likelihood of divorce. What is the risk that a marriage will end? This is a more complex question, and it relies on complex demographic estimates to answer. The most recent estimates suggest that 40 percent of women married to men will divorce before their 15th anniversary (Figure 6.2; Copen et al., 2012). Even this statistic, however, masks a complex reality. The risk of divorce varies widely by population group—education, age at marriage, race, and other sociodemographic characteristics shape who is most at risk for divorce and who is not. That estimate of 40 percent applies to the population as a whole, but it masks significant variation within it.

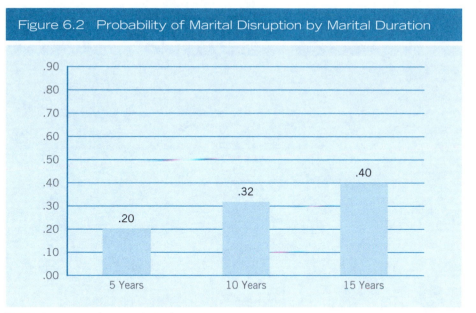

Figure 6.2 Probability of Marital Disruption by Marital Duration

Source: Copen, Daniels, Vespa, & Mosher, 2012.

Note: Data for women aged 15 to 44 years in first marriages.

Education: One primary correlate of divorce is education. As discussed in the previous chapter and shown in Figure 6.3, women with a Bachelor's degree have a significantly lower risk of divorce than women without a college degree. Women with a high-school degree or less are more than twice as likely to divorce than women with a college degree.

Race-Ethnicity: Figure 6.4 shows the risk of divorce by race-ethnicity. Asian American women have the lowest risk of divorce, and African American women have the highest. Risks for White women and Latinas are in between. As discussed in the previous chapter, educational inequalities can help explain these differences. A high percentage of Asian Americans have college degrees, which reduces the risk for divorce. And the lower percentage of African Americans with college degrees increases their risk for relationship dissolution.

Family of Origin: Figure 6.5 shows the risk of divorce by characteristics of one's family of origin. Women who lived with both biological or adoptive parents at age 14 are about one third less likely to divorce within 15 years than women who grew up in some other living arrangement. In other words, family structure as a child is associated with marital instability as an adult. Growing up with continuously married parents lowers one's risk of divorce.

Figure 6.3 Probability of Marital Disruption Within 15 Years by Education

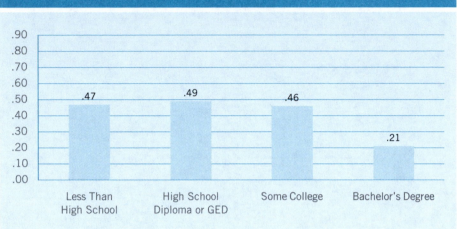

Source: Copen et al., 2012.

Note: Data for women aged 15 to 44 years in first marriages.

Figure 6.4 Probability of Marital Disruption by Race-Ethnicity

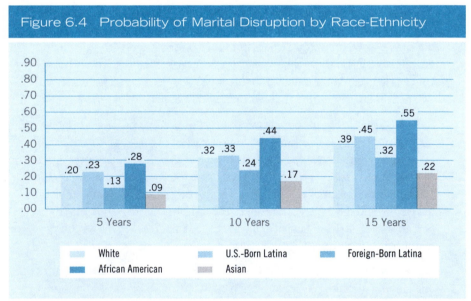

Source: Copen et al., 2012.

Note: Data for women aged 15 to 44 years in first marriages.

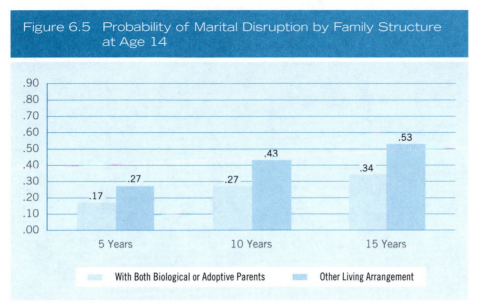

Figure 6.5   Probability of Marital Disruption by Family Structure at Age 14

Source: Copen et al., 2012.

Note: Data for women aged 15 to 44 years in first marriages.

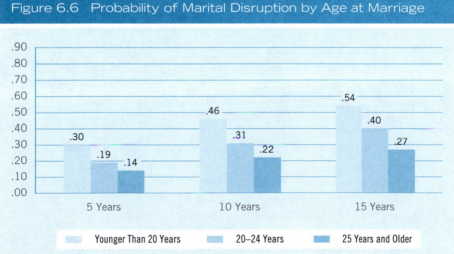

Figure 6.6   Probability of Marital Disruption by Age at Marriage

Source: Copen et al., 2012.

Note: Data for women aged 15 to 44 years in first marriages.

Figure 6.7   Probability of Marital Disruption Within 15 Years by Timing of First Birth

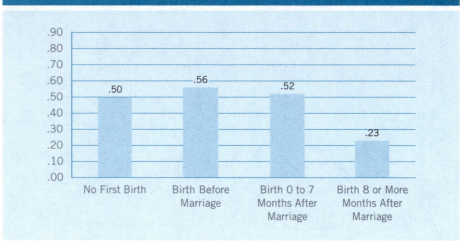

Source: Copen et al., 2012.

Note: Data for women aged 15 to 44 years in first marriages.

Age at Marriage: Older age at marriage is also associated with lower risk of divorce. Greater than 50 percent of women who married before age 20 will divorce in 15 years, compared with 40 percent of those married between ages 20 and 24, and less than 30 percent of those who married at age 25 or older (Figure 6.6). And as you learned in the previous chapter, couples who started living together at a young age, and later married, are also at higher risk of divorce (Kuperberg, 2014).

Timing of First Birth: Figure 6.7 shows the probability of divorce by timing of first birth. Women who gave birth to their first child before marriage or within the first few months of marriage (suggesting she was pregnant at the wedding) have a higher risk of divorce than women who had their first child at least 8 months after marriage. Only 23 percent of women who had their first child after marriage are divorced within 15 years, compared with more than half of those who had their first birth prior to marriage. Women who have no children also have a high risk of divorce, with 50 percent divorcing within 15 years of marriage.

Studio-Annika/iStock

Women who are pregnant when they get married have a higher risk of divorce.

Heterogamy: Couples who differ on socially important characteristics are more likely to divorce than those who are homogamous. For example, the probability of marital disruption for a woman whose spouse is of a different race is almost 18 percent higher than it is for those whose spouse is of the same race (Bramlett & Mosher, 2002). In addition, the risk of divorce varies by the racial-ethnic makeup of the couple. For example, a marriage between an African American and a European American has a higher risk of divorce than one between a European American and an Asian American.

Remarriages: Second and higher order marriages are more likely than first marriages to end in divorce. The more complex life histories of those in remarriages, including marital and cohabitation history and having children with previous partners, as well as their demonstrated willingness to divorce, increases the risk of marital dissolution (Teachman, 2008). This pattern is discussed in more detail later in the chapter.

The Process of Uncoupling

Although a breakup is usually thought of as an event, it is better characterized as a process. In 1986, sociologist Diane Vaughan coined the term *uncoupling* to

Marriage is a legal contract, and divorce is the severing of that contract.

describe the complex process that married and cohabiting couples go through when relationships end, describing it not simply as a breakup but as a "transition to a different life" (Vaughan, 1986, p. 44). The uncoupling process is fraught with legal, parental, financial, social, and emotional components. Legally, and as parents, couples negotiate how to divide the family's financial resources and how best to care for children. Socially, former partners disentangle their social networks and negotiate new relationship boundaries with in-laws and shared friends. Emotionally, individuals deal with the pain of loss and work to establish a new identity as a single person. The signing of divorce papers is just one part in a complex process, one that begins long before and continues long after a marriage is legally terminated.

Legal Divorce

At its most basic level, marriage is a legal contract, regulated by the government. Statutes define who is eligible to marry and under what circumstances, the rights and responsibilities of spouses to each other, and the conditions under which the contract can be terminated. Thus, divorce is, in essence, a severing of a legal contract. The legal requirements for this severance vary over time and from state to state. For example, some states require a waiting period before a divorce will be granted and others do not. Despite this state-level variation, the general legal history of divorce in the United States is one of expansion (Amato & Irving, 2006). In the Colonial period, divorces were granted rarely and only for extreme circumstances like desertion and adultery. Over time, the grounds for divorce expanded as, for example, cruelty came to encompass not just extreme physical abuse, as was the case in earlier periods, but also mental and emotional cruelty.

This expansion of the legal criteria for divorce eventually led to no-fault divorce laws, first enacted in California in 1970, which allow couples to split without having to prove that one spouse was adulterous, abusive, or otherwise at fault. With this change, "irreconcilable differences" and "irretrievable breakdown" became legally justified reasons to end a marriage. By 1985, all states except New York had enacted similar laws; New York changed its law in 2010. No-fault divorce is often blamed for the rise in divorce in the 1970s and 1980s. However, as you can see in Figure 6.1, the divorce rate started its steep late-20th-century climb in the early 1960s, well before the legal changes became widespread. Most scholars now agree that no-fault divorce was a consequence of increased demand for divorce rather than a cause of it.

A few states have tried to reverse (or at least slow down) the long-term pattern of expanding legal grounds for divorce by enacting a two-tiered marriage system. Couples in Louisiana, Arizona, and Arkansas can choose to enter into either a standard marriage or a **covenant marriage**. Covenant marriage requires couples to undergo premarital counseling, and these marriages can be dissolved on limited grounds. Essentially, covenant-married couples waive their right to no-fault divorce, and instead divorce can be granted only for adultery, abandonment, abuse, felony conviction, or other serious offenses. Couples who cannot prove these offenses may divorce after a lengthy waiting period.

In the almost 20 years since these laws were first passed, covenant marriage has not proven to be a popular option. In Louisiana, only about 1 percent of couples choose covenant marriage. In Arkansas, it is less than that (Felkey, 2011). Steve Nock, Laura Sanchez, and James Wright (2008) found that couples in Louisiana who choose covenant marriage are significantly more religious than are those choosing standard marriage and that, once religion is taken into account, they are just as likely to divorce as standard-married couples. Their research also found no differences in marital quality between standard-married and covenant-married couples.

Although divorce can be perceived by the public as too easy to access (Smith, 1999), few who have gone through the process would describe it as such.

More couples are using mediators to negotiate divorce agreements in order to minimize conflict.

The legal process of divorce is often a messy one. The U.S. legal system is adversarial as parties advocate for their case and work to undermine the case of the other. It is a zero-sum process that declares a winner and a loser. Unfortunately, this adversarial process is counterproductive in divorce as it encourages conflict and bad feelings between spouses rather than minimizing them, which leads to more adjustment difficulties for both adults and children. Recognizing this, alternative legal processes, such as mediation and collaborative divorce, have been developed to encourage a less adversarial process (Demo & Fine, 2010).

Parental Divorce

One of the primary legal decisions that must be made during a divorce is how to care for children. Custody decisions involve two dimensions: physical custody (i.e., where the child will reside) and legal custody (i.e., who has the legal rights and responsibilities to make decisions regarding the child's behaviors and well-being). In the past, both physical and legal custody tended to go to only one parent. Before the 19th century, in the rare cases of divorce, custody was awarded to fathers. Because fathers, not mothers, held legal and moral responsibility for childrearing, this responsibility continued when a marriage dissolved.

With the rise in separate spheres in the 19th century, ideologies of childrearing changed so that children were seen as needing the care of their mothers to thrive; this *tender years doctrine* took hold in the courts in the late 19th century, and custody was generally awarded to mothers based on this idea. This doctrine shaped custody decisions until the 1970s when the gendered nature of family law was being challenged on multiple fronts and the tender years doctrine fell out of favor to be replaced by the *best interests of the child* standard. This standard established a custody arrangement that would best meet the needs of the child as determined by the court. Although the move to put children's needs above adult needs was a move in the right direction, this doctrine was far from perfect. Decisions about best interests varied from judge to judge and, thus, were unpredictable and subject to bias; to parents, the decisions often felt arbitrary. Plus, in families with two caring parents, the child's needs could be met by either parent.

Four recent changes in custody practices have tried to bring more certainty to the process (Demo & Fine, 2010). First, standards now advocate that "each parent's postdivorce parenting responsibilities be determined on the basis of each parent's predivorce involvement with the children" (p. 67). This model tries to ease children's adjustment after a divorce by minimizing disruption to their routines and care. Second, joint custody, both legal and physical, has become more common. The most common custody arrangement is legal custody shared between parents and primary physical custody with the mother (Kelly, 1994), although joint physical custody is also on the rise. In a Washington State study of postdivorce residential plans, for example, 58 percent of children spend most of their time living with mothers, 28 percent spend about half of their time living with each parent, and 15 percent spend most of their time living with fathers (George, 2010). Similarly, in their analysis of custody decisions in Wisconsin, Maria Cancian, Daniel Meyer, Patricia Brown, and Steven Cook (2014) found that between 1988 and 2008, equally shared custody grew from 5 to 27 percent of cases.

A third change in custody practice is that some states have limited the factors that can be considered in determining custody, including parent sexual orientation, religion, or race. Other states, however, do allow judges to take these factors into account. A judge who is biased against a gay parent or an atheist parent, for example, can deny or limit custody on those grounds. Fourth, many states now require parents to take parenting education classes and to develop parenting plans to encourage effective and consistent parenting during and after the divorce process.

Even when parents act with the best intentions, shared parenting after a divorce is challenging. A couple that could not get along in marriage will often have a difficult time getting along in divorce, particularly in the first few years. In their large study of almost 1,000 postdivorce families, Hetherington and Kelly (2002) found that co-parents fell into one of three categories: *conflicted*, *cooperative*, and *parallel*. The conflicted co-parents were disparaging of the other parent, fought in front of the children, and tried to undermine the children's relationship with the other parent. This kind of behavior can undermine child well-being; as Hetherington and Kelly put it: "[T]he only childhood stress greater than having two married parents who fight all the time is having two divorced parents who fight all the time" (pp. 136–137). Fortunately, conflicted parents were a minority in their sample, about 25 percent.

Not so fortunately, cooperative co-parents were also in the minority, at about 25 percent. These parents could put aside negative feelings from the divorce and work together in their parenting—talking regularly, adapting to children's needs, and maintaining consistent rules and expectations across households. Many married couples struggle to parent in this way, so divorced couples who can do this are especially unusual.

The largest group of parents in Hetherington and Kelly's (2002) sample, about half, were the parallel co-parents. These parents avoided fighting with each other, but they also avoiding talking with each other. Each parent enacted positive parenting behaviors with the children, but they did not do so in a coordinated way. Mom did her thing, Dad did his thing. Although not ideal, especially for very young children who benefit from consistency, this arrangement minimized conflict between parents, to the benefit of children and adults, and most children could adapt to the two parenting styles without much difficulty.

Financial Divorce

Marriage is not only a legal relationship, but it is also an economic one. Although most couples are financially interdependent, with both partners relying on the income of the other to maintain their current living standard, greater than 60 percent of wives still earn less than their husbands. An important part of the divorce process is disentangling this interdependence while taking into account partners' unequal financial resources.

The negative economic consequences of divorce for women are well documented. Although specific estimates vary by data source (Sayer, 2006), on average, women's family income declines about one third after a divorce. These economic consequences are less severe today than they were in the past because women are earning more relative to men and are more likely to receive child support (Tach & Eads, 2015). The economic consequences of relationship dissolution are also high for women in cohabiting relationships, and these consequences have increased over time.

For men, the economic consequences of divorce are more varied (McManus & DePrete, 2001). Men who were the primary earners in their families tend to experience a higher standard of living after divorce as they bring their high earnings into a single-person household. But men whose wives earned incomes similar to theirs often experience a drop in their standard of living after divorce, although the decline tends to be smaller than it is for women.

Historically, men were expected to financially support their ex-wives by paying alimony. Separate spheres ideology was so entrenched that men were held responsible for providing for their spouse even after a divorce. This had an economic logic—middle-class women had limited opportunities in the labor market—as well as a moral one, as it was meant to discourage divorce and even to punish spouses who behaved poorly in their marriages.

Alimony is granted in only a small minority of cases, and when granted, awards vary widely. Most divorce settlements are decided by negotiations between lawyers, and alimony is just one chip in the complex bargaining process that legal divorce entails, so there is little consistency in how alimony is awarded. Alimony rules also vary state to state. Generally, however, the following factors are considered: "length of marriage; age and health (both physical and emotional) of the parties; distribution of property; education level of each party at the time of the marriage and at the time divorce proceedings are begun; . . . child care and homemaking services and contributions to the career or career potential of the other party[; and] . . . the earning capacity of the recipient" (Shehan, Berardo, Owens, & Berardo, 2002, p. 310). No longer viewed as punishment for wrongdoing or an ongoing obligation for husbands to support their former wives, alimony is now intended to help spouses transition to economic independence. Most alimony awards are temporary—providing support for a specified time period to facilitate a former spouse's transition to economic self-sufficiency, such as to complete education or to find a job.

Emotional and Social Divorce

In a 1964 article, Peter Berger and Hansfried Kellner applied the theory of symbolic interactionism to analyze the "social construction of marriage," as described by sociologist Diane Vaughan (1986) in her book *Uncoupling*:

> Marriage [is] a process in which two individuals renegotiate who they are with respect to each other and the world around

them. They restructure their lives around each other. They create common friends, belongings, memories, and a common future. They redefine themselves as a couple, in their own eyes and in the eyes of others, who respond to the coupled identity they are creating. They are invited out as a twosome, mail comes addressed to both, the IRS taxes them jointly. Single friends may hesitate to call, while the two people are readily incorporated into the social world of those who also are coupled. (p. 4)

Divorce is this process in reverse—two individuals renegotiating who they are independent of each other. It means restructuring one's life without the other: creating new friendships and ending old ones; separating belongings and memories; and imagining a future without the other. Married friends hesitate to call, while one is more easily invited into the social world of those who are single. And, often, the mail continues to come addressed to both, which is a daily reminder of the union that is no longer.

Newly divorced people ask "who am I?" as they renegotiate their identities and social relationships postmarriage.

Although the practical matters of custody, finances, and legally terminating a relationship are given most of the attention in the sociological research on divorce and relationship dissolution, the emotional and social divorce—the process by which a partner disengages from a relationship and develops a new social identity as a single person—is a vital part of the process. Vaughan (1986) was one of the first to study this process from a sociological perspective. She focused on breaking up as a redefinition of self, a process of creating a new identity: "Uncoupling is complete when the partners define themselves and are defined by others as separate and independent of each other—when being partners is no longer a major source of their identity" (p. 173).

A central idea in the theory of symbolic interactionism is that our identities are created and reinforced in our environments and in our interactions with others. Breakups often lead to changes in physical appearance, such as losing weight or getting a tattoo, and to changes in one's physical environment, such as rearranging the furniture or buying a new car (Gregson & Ceynar, 2009; Vaughan, 1986). These external changes both create and reinforce an independent sense of self, symbolizing and facilitating the internal changes that uncoupling requires. In the absence of socially recognized rituals to mark the transition to this new stage of life, individuals use physical changes to create these rituals for themselves.

Uncoupling also requires a renegotiation of social networks. Most partners have significant overlap in their social networks, and when the relationship ends, "the shared network is likely to be pulled apart to some extent, sometimes by choice, sometimes not" (Rands, 1988, p. 128). In general, relationship dissolution leads to less interaction with the former partner's kin and the friends he or she brought to the relationship (Rands, 1988). One tends to fall out of contact with some friends, especially those who are coupled, and to develop relationships with new, often single, friends (Greif & Deal, 2012; Rands, 1988). This shuffling of social networks has consequences for how easily adults and children adjust to the breakup as those with stronger social supports get through the crisis period more easily than those without them (Wang & Amato, 2000).

Relationship Dissolution and Children

For both researchers and the general public, one of the primary concerns about divorce and relationship dissolution is how it affects children. Research has consistently demonstrated that compared with children with continuously married parents, children who experience a parental breakup "score lower on a variety of emotional, behavioral, social, health, and academic outcomes" (Amato, 2010, p. 653). In addition, adults with unmarried parents "tend to obtain less education, have lower levels of psychological well-being, report more problems in their own marriages, feel less close to their parents (especially fathers), and are at greater risk of seeing their own marriages end in divorce" (Amato, 2010, p. 653). These are robust results, having been replicated using a variety of datasets over multiple years. They also apply to children whose unmarried parents split up.

Because the circumstances surrounding a divorce vary so widely, responses to divorce vary as well. For some children, divorce can have negative consequences, such as a decreased standard of living and a less intimate relationship with a noncustodial parent, usually the father. For other children, the consequences can be positive, including less conflict in the home and happier and more effective parents. In addition, even children of married parents exhibit a wide range of outcomes on any specific measure. Research that focuses only on average and small differences between children of divorced and married parents obscures these complexities.

To illustrate, take a look at Figure 6.8. This shows two distributions on a hypothetical measure of children's well-being—one for children whose parents are married ("intact") and one for children whose parents are divorced. If we look at the averages (the peak of each curve), we can see that children with divorced parents have a lower score on this (again, hypothetical) measure of well-being. Most discourse on the effects of divorce on children focuses on this small difference in averages and ignores the wide variation in outcomes for children in both types of families, which is illustrated by the full distribution of the curves.

Fortunately, researchers are starting to pay more attention to this variability in both quantitative and qualitative research. For example, in their analysis of two nationally representative datasets, Paul Amato and Christopher Anthony (2014) find that after a divorce, some children decline on measures of well-being, slightly fewer children improve on measures of well-being, and that most

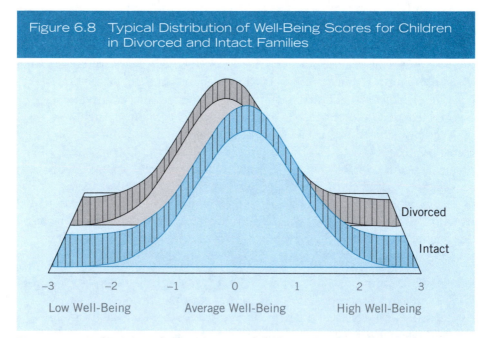

Figure 6.8 Typical Distribution of Well-Being Scores for Children in Divorced and Intact Families

Source: Amato, Paul R. 1994. "Life-Span Adjustment of Children to Their Parents' Divorce." *The Future of Children* 4(1):143–164. (http://www.princeton.edu/futureofchildren/publications/docs/04_01_08.pdf)

children experience no change in these measures at all. For example, they found that 18 percent of children whose parents divorced experienced an increase in behavioral problems at school, including fighting and acting impulsively, and 14 percent exhibited fewer of these problems. The remaining children—68 percent—experienced no change on this measure before and after their parents' divorce.

Similarly, Kathleen Gerson (2011) found in her interviews with young adults that parent's decisions to divorce or stay together were less important in shaping adults' reflections on their childhoods than "*why* they made the decision and *what consequences* it held for all" (Gerson, 2011, p. 33, emphases in original). Most young adults recall experiencing sadness and confusion at the time of their parents' breakup, but many also recognized the benefits. Almost half reported that the breakup was for the best. One respondent said, "It was very sad, but I remember feeling a sense of relief that the tension, the stress, the fighting, the fear of what was going on with my parents was over" (Gerson, 2011, p. 32).

Another methodological challenge in studying how divorce affects children is determining the appropriate comparison group. Research that simply compares children of divorced parents with children of married parents does not account for selection effects—differences in families that exist before a divorce takes place. For example, parental conflict tends to reduce child well-being. Some of the negative effects of divorce on children can be attributed to the conflict that they experienced *before* a divorce took place. Even if these high-conflict couples stay married, children would still experience negative outcomes. As Frank Furstenberg and Andrew Cherlin (1991) put it, "We do not doubt that many young adults retain painful memories of their parents' divorce. But it doesn't necessarily follow that these feelings will impair their functioning as adults. Had their parents not divorced, they might have retained equally painful memories of a conflict-ridden marriage" (p. 68).

One way to account for this selection is to follow large groups of children in various family structures over time, which is called **longitudinal research**. This allows researchers to take measures on several dimensions of well-being—emotional health, academic achievement, behavioral difficulties—over time as the children grow and as their family conditions change. Essentially, a child serves as his or her own comparison. Studies like these find that children whose parents eventually divorce tend to experience more challenges than other children well before the divorce takes place (Strohschein, 2005). In addition, children in high-conflict families whose parents remain married experience negative outcomes similar to children whose parents are divorced (Amato, 2005).

Another issue relates to how results are interpreted. For example, say that 20 percent of children whose parents are divorced and 10 percent of children whose parents are married experience behavioral or mental health challenges. We can interpret this finding in two ways. One, we can emphasize the difference between the two groups of children, stating that children of divorce are twice as likely as other children to experience negative outcomes. Or we can emphasize the fact that four out of five children whose parents are divorced do not experience negative outcomes as a result. Both are true; it is simply a matter of emphasis.

Relationship Dissolution Among Unmarried Parents

Most of the existing research on relationship dissolution and child well-being has focused on the dissolution of married relationships. However, in the last decade or so, the rise in nonmarital fertility has shifted attention to these fragile families (Carlson, McLanahan, & England, 2004). More than 40 percent of births in the United States are to unmarried mothers, and 80 percent of these mothers are romantically involved with the father at the time of the child's birth. Most of these couples have high hopes for the future of their relationship: Reported relationship quality is high, half are living together, and three quarters plan to marry (McLanahan & Beck, 2010). However, most couples do not get there, with only 15 to 20 percent marrying within 5 years (Gibson-Davis, 2014; McLanahan, 2011) and two thirds breaking up. On-again and off-again relationships are also common (Reed, 2007), which can reinforce instability for children.

Parenting practices in fragile families vary widely. Without a legal process to determine custody, nor clear role expectations for nonresidential parents, parents rely on informal negotiations for visitation and support. In almost all cases, children live with their mothers and the father's relationship with the children depends on a variety of factors, including education, age, earnings, child gender, payment of child support, years since relationship dissolution, drug and alcohol use, incarceration, race (African American fathers are more involved than fathers of other races), and the father's relationship with the child's mother. Note that these are the same factors that influence divorced father's involvement with their children.

Analysis of data from the Fragile Families study finds that 63 percent of nonresident fathers saw their 1-year-old child in the last month, although this declines to less than half once the child is 3 and 5 years old (Carlson,

McLanahan, & Brooks-Gunn, 2008). For those who are involved with the child at age 5, fathers see the child, on average, about nine days per month. When unmarried parents form new romantic relationships and have additional children with a new partner, father involvement declines, although it is mother's new relationships and new children that play the larger role in limiting father's involvement than his own.

This speaks to the complexity of multipartner fertility, having a biological child with more than one partner. In general, the more unstable parents' romantic relationships are and the more frequently parents repartner, the more likely they are to have children with multiple partners. Karen Guzzo and Frank Furstenberg (2007) analyzed data from a national sample of men and found that 16 percent of men aged 35 to 44 have children with more than one partner and that 30 percent of fathers with two or more children had them with multiple partners. Analysis of data from a national sample of births to unmarried mothers in U.S. cities found that in almost 60 percent of the couples, at least one partner already had a biological child with someone else; among married couples, it was only one in five. Multipartner fertility is more common among groups that have high rates of relationship instability, namely, African Americans and those who are economically disadvantaged.

There is also a feedback loop between relationship instability and fertility: Ending a relationship increases the likelihood you will enter a new one and have another child, while the presence of children from other relationships decreases the stability of the new one (Monte, 2007). Conflict and jealousy between former and new partners is common. There is also tension around the distribution of men's financial resources: Money that is given to the mother of one child is money not being given to another. Since money is tight for most of these families, fathers are left spreading meager resources over multiple households and leaving partners needing and wanting more.

Supporting Children When Parents Break Up

The complexity of children's responses to their parents' relationship instability has led to new questions. Increasingly, researchers are investigating the factors that can minimize the risk of negative outcomes for children who experience a parental breakup. In general, the correlates of the negative consequences of parental relationship dissolution are similar whether parents are married or cohabiting; children in families with fewer financial resources, more conflict, less effective parenting, weaker relationships with nonresident fathers, and frequent transitions are at higher risk of negative outcomes. The rub is that children born to unmarried parents are more likely than their peers in married families to be exposed to one or more of these risk factors, making them especially vulnerable. That children in minority and low-income families are disproportionately exposed to family instability is also a central mechanism in the reproduction of inequality (Osborne & McLanahan, 2007).

Economic Support

The economic consequences of relationship dissolution are well documented, and the loss of economic resources can account for many of the challenges that children experience (McLanahan & Sandefur, 1997), especially for formerly married parents. Several researchers have found that when socioeconomic status is taken into account, the gap between children whose parents divorce and those who remain married is reduced or disappears all together (Barber & Demo, 2006). Thus, one way to improve child well-being after relationship dissolution is to support a family's economic stability. This stability can be achieved in two ways: (1) ensuring that noncustodial parents contribute to the financial support of the child and (2) ensuring that custodial parents are economically self-sufficient (Amato, 1994).

As discussed, mothers, who are more likely than fathers to be a custodial parent, experience a drop in their standard of living after a divorce or end to a cohabiting union. Not only do they lose their partner's income, but many also receive little-to-no child support. In 2011, 44 percent of custodial mothers received the full child support that they were due and another 25 percent did not receive any (Grall, 2013). Of those who received support, the average amount received was $3,770 per year.

Recognizing how important these financial contributions are to child well-being, federal and state governments have improved child support enforcement to make the payments "compelled and automatic" rather than "discretionary" (Huang & Han, 2012, p. 623). In 2009, federal and state governments spent $4.6 billion on child support enforcement (U.S. House of Representatives, 2012) for both divorced and never married parents. A variety of tactics are used, including wage garnishing, withholding tax refunds, and credit bureau reporting.

In addition to increasing the amount of child support received from noncustodial parents, children's well-being is also improved when their custodial parent is economically self-sufficient. Women still earn only $0.78 for every $1 earned

Children benefit when their parents minimize conflict—before, during, and after a relationship dissolves.

by men, and a large part of this discrepancy is the lower wages earned by workers in female-dominated professions. Women who have dropped out of the workforce to care for children, as many mothers of young children do, are also at a disadvantage when going back to work. Low-income women are especially vulnerable as they are unlikely to be able to earn enough to support themselves and their children. Subsidized childcare and job training would be especially useful for women in this social location (Amato, 1994).

Current child support practices for women and children on public assistance also undermine economic stability. When a noncustodial parent pays child support for a child on public assistance, that support is processed through the state. Current practice allows states to keep some or all of that money as it is considered reimbursement for welfare payments received by a custodial parent. Thus, child support paid by fathers of children on public assistance does not go to the children; it goes to the government instead. Giving this money to families instead of considering it repayment for welfare receipt would be one way to increase a family's access to financial resources.

Reducing Conflict

Another major factor that shapes child well-being—before and after relationship dissolution—is the level of family conflict. High levels of conflict are one of the major reasons why children whose parents break up have a higher risk of negative outcomes. It is also the reason why many of these children show evidence of problems long before the breakup takes place. When relationship dissolution reduces conflict between parents, and between parents and children, a breakup can actually improve child well-being.

For many parents, however, conflict continues after a breakup. Mavis Hetherington and John Kelly (2002), for example, found that 20 to 25 percent of divorced couples continued to engage in conflict six years after a divorce. This ongoing conflict puts pressure on children, who feel caught in the middle between conflicting parents and feel forced to choose between them. Parents who are able to cooperate or, at the least, maintain civility increase their children's ability to adjust.

Effective Parenting

Children benefit when their parents can maintain effective parenting practices before, during, and after a breakup. This includes consistency, warmth, and authoritative parenting practices like setting and enforcing clear rules. Children also benefit when they experience appropriate levels of parental control and supervision. Adolescents, in particular, are vulnerable to changes in parental supervision. The shift to a single-parent family often gives an adolescent more autonomy and responsibility. If this responsibility is age appropriate and is provided in a context of authoritative parenting, adolescents can gain confidence and pride in their contributions to the family (Barber & Demo, 2006). However, if the child is not developmentally ready for this responsibility, due to age or personality, and he or she lacks adequate monitoring, it can lead to poor outcomes (Barber & Demo, 2006).

Relationships With Fathers

Fathers are more involved in their children's lives after a breakup than used to be the case. Jacob Cheadle, Paul Amato, and Valerie King (2010) recently analyzed the trajectory of father involvement 12 years after moving out of the family home; the data include formerly married and never married fathers. They found that the largest group of fathers—38 percent—had frequent and stable involvement with children over the 12-year period. Thirty-two percent of fathers had low involvement during the 12 years; 23 percent were highly involved in the years after the breakup, and then involvement declined over time; and 8 percent increased their involvement during the 12 years. Paul Amato, Catherine

Meyers, and Robert Emery (2009) found that 22 percent of fathers have no contact with their noncustodial children. Generally, fathers who were active in childrearing during the marriage are more likely to stay that way after divorce (Kalmijn, 2015). Fathers who do stay involved can improve child well-being as long as that involvement is positive, authoritative, and low-conflict (Braver & Lamb, 2013).

Fewer Transitions

Finally, children benefit from stability. The more that families can create stability for children such as by minimizing residential moves, maintaining relationships with friends and extended family, and avoiding introducing new romantic partners into children's lives too soon or too frequently, children's adjustment to a parental breakup is supported. Transitions are stressful for children and increase their risk of negative outcomes (Cherlin, 2009; Demo & Fine, 2010). A single transition in a mother's relationship status has a modest negative effect on child well-being, but each subsequent transition has a cumulative effect. Children born to unmarried parents are more likely to experience frequent transitions, which has a significant impact on their well-being.

Remarriage and Blended Families

"Second marriage is the triumph of hope over experience," an oft-heard quip attributed to both Samuel Johnson and Oscar Wilde. That about one in three marriages in the United States are remarriages for at least one partner (Lamidi & Cruz, 2014) certainly reinforces the culture of marriage, although remarriage rates have declined in the past few years as more couples cohabit rather than marry.

Remarriage has always been a central part of the U.S. family system. Before the 20th century, remarriage almost always involved a widow or widower rather than a divorcee. High death rates meant that it was not uncommon for one's spouse to die well before old age, and most people remarried relatively quickly because the labor of both husbands and wives were required to support the family. Even in the 1920s, most remarriages included widows and widowers rather than divorcees. Over the course of the 20th century, as death rates declined and divorce rates rose, remarriage after divorce became more common than remarriage after widowhood.

About two thirds of divorced women and three fourths of divorced men remarry, and most will cohabit prior to remarriage (Sweeney, 2010). Remarriage is more common among Whites than among African Americans and more common for Asian Americans and Latinos than it is for Whites (Lamidi & Cruz, 2014).

Remarriage is less common for those with lower levels of education (Lamidi & Cruz, 2014) and in communities with high rates of poverty and unemployment (Bramlett & Mosher, 2002). Both men and women with children are more likely to marry someone who also has children than they are to marry a childless person (Sweeney, 2010).

In 1978, Cherlin described remarriage and stepfamilies as **incomplete institutions**. He was not using the term "incomplete" as a value judgment; rather, he meant that the behavioral norms in remarriage and stepfamilies were not as fully developed as they are in first marriages. Remarriage and stepfamilies, as institutions, lacked clear guidelines for behaviors and identities within them. He cited two areas that demonstrated this absence of norms—language and the law. First, in regard to language, think about the variety of ways that children refer to their stepparents. Some use "mom" or "dad," some use first names, and some use a name like "papa" and reserve "dad" for a biological parent. This variety indicates a lack of social consensus about how to refer to the person occupying this role. The ambiguity in the role reflects the incomplete institutionalization of the family type.

The law is also inadequate in its treatment of stepfamilies. Stepparents cannot legally adopt their stepchildren if the children maintain legal ties to both biological parents, as most children do now that joint legal custody is commonplace. This means that a stepparent has no legal relationship to a stepchild. Even if this stepparent acted as a primary parent—tucking the child in at night, getting her ready for school, and contributing finances to her upbringing—the stepparent is a legal stranger to the child. Almost 40 years after Cherlin (1978) wrote his article, neither language nor law has caught up to capture the complex family relationships that remarriages entail.

Stepfamily structures have become only more complex. Increases in premarital cohabitation, postmarital cohabitation, and nonmarital fertility have diversified the pathways to stepfamily living. The narrowest definition of a stepfamily refers to a married couple living with at least one child who is not biologically related to both spouses. But there are also cohabiting stepfamilies, where a cohabiting couple is living together with children related to only one partner; these types of stepfamilies are becoming more common. These definitions are also household dependent. A child whose nonresidential father has remarried a woman with children is not considered part of a stepfamily under this definition because the child is not living with the father and stepmother.

Sociological data on remarriage and stepfamilies are not as strong as they are for other family types (Sweeney, 2010). National level datasets that capture the complexity of these family relationships are scarce, and those that do exist are outdated. In addition, stepfamilies are very "diverse in structure, processes, and outcomes" (Sweeney, 2010, p. 679), so it is difficult to identify general patterns. Research on stepfamilies also tends to show inconsistent results, reflecting the complexity of this family form relative to others.

The sociological research on remarriage and stepfamilies that does exist has focused on the effects on children. In general, children in stepfamilies are similar to those in single-parent families in terms of academic, behavioral, and mental health outcomes; that is, children in stepfamilies fare worse than those living with two married biological parents (Sweeney, 2010). Like the research on single-parent families, however, most differences between children in remarried and first married families are small and most children in stepfamilies do just fine. In addition, children's outcomes vary widely.

Remarriages have higher rates of dissolution than first marriages. Three different explanations have been proposed to account for this higher rate. First, the incomplete institutionalization of remarriage and stepfamilies means that families lack clear roles and rules for how to behave as a family. They are left to negotiate their roles and responsibilities on their own, and this uncertainty can create tensions and miscommunications that undermine family solidarity. A second explanation for the higher rate of divorce for remarried couples is that the complex kin relationships that often result from remarriage, with various combinations of stepparent, stepsibling, half-sibling, and extended family relationships, are more difficult to navigate than the kin relationships in first marriages, and this complexity, again, can undermine marital stability. Finally, a selection effect is also used to explain the higher rates. People who remarry have already demonstrated a willingness to divorce and may exhibit personality or behavioral traits that make marital stability difficult to attain.

Change, Continuity, and Diversity in Divorce and Relationship Dissolution

Divorce is another part of family life where we can see both continuity with and change from the past; we can also see how a family's social location influences the risks and consequences of divorce and relationship dissolution. Continuity is evident in the long increase in divorce over the past 150 years. As Cherlin (2009) put it, "the seed of divorce was planted in the soil of the northern [American] colonies" (p. 49), and this seed has continued to grow ever since. The sociodemographic risk factors for divorce and relationship dissolution, such as age at union formation, years of education, and parents' marital status, have remained consistent over time, although we also see change in the growing divorce gap between the most and least educated Americans. And although laws around divorce have changed over time, the underlying logic of these legal changes has been fairly consistent—expanding the grounds for which divorce can be granted.

Relationship instability increases children's risks of negative outcomes. Legal changes in the divorce process that reduce conflict between parents and help children maintain healthy ties to both parents have tried to minimize these risks. Children of unmarried parents are especially vulnerable: These relationships are less stable than marriages and they are more likely to have other risk factors including access to fewer financial resources. Although relationship instability increases children's risk, children also vary widely in their responses. Frequent transitions in a child's family and living arrangements seems to be the biggest risk factor; families that can maintain stability, even when a relationship dissolves, offer the best support for children.

MAIN IDEAS

- Relationship instability is built into our marriage system.

- Divorce started its rise in the late 19th century and has declined since the mid-1980s.

- Divorce rates vary by sociodemographic characteristics, including education, race-ethnicity, family structure, age at marriage, timing of first birth, heterogamy, and remarriages.

- Uncoupling is a complex process that includes legal, parental, financial, social, and emotional processes.

- On average, parental relationship dissolution has negative effects on children, although children also vary widely in their responses. Relationship instability in unmarried families is especially high.

- Children's well-being is supported when their families have adequate economic resources, minimal conflict, effective parenting, stable relationships with fathers, and few transitions.

- Most people who break up with a romantic partner form new relationships, both remarriages and cohabitation, creating complex blended families.

CHAPTER

7

Parents and Children

In July 2014, a mother in South Carolina was arrested and charged with felony child neglect for allowing her 9-year-old child to play in a neighborhood park while she was at work at a nearby McDonalds. That same month, a mother in Florida was arrested for allowing her 7-year-old child to walk half a mile to the park near their home. And later that year, a married couple was under investigation by Maryland's Child Protective Services for allowing their 10-year-old and 6-year-old to walk home from a park about a mile from their home.

These three cases, all taking place within six months of each other, highlight a few things about parenting and childrearing in the contemporary United States. First, they illustrate how children are seen as vulnerable, in need of adult protection and supervision, and unable to care for themselves. A generation or two ago, it wouldn't have been unusual for school-aged children to play at a park on their own; children walked or rode their bikes to and from school, ran errands for their parents, and spent their summers playing freely all over the neighborhood, returning home only when it started to get dark (Rutherford, 2011). Today, parents who allow this put themselves at risk of police intervention even though violent crime rates are two thirds lower today than they were 40 years ago.

Because children are seen as vulnerable, expectations about parenthood have changed as well. Intensive parenting—parenting that is "child-centered, expert-guided, emotionally absorbing, labor-intensive, and financially expensive" (Hays, 1996, p. 8)—has become the dominant norm. Parents are expected to have their eyes on their children at all times. Anything less is a sign of neglect. The case of the South Carolina mom also illustrates the tensions between wage earning and caregiving in the United States, where institutional supports for these competing roles are minimal. Parents are expected to financially support their children through paid employment; yet they are also expected to supervise their children 24 hours a day. These competing ideologies put parents in a bind, especially working-class single parents like the mother in South Carolina.

This chapter will explore the ideologies of childhood, motherhood, and fatherhood: how they have changed over time and how today's ideologies are rooted in those of the past. We will examine data on fertility and on how much time parents spend with children and consider how parenting ideologies and experiences vary by gender, class, immigration status, and sexuality. We will also learn about adults who choose to remain childfree. As we explore these themes, it is important to keep in mind the distinction between ideology and experience. Just like the ideology of separate spheres masked wide variation in how families balanced market and domestic needs in the 19th century, the experiences of children and parents rarely live up to the dominant ideal.

Children and Parents in Historical Context

Like all ideologies, ideas about childhood, motherhood, and fatherhood are products of a particular context. And like all ideologies, they change and morph as that context changes. As you will recall from Chapter 1, the shift from an agrarian to an industrial economy in the 19th-century United States fundamentally changed family life. Among those changes were new ideas about childhood, fatherhood, and motherhood. These changes, however, did not affect all children, fathers, and mothers in the same way.

Childhood: Economically Useful to Emotionally Priceless

In the agrarian economy of the 18th century, households were large, fertility and mortality were high, and family relationships, although often loving and affectionate, were more instrumental than sentimental. During this period, "we find no notion of childhood innocence, no protected place for children, no separate children's toys or games" (Hays, 1996, pp. 26–27). Family life was organized around productive labor, and children were an important part of that productivity. Children of all races were put to work at very young ages—as young as seven to eight years old—with sons assisting fathers with their work and daughters assisting mothers with theirs. Some Puritan families sent their children to another household to live and work, accepting another family's child into their household as an apprentice.

Children were valued primarily as economic assets—as laborers and as support for parents in their old age (Zelizer, 1985). This instrumental view required that children be raised with strict discipline and obedience. Children were "consciously molded by means of physical punishment, religious instruction, and participation in work life" (Hays, 1996, p. 27). Children also had considerable autonomy. Far from being doted on, they were left on their own to work and play. "Beyond infancy, children were not understood

In an agrarian economy, fathers, mothers, and children were involved in productive labor to support the family.

as being particularly fragile, innocent, or vulnerable. . . . Instead, the defining characteristics of useful children were sturdiness and an early capacity for responsibility" (Farrell, 1999, p. 22).

Over the course of the 19th century, views toward childhood changed. Families were having fewer children and devoting more attention to each one. Childhood came to be understood as a series of distinct developmental stages. At each stage, a child had different needs, and mothers were expected to be in tune with those needs, providing constant care and attention. Childhood became increasingly sentimentalized as children were viewed as vulnerable, precious, and emotionally priceless. Children needed love, not discipline.

Not all children experienced these shifting ideologies about childhood at the same time or in the same way. Class, race, and regional diversity in family patterns in the 19th century differentiated children's experiences into three broad clusters (Farrell, 1999). The first cluster is made up of children in prosperous families who were the first to experience these new ideologies about childhood.

These were White children of professionals in the Northeast, wealthy farm families throughout the North and Midwest, and plantation owners in the South. These children had fewer siblings, had access to expanding educational opportunities, and experienced extended, sheltered, and supervised childhoods.

The second group of children were not so privileged. Children living on small farms throughout the country and in working-class families in urban areas continued to contribute to the family economy throughout the 19th century. They spent less time in school and at leisure, and instead, they helped to support their families by working in factories, domestic service, agriculture, and the informal economy. This group of children included native-born White children, free Black children, and children of immigrants from Southern and Eastern Europe, of Chinese and Japanese immigrants in the West, and of Mexicans in the Southwest, who lived in areas that were incorporated into the United States after 1848.

The third cluster of childhood experiences in the 19th century reflects the harsh conditions faced by Native American and enslaved African American children. Native American children faced disease, forced relocation, and the deliberate elimination of their communities and cultures. In the late 19th and early 20th centuries, many Native American children were taken from their families and enrolled in government boarding schools, where they were forbidden from speaking their native language or practicing their religion. These schools were intended to "civilize" Native American children and assimilate them into dominant White culture, stripping them of all connection to indigenous cultures and communities.

The new ideologies about priceless children were also not applied to enslaved African American children, who faced dangerous and degrading conditions and were put to work at very early ages. Most received little or no education. Parents and other adults did their best to protect children from the worst cruelties of slavery, but they were at the mercy of their masters and overseers. Even after emancipation, most African Americans continued to work in southern agriculture, and children's labor was an important part of this family economy.

Although the new ideologies about childhood started to gain ground in the mid-19th century, the ideologies were not relevant for most families until decades later. By the 1930s, the sentimentalization of childhood that had begun for middle-class children in the previous century had spread to the working class. In response to child labor laws and compulsory education, more children attended public schools and attended for longer periods, fewer children worked in paid employment, and families were increasingly child-centered. Zelizer's (1985) analysis of wrongful death settlements during this period demonstrates

Children were not always seen as vulnerable as they are today.

how views toward children had changed. When a child was killed in an accident in the late 1800s, the parents could sue to receive compensation for the child's lost wages as the child was no longer able to contribute to the family economy nor care for the parents in old age. By the 1920s and 1930s, parents who lost a child received even larger financial settlements to compensate for the mental pain and suffering they experienced at the loss of their child. No longer valued for their economic contributions, children had become priceless.

Fatherhood: Moral Overseer to Breadwinner

White fathers in the 18th century were the legal and moral heads of households. They held patriarchal authority over their households, and fathers were responsible for teaching their children religious values and a strong work ethic. Parenting advice during this era was directed to fathers and was concerned primarily with a child's moral development.

In an agrarian economy, work and home were one, so fathers were a regular daily presence in children's lives. Whereas tasks like dressing and feeding children were left to mothers and older siblings, fathers provided literacy, mathematics, and religious instruction to both sons and daughters and worked side by side with their sons on the farm. Far from the distant father figure that dominated in later years, fathers were an active, regular part of children's lives: Fatherhood was "woven into the whole fabric of domestic and productive life. . . . Fathers were a visible presence, year after year, day after day. . . . Fathering was thus an extension, if not a part of, much routine activity" (Demos, 1982, p. 429).

As the economy industrialized in the 19th century, traditional family life was disrupted. More men worked for wages in manufacturing, and fewer worked in agriculture. Because paid work took them away from home, fathers were spending less time with their children, and patriarchal authority in the family lessened as home life was redefined as a feminine space (Coltrane, 1996). As this economic context shifted, so did ideologies about fatherhood. No longer a moral overseer, the ideal father and husband was now a breadwinner; his responsibility was to earn money in the market economy to support his wife and children, who were to be safely ensconced in the domestic sphere. In the 19th century, fatherhood became synonymous with the **provider role**.

Of course, class and race inequalities meant that not all men were able to live up to this new fatherhood ideal. Middle-class and skilled workers had new professional opportunities in white-collar occupations and skilled manufacturing, but men without these skills, education, or connections faced economic insecurity (Coontz, 2010). African American men were denied access to most occupations outside of agriculture, and immigrant men from Europe occupied the lowest paid jobs in manufacturing and service. Unable to earn a **family wage**, lower- and working-class men of all races had a harder time living up to the breadwinner ideal.

Motherhood: Productivity to Domesticity

In the agrarian, household-based economy of the 18th century, mothers were a crucial part of household production. Women's primary responsibility was productive labor around the household—tending animals and a vegetable garden, preparing meals, preserving food, sewing clothing—rather than childcare. Mothers did provide most of the direct physical care for young children, but older siblings took on that responsibility as soon as they were able. Like fathers and their sons, mothers oversaw the household labor of their daughters.

Industrialization led to sharp changes in expectations for motherhood. Like childhood, motherhood became idealized and sentimentalized. Rather than focusing on productive labor as they did in the previous era, mothers were expected to devote their energies to childrearing and homemaking. A good mother was now primarily concerned with the emotional development and comfort of her children. These new mothering ideologies, which historian Barbara Welter (1966) called the "cult of true womanhood" or "cult of domesticity," glorified motherhood and redefined homemaking and childrearing as acts of piety, submissiveness, and love, not of labor.

Mothers were expected to create a home that was child centered, creating the foundation for **intensive mothering** ideologies that continue today:

Mothering was redefined to be child centered.

> Child rearing came to be understood as a task that was best done primarily by the individual mother—without reliance on servants, older children, or other women. The mother was instructed to bring all her knowledge, religious devotion, and loving capacities to bear on the task, and she was urged to be consistently affectionate, constantly watchful of her own behavior, and extremely careful in guiding the child. Child rearing had become expensive as well: the child not only needed the right toys, books, and clothes but also had to be kept out of the labor force and supported through school. (Hays, 1996, pp. 32–33)

These ideologies—that childrearing is best done by mothers; that mothers should be devoted, affectionate, and watchful; and that childhood is simultaneously expensive and separate from the market economy—are familiar to us today. But in the 19th century, they were radical changes from the previous era.

These new standards for motherhood were developed by the White urban middle classes. Working-class families, rural families, and families of color continued to rely on the productive labor and wage-earning of both mothers and children. It is only when laws were passed in the early 20th century that limited children's labor and required them to attend school that working-class families no longer relied as heavily on children's economic contributions. Mothers' economic contributions, however, continued (which you will read more about in the next chapter).

Issues in Contemporary Childrearing

The ideologies of motherhood, fatherhood, and childhood that developed in the 19th century continue to shape contemporary expectations of childrearing.

Fathers still identify strongly with the provider role even as they now spend more time with their children than they did for most of the 20th century. Mothers are expected to be the primary caregiver and to organize their day-to-day lives around children's needs even as most are also employed in the labor market. And views of children as vulnerable, unique, and priceless structure almost all aspects of contemporary childrearing.

Demographic Patterns in Fertility

In 2013, the total fertility rate in the United States was 1.9, meaning that the average woman will have 1.9 children during her lifetime. This is slightly lower than the 2.1 children that are generally considered necessary to maintain the size of the population, called **replacement level fertility**. However, because of our relatively high rates of immigration, the United States does not need to worry about declining population. This is far from the case in many other developed countries (Figure 7.1). In Spain, for example, the total fertility rate is only 1.3 children per woman, which is well below replacement. Most other European countries also have low fertility rates, as do Japan, Canada, and Australia. These low fertility levels,

Figure 7.1   Total Fertility Rate, 2013, Select Countries

Spain	1.3
Germany	1.4
Italy	1.4
Japan	1.4
Canada	1.6
Australia	1.9
Norway	1.9
United States	1.9
United Kingdom	1.9
Ireland	2.0
France	2.0
Mexico	2.2

Source: The World Bank, 2015.

coupled with long life expectancies, result in an older population structure, with small working-age generations caring for larger retired generations.

Although the total fertility rate for all women in the United States is 1.9, there is variation by race-ethnicity. As shown in Figure 7.2, American Indian women have fewer children than other racial-ethnic groups, and Hispanic women have more. When the Hispanic category is disaggregated, we also see variation. For example, women of Mexican descent have a total fertility rate of 2.1 compared with 1.7 for women of Puerto Rican descent, 1.4 for women of Cuban descent, and 2.8 for women from other areas of Latin America (Martin, Hamilton, Osterman, Curtin, & Matthews, 2015).

Women are having fewer children than in the past and having them later. In 2013, the mean age at first birth was at a historic high of 26 for women (Martin et al., 2015), which was up from 21.4 in 1970 (Mathews & Hamilton, 2009). As shown in Figure 7.3, the mean age at first birth is highest for Asian Americans/Pacific Islanders at 29.4 years, which is mainly a result of higher levels of education, later ages at marriage, and low rates of nonmarital childbearing. The lowest age is among Native Americans.

Another important demographic difference in fertility patterns is the relative proportion of marital and nonmarital fertility and how these vary by social

Figure 7.2 Total Fertility Rate in the United States, 2013

All women	1.9
Non-Hispanic White	1.8
Non-Hispanic Black	1.9
American Indian	1.3
Asian and Pacific Islander	1.7
Hispanic	2.1
Mexican	2.1
Puerto Rican	1.7
Cuban	1.4
Other Latin American	2.8

Source: Martin et al., 2015.

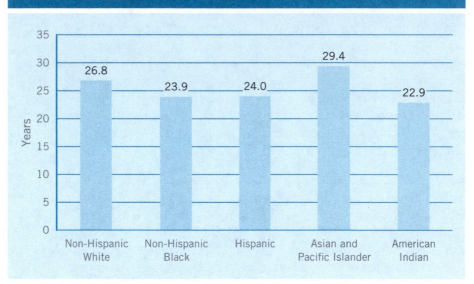

Figure 7.3 Mean Age at Women's First Birth, 2013

Source: Martin et al., 2015.

class. Currently, 40.6 percent of all births are to unmarried mothers (Martin et al., 2015), most of whom are cohabiting with a partner. Yet, the patterns differ greatly when we differentiate by social class, as you learned in Chapter 5. Only 9 percent of college-educated women who gave birth in 2013 were not married; compare that with 49 percent of women who have a high-school degree and 57 percent of women with less than a high-school degree. Education level has become a primary determinant of fertility patterns in the United States.

Time With Children

When mother's labor force participation started rising in the 1970s and 1980s, one primary concern was that children would fail to get the care and attention they needed. These fears proved to be unfounded. Because of new norms around intensive parenting, both mothers and fathers spend more time providing physical care, more time interacting with and playing with children, and more time managing children's schedules and getting them where they need to be. In fact, today's employed mothers spend more time with their children than nonemployed mothers did in the 1970s. And fathers have significantly increased the time they spend with their children, almost tripling the time they spend in childcare between 1965 and 2008 (Bianchi, 2011b).

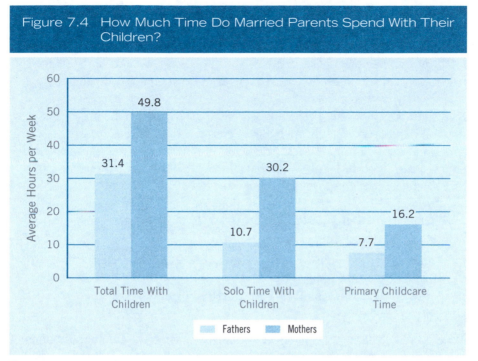

Figure 7.4 How Much Time Do Married Parents Spend With Their Children?

Source: Raley et al., 2012.

What differentiates how much time parents spend with children? Three factors stand out. First, and most significant, is gender: Mothers spend more time with their children than fathers do. Figure 7.4 shows that married mothers spend almost 50 hours per week with children compared with the 31 hours fathers spend; this includes both active time with children and passive time, when parents are available for children but not directly interacting with them. Mothers also spend three times more solo time with children—time when another adult is not present—and about twice as much time doing primary care (Raley, Bianchi, & Wang, 2012).

A second factor that affects how much time parents spend with children is women's employment. Because most fathers remain highly attached to the labor market, their work characteristics have little effect on their childcare time. What does matter is the work characteristics of their wives (Raley et al., 2012). Married fathers whose wives are employed spend more one-on-one time with children; fathers with higher earning wives spend more time on physical care of children; and fathers whose wives work longer hours spend more time managing children's schedules. In contrast, a mother's time with her children is affected by her employment status, rather than that of her husband: Employed mothers spend less time with children than nonemployed mothers do (Bianchi, 2011b).

A final factor that influences time with children is marital status. "Single mothers spend less time in childcare than married mothers—less total childcare, less routine care, less time playing with and interacting with their children, and less total time with children" (Bianchi, 2011b, p. 30). Single parents have, on average, fewer economic resources and fewer time resources than married parents: "[T]hey may have as many demands on their time as married parents but half as many adults to meet those demands" (Bianchi, 2011b, p. 30). Because the time that married parents spend with children continues to increase, the gap between single and married parents is also widening. In other words, it is not that single parents spend less time with children than parents did in the past; instead, it is that married parents are spending more time.

Parenting as a Gendered Practice

Parenting has always been and continues to be a gendered practice. Even as more mothers engage in wage-earning and more fathers are involved with the direct care of their children, the practice and ideologies of mothering differ from those of fathering. In other words, mothering and fathering are socially constructed as distinct.

The dominant parenting ideology in the United States continues to put mothers at the center of successful childrearing, resulting in what Sharon Hays (1996)

© Hero Images/Corbis

Fathers are spending more time with their children and taking care of more everyday tasks like making breakfast.

calls an ideology of *intensive mothering*. Intensive mothering has three main tenets. First, it assumes that a child should be nurtured primarily and solely by his or her mother. Other caregivers, including fathers, are seen as second best. A second tenet of intensive mothering is that it requires mothers to "lavish copious amounts of time and energy on their children" (O'Brien Hallstein, 2006, p. 97). A good mother thinks about her children constantly and is preoccupied with their well-being. In fact, worrying about a child is in itself evidence of successful mothering; as one father said in reference to his wife: "She is a very good mother. She worries a lot" (Walzer, 1998, p. 34). The third tenet of intensive mothering is that it requires mothers to be selfless and self-sacrificing, putting the needs of others before their own, a continuity with 19th century's cult of true womanhood.

Walzer (1998) used the term **mother worry** to describe the mental labor that mothers do to manage the high expectations of being a good mother. Many mothers internalize these expectations, and others hold them accountable to them. One new mother in Walzer's study told the story of a recent visit to her parents when her infant son Jimmy was being clingy: "[H]e wouldn't go to anybody else but me. My father said, 'Look at her, she's spoiling him.' And my mother said, 'be quiet . . . she ought to be glad he knows who she is.'" (Walzer, 1998, p. 47). This mother was simultaneously being criticized for giving too much attention to her child—"she's spoiling him"—and for not spending enough time with him because she was employed—"she ought to be glad [her son] knows who she is." No matter what they do, mothers can't win.

Most mothers in the United States engage with the ideology of intensive mothering in some way, either by trying to live up to it, feeling guilty about not living up to it, or actively resisting and critiquing its assumptions about gender, class, and family life. Not all mothers, however, feel accountable to this ideal. Dawn Marie Dow (2016) coined the term *integrated motherhood* to describe the mothering ideologies of African American mothers in professional occupations whom she interviewed. Unlike women who either ascribe to or actively resist intensive mothering ideology, these women do not worry about this ideology at all. Instead, the mothers articulated an alternative ideology that assumed that mothers should be employed; that childcare was a shared responsibility of mothers, family members, and the community; and that economic self-reliance, not domestic dependence on a spouse, was a central feature of womanhood. Even though these mothers occupied a privileged class location, they did not feel the same pressures to live up to intensive mothering ideals that many White mothers in similar class locations feel. Instead, they framed an alternative ideology that better reflected both the ideals and the reality of their family lives.

Like mothers who feel accountable to intensive mothering ideals, fathers face a similar accountability to norms around breadwinning and economic providership. Like most women who continue to identify with caregiving, breadwinning remains central to most men's identities as fathers. Some fully embrace it, and they work as long and as hard as possible to provide for their families. These fathers don't spend a lot of time with their children and usually have stay-at-home wives. They sacrifice time with their children to provide for them the safety, security, and opportunity that economic resources can offer (Townsend, 2002). For many of the fathers whom Nicholas Townsend (2002) interviewed, for example, earning enough to provide their children a stay-at-home mother became a symbol of fathers' commitment to their children even though it often meant sacrificing their time with them.

Other fathers feel conflicted about how best to balance their work and home responsibilities (Kaufman, 2013). They make some small adjustments to their work schedules to spend time with their children, such as limiting overtime and traveling less often, but they remain firmly attached to the labor market. A third group of fathers also feels this conflict, but these fathers resist the ideology that fatherhood equals providership by embracing caregiving and making significant changes in their work lives, including changing jobs, reducing their hours, or working from home, to spend more time caring for their children (Kaufman, 2013). But even these men remain accountable to the breadwinning ideal in their interactions with peers, co-workers, and family members. In other words, even in their resistance to these expectations of fathering, they are forced to negotiate and engage with them, providing justification for why they are choosing an alternative path.

This gender dynamic in parenting is not natural but created by social structure. On the individual level, parents tend to internalize the messages about what makes a good mother and a good father and try to live up to these ideals. On the interactional level, peers, co-workers, and family members communicate these same expectations and hold parents accountable. The dominant ideology judges mothers who are committed to their careers as selfish and unfeminine; fathers who take time off for caregiving are seen as weak and failed providers.

Institutionally, gendered patterns in family leave also reinforce women's orientation toward caregiving and men's orientation toward breadwinning. After a birth or adoption, mothers take time off work; for some it is only a few weeks, whereas for others it is a few months or a few years. Two in five new mothers are out of the labor market for at least one year (Laughlin, 2011). Fathers, on the other hand, rarely take extended leave. They may patch together some unused vacation time or sick time, but even that option is available only to men whose jobs offer those kinds of benefits. And that rarely lasts for more than a couple weeks. Instead, a birth tends to reinforce men's commitment to employment as he takes on a more intensive role as provider.

The only way to learn how to parent is to do it, and new parents experience a steep learning curve around how to care for an infant. Because mothers take more time off from work, they do more of the hands-on care from the beginning. This gives them more opportunities than fathers have to learn the skills necessary to care for a child, and thus, mothers become the experts and fathers the helpers. This distinction then continues throughout the child's life. One father interviewed by Erin Rehel (2014) describes this learning process well:

> Because or else it becomes a routine, where the mom does the everyday necessities with the child and the dad comes home at night, spends a little time, plays with him, and that's it. But I find that if you're in there, every day with the child, taking care of him, making his meals in the morning, at lunch, putting him to sleep, like, all the little details, you'll become attached just as much as the mom. Then it no longer seems like just the mom who has the initiative to look after all these things. It becomes the dad and the mom together. (pp. 123–124)

The influence of structure on parenting behaviors can be seen among men who do act as primary parents. Single fathers and stay-at-home dads, for example, tend to parent similarly to the ways most mothers do. Occupying the role of primary parent requires certain kinds of behaviors and cognitive strategies. Women usually take on this role, and their skills are typically interpreted as naturally feminine, a "maternal instinct." But men who are primary parents tend to behave and think in ways that mirror that of mothers, suggesting that parenting ideologies and behaviors are socially constructed, not innate.

Parenting Ideologies and Social Class

Social class differences in childrearing have long been of interest to researchers and social reformers. In the early 20th century, child labor laws and compulsory schooling were enacted in response to pressures from middle-class reformers who disapproved of the way that working-class families were raising their children. These different orientations toward childrearing were not simply a question of cultural values but of social location. Working-class families in the early 20th century kept their children out of school and put them to work not because they didn't value education, but because they needed the wages that children could earn to feed, clothe, and house the family. Similarly, today's working-class and poor families emphasize teaching their children respect for authority and a strong work ethic because this is what will keep them safe and will best prepare them for employment in working-class occupations.

Sociologist Annette Lareau has spent many years investigating social class differences in parenting and how these differences are experienced in social institutions. Based on her fieldwork with Black and White families at various class levels, Lareau (2003) identified two distinct childrearing logics that differed by social class. The first she called "concerted cultivation" and was practiced by middle-class parents, both Black and White. It is organized around cultivating each child's unique talents, opinions, and skills. This is accomplished through adult-organized activities like sports, scouting, and music and dance lessons, as well as by regular negotiation and dialogue between parents and children about their activities, their school days, and even about what to have for dinner. This childrearing strategy requires large investments of time, energy, and money, as well as educational resources and social connections. The rhythm of daily family life is dominated by children's schedules often in a way that creates extra stress and burdens for parents, especially mothers.

In contrast, working-class and poor families tend to use a childrearing logic that Lareau (2003) called "accomplishment of natural growth." Under this model, parents provide care for children and meet their needs for safety, security, health, and overall well-being, but they do not explicitly seek to nurture children's talents and opinions. They provide loving care for children and simply allow them to grow, develop, and mature. These children are involved in few, if any, organized activities and are not encouraged to articulate or negotiate for their desires. Rather, children are expected to respect adult authority and mind what parents and other adults instruct them to do.

Neither one of these childrearing logics is inherently better than the other; in both, children are loved and well cared for. Where inequality emerges is in social institutions, which tend to be built on and value middle-class norms. For example, schools continue to rely on a middle-class logic that values a particular type of parental involvement in education—volunteering in the classroom, being part of the parent–teacher association (PTA)—while ignoring other ways that parents contribute to their children's education, such as by ensuring they are well rested, well fed, and ready to learn (Lopez, 2001). Teachers and principals view working-class parents as indifferent toward their children's education because the parents tend to focus on the latter, traits that do not count as parental involvement according to middle-class standards (Lareau, 2000). In turn, because their parents are perceived as uninvolved, teachers and principals have lower expectations for working-class students' academic achievement. Lareau's research demonstrates that the consequences of class differences in parenting result not from one type being inherently better than the other but from the ways that institutions apply middle-class standards to working-class parents.

Immigrant and Transnational Parenting

In 2010, 13 percent of the U.S. population was foreign born, slightly less than the 15 percent at the peak of immigration to the United States in 1890. Although the overall rate of immigration mirrors that of a century ago, what has changed are the countries of origin for these immigrants. In 1900, 86 percent of immigrants were from Europe; in 2010, 53 percent were from Latin America, including Mexico, and 28 percent were from Asia (Singer, 2013). Thus, when we are discussing immigrant children and parents, we are primarily talking about Latinos and Asians, although even within these groups, there is wide variation in experiences.

In 2013, 24 percent of children in the United States were part of immigrant families. By *immigrant family*, I am referring to families that include children who are foreign born or who live with at least one foreign-born parent. Most of these children—89 percent—are U.S. citizens (Kids Count, 2015). Children in immigrant families are more likely to be poor than those in U.S.-born families

John Moore / Getty Images

Activists are raising awareness about the challenges faced by undocumented and mixed-status immigrant families.

(27 percent vs. 21 percent) even though they are also more likely to live with married parents. This poverty is highest among children whose families are from Latin America or who came to the United States as refugees or as asylum-seekers. Poverty rates are lowest for immigrants from China, Korea, India, and the Philippines, as well as for White immigrants from Canada and Europe. Immigrants from these countries tend to have higher levels of education and to work in well-paid occupations such as health care and technology.

Most undocumented immigrants living in the United States are living in families (Pyke, 2014). Many of these are **mixed-status families** in which family members differ in their immigration status. Three quarters of children living with parents who are undocumented are citizens. Because undocumented immigrants are marginalized in the economy, education, housing, health care, and the law, the entire family is at risk even if children are citizens. Parents may be reluctant to seek services for which their citizen children qualify for fear of their own status being discovered. The fear of deportation has a negative effect on family well-being, and children whose parents are undocumented fare worse on educational and cognitive outcomes than children whose parents have legal status.

Much of the research on immigrant families focuses on the conflicts and tensions that emerge as a result of **generational dissonance** between parents and children (Foner & Dreby, 2011). Parents tend to hold the values and behavioral expectations of their country of origin, whereas U.S.-born and -raised children are more fully immersed in mainstream American culture. As a result, parents and children often have different ideas about discipline, education, parental authority, religion, dating, sexuality, and finding a marriage partner. Another tension emerges when children, who are often more proficient in English than their parents and are more familiar with navigating U.S. institutions, serve as interpreters and mediators for parents in schools, government, and health care. This upends traditional lines of authority and often gives children more responsibility than they otherwise would have.

In many ways, children in immigrant families are cultural innovators, combining aspects of their parents' home culture with those of U.S. culture. Parents do the same, adapting and compromising their expectations within this new context. Mexican fathers living in the United States, for example, report that they are raising their children more strictly than they would in Mexico, given what they see as the looser morality in the United States around sexuality, drug use, and alcohol use (Behnke, Taylor, & Parra-Cardona, 2008). Research among immigrant parents in Canada found that parents adapted their parenting styles to their new context by spending more time with their children than they would have in their home country and renegotiating lines of communication and authority between parents and children (Ochocka & Janzen, 2008). These examples remind us that culture is never static; it is always rooted in a structural context. Parents and children adapt their cultural values and ideals to this new context.

Many immigrant families are transnational, which means that the nuclear family is spread across two different countries. Most often it is fathers who migrate, leaving wives and children behind. This pattern is not new as it was also typical among European migrants more than 100 years ago. What is new is the frequency of transnational mothering. Some women migrate leaving husbands and children in their home country; some are unmarried and leave just their children; and some join husbands already in the United States, leaving children behind (Dreby, 2010). Dreby (2010) found that Mexican mothers who immigrate to the United States face challenges that fathers in similar circumstances do not. Because the provider role is central to fathering, men who move to the United States to provide financial support to their children are fulfilling their role as fathers. Fathers are dearly missed at home, but everyone in the family understands that the father is sacrificing for the economic well-being of his family, as good fathers are expected to do. Mothers, however, are judged more harshly. Even though they engage in the same behavior as fathers—migrating to provide better economic opportunities for their children—they are not judged by the same standards. A good mother provides daily care and nurturing for her children. A mother who lives abroad cannot do this, and so she is failing to live up to the good mother ideal.

In addition to the increasing frequency of transnational mothering, it is also becoming more common for children to migrate on their own. Children of privilege move to the United States to pursue educational opportunities in high school and college. Less privileged children come to the United States fleeing violence at home, as was the case in 2014, when more than 60,000 unaccompanied minors, mostly from Honduras, El Salvador, and Guatemala arrived in the United States (Chishti & Hipsman, 2014).

One thing that has changed for today's immigrant families compared with earlier generations is that it is much easier to stay in touch with home countries. Internet, cell phones, and relatively inexpensive international calling makes frequent contact more accessible than it was 100 years ago when handwritten letters that would take weeks to arrive were the only way to keep in touch across long distances. The relative ease of international travel (e.g., an airplane, train, or bus ride instead of a berth on a transoceanic ship) also makes visits easier, at least for those with legal authorization to return to the United States. For those without documents, more restrictive immigration policies and increased border security in recent years has made travel more difficult. This has decreased the frequency of travel back home and lengthened their stays in the United States. Because it is too risky to return home and to try to cross the border again, they remain in the United States and forgo visits to children and family members at home.

Gay and Lesbian Parenting

A generation or two ago, most lesbians and, especially, gay men, did not expect to have children. A same-sex couple raising a child together was rare. If a gay man or lesbian wanted to parent, he or she would have entered a heterosexual marriage, as many did. What was 20 years ago a radical and rare act is now much more widely accepted. According to Gallup, in 1992, only 29 percent of Americans thought that gays and lesbians should be able to adopt children; that is now up to 63 percent, slightly higher than the proportion supporting same-sex marriage (Swift, 2014).

Almost one in four lesbian-couple households and one in ten gay-couple households include children (U.S. Census Bureau, 2013a). In addition, among gays and lesbians without children, 52 percent of gay men and 41 percent of lesbians say that they would like to have children. Although substantial, this is lower than the rates for childless heterosexuals (Gates, Badgett, Macomber, & Chambers, 2007).

MarcelaC/iStock

Almost one in four lesbian households include children.

Gay men and lesbians become parents through both biological and legal pathways. Until recent years, it was most common for gays and lesbians to have a biological child the old-fashioned way—through a relationship with an opposite-sex partner. This is common among older parents, among those whose communities are less accepting of same-sex relationships, and among those who did not enter into same-sex relationships until later in life. Other biological pathways to same-sex parenting include reproductive technologies like alternative (artificial) insemination, *in vitro* fertilization, and surrogacy.

Other gay men and lesbians become parents through adoption. Some go through a public or private agency to adopt a child. Others have what is called a second-parent adoption when a nonbiological parent adopts his or her partner's biological child. Without a second parent adoption, the nonbiological parent has no legal relationship with the child. Thus, second-parent adoptions are important to "protect the rights of both parents and allow both of them to claim their child as a dependent for tax purposes, to provide health insurance to their child from their employers, to take their child to the hospital for emergency care, and to share child custody and support in the event that their relationship dissolves" (Goldberg, 2010, p. 64).

Before the U.S. Supreme Court ruling in *Obergefell v. Hodges* that struck down state bans on same-sex marriage in 2015, many states did not allow adoption by same-sex couples nor second-parent adoption. April DeBoer and Jayne Rowse, the couple at the center of the court case that challenged Michigan's ban against same-sex marriage, are a case in point. They have four adopted children; because Michigan did not allow two unmarried people to adopt a child jointly (nor would it allow them to marry because they were of the same sex), each parent legally adopted two of them. The other parent had no legal relationship to the children her partner had adopted. If either parent died, a judge could have had the deceased parent's legally adopted children removed from the home and sent to foster care. As DeBoer describes it, "It was scary. . . . All along we thought we could protect our children, and we couldn't" (Bosman, 2015). This is what motivated them to challenge the marriage ban. Since the *Obergefell* ruling in 2015, all states have started to allow same-sex adoption.

The legalization of same-sex marriage did not remove all barriers to parenting. Reproductive technologies typically cost tens of thousands of dollars and are not covered by most health insurance plans, making them available only to the most privileged. Private adoption, both domestic and international, is also expensive. Legal barriers to same-sex adoption can also be significant, and they vary widely by agency and jurisdiction. In some states, judges can use a parent's identity as gay or lesbian to determine fitness for custody and visitation. In addition, many private adoption agencies, especially those that place infants, do not accept applications from same-sex couples (Brodzinsky, 2012).

The legal barriers to same-sex parenting are rooted in the perception that children are harmed by being raised by gay or lesbian parents. This was a primary argument used to defend bans on same-sex marriage. However, all the reliable scientific evidence points to the opposite conclusion: "[C]hildren living with two same-sex parents fare as well as children residing with two different-sex parents" (Manning, Fettro, & Lamidi, 2014, p. 486). Reviewing studies that looked at a variety of child outcomes, including academic performance, cognitive and social development, psychological health, early sexual activity, and substance abuse, these researchers found no evidence that children of same-sex parents differ from those of different-sex parents on these outcomes.

Same-sex parents do differ from different-sex parents in two important ways. First, to the extent that gay and lesbian parents model different gender expectations than do heterosexual parents, their children may have more flexible gender ideologies (Biblarz & Savci, 2010). For example, children's interests are less gender stereotypical when their parents have a more egalitarian division of labor. Because same-sex couples tend to have more egalitarian partnerships than do straight couples, this egalitarianism will influence children's gender ideologies. Some evidence also suggests that same-sex parents, particularly lesbian parents, are less likely to promote gender stereotypical behaviors in their children (Biblarz & Stacey, 2010). For example, Kate Henley Averett (2016) found that the gay and lesbian parents she interviewed intentionally exposed their children to a "gender buffet," a range of toys and activities that are not limited to those typically associated with the child's gender.

A second difference between same-sex and different-sex parents is the stigma and discrimination faced by the former. Same-sex parents are aware of their status as a stigmatized minority and make parenting choices based on this awareness. For example, both Averett (2016) and Kane (2012) found that gay and lesbian parents worried about being held accountable for their children's gendered behaviors; they feared that others would perceive a gender-nonconforming child as evidence that they are unfit parents. Same-sex parents also face both informal and formal discrimination from other parents, schools, religious institutions, and healthcare providers.

Opting Out of Parenthood

Although most people see children as central to family life (Powell, Bolzendahl, Geist, & Steelman, 2010), some Americans are not having children at all. In 2012,

15 percent of women aged 40 to 44 (typically seen as the end of the childbearing years) had never had a child compared with 10 percent in 1976 (U.S. Census Bureau, 2014a). The rate is highest for White women (16 percent) and African American women (15 percent) and lower for Asian American women (13 percent) and Hispanic women (11 percent) (Monte & Ellis, 2014). People who do not have children tend to be more highly educated, less religious, and less gender traditional than those with children, and they are more likely to live in urban areas and be in professional occupations (Blackstone, 2014). These same demographic groups also tend to have more positive attitudes toward childlessness as do women compared with men (Koropeckyj-Cox & Pendell, 2007).

Although fertility was much higher in the past than it is today, childlessness was not uncommon (Morgan, 1991). In fact, over 20 percent of White women born in the 1880s never had children. Childlessness was even more common among women born in 1910: 25 percent. The rate dropped during the baby boom years when fertility was on the upswing, but even then, 10 percent of women did not have children.

Although counting the number of women who do not have children is relatively straight-forward (and the overwhelming majority of this research is on women, not on men), figuring out *why* they do not have children is more complicated. In general, there are three categories of childlessness: the *voluntarily childless*, who can have children but choose not to (this group is also referred to as *childless-by-choice* and *childfree*); the *involuntarily childless*, who would like to have children but cannot as a result of infertility or other health concerns; and the *temporarily childless*, who do not currently have children but who plan to have them in the future. Most datasets do not distinguish between these categories, so it can be difficult to assess how many of the childless are within each group. However, Joyce Alba and Gladys Martinez (2006) estimated that among 40- to 44-year-old women without children in a national dataset, 44 percent were voluntarily childless, 40 percent were involuntarily childless, and 16 percent were temporarily childless.

Another difficulty in analyzing the reasons behind childlessness is that birth intentions are not static. Twenty-somethings who plan to have children may change their minds later when they realize that they are happy as they are and don't want to make the sacrifices that parenting entails. Others might be planning to remain childfree only to become involved with romantic partners who change their minds. Tim Heaton, Cardell Jacobson, and Kimberlee Holland (1999) find that changing birth intentions is not uncommon. About one in five respondents in their national sample changed their childbearing intentions in the six years between interviews—13 percent moved from intending to have children to not intending them, and 6 percent shifted from intending to be childfree to intending to have children. And this was only a six-year time period! Imagine how one's intentions might develop over a longer period, such as from one's early 20s to mid-30s. In addition, not all people who are childless made a conscious decision to stay that way: "Though some respondents make an early and permanent decision to be childless, others simply postpone having children until age, career, education, established lifestyle, and related factors significantly reduce the possibility of having children" (Heaton et al., 1999, p. 539).

Qualitative research on those without children has provided more nuanced understanding of these choices. Amy Blackstone (2014) finds that for women, the choice to remain childfree is often related to a desire to focus on career, whereas men are more likely to express concerns about the financial costs of childrearing. Both men and women report that they do not want to change their lifestyle in a way that intensive parenting requires, or to risk losing emotional and sexual intimacy with their partner. Others refer to the environmental consequences of population growth and to the desire to limit human impact on the Earth. Being childfree, especially when one is in a committed partnership, is not without stigma. People without children, particularly women, are often perceived as selfish, shallow, lonely, and cold. Contrary to these perceptions, however, people who are childfree have more time and energy to devote to community-building and are more civically and community engaged than are parents (Blackstone, 2014).

Change, Continuity, and Diversity in Parenting and Childhood

Ideologies and experiences of parenting and childhood in the United States have changed over time, but many of today's practices and ideals are rooted in the past. Contemporary fathers, for example, who play a more visible and active role in children's day-to-day lives, are more similar in this way to fathers in the 18th century than they are to the distant fathers of the 19th and early 20th centuries. Today's expectations of intensive mothering are also rooted in the cult of true womanhood that started developing in the 19th century. That most fathers continue to prioritize breadwinning and most mothers continue to prioritize caregiving is also rooted in separate spheres ideologies of the 19th century.

Ideologies of childhood have also grown from those in the past, with each era adding new expectations for what children need. In the Colonial period, parents were expected to provide for the physical care of children. Later, children's psychological and emotional health became a central part of childrearing as childhood was redefined as a time of vulnerability. Today, in addition to physical and psychological care, parents are expected to provide for children's cognitive development, raising expectations for parents to follow intensive parenting practices and reinforcing inequalities between families who have the cultural capital to provide this kind of care and those who do not.

The influences of gender, class, sexual orientation, and immigrant status on parenting are not new, although the specific challenges and opportunities for parents in these social locations do vary. Childlessness, for example, is less common now than it was in the early 20th century. Mothers and fathers continue to be held to distinctly gendered parenting expectations. More gays and lesbians are pursuing parenthood outside of the confines of heterosexual relationships, and the recent legalization of same-sex marriage has created a new legal context for same-sex parenting that may shape whether and how gay and lesbian couples parent. The challenges of immigrant and transnational families also have continuities with the past, even though these families are from different parts of the world than they were 100 years ago.

MAIN IDEAS

- Industrialization shifted ideologies of childhood, fatherhood, and motherhood. Children moved from being economically useful to emotionally priceless; fathers from moral overseers to breadwinners; and mothers from productivity to domesticity.

- Fertility rates vary by race-ethnicity, and women are having their first child at older ages.

- Parents today spend more time with their children than parents did in the past even though they are also spending more time in paid employment.

- Parenting is a gendered practice with higher expectations for mothers than fathers.

- Parenting ideologies vary by social class with middle-class families focused on cultivating their children's unique talents and working-class families allowing their children to grow and thrive naturally.

- One quarter of children are in immigrant families and face unique challenges.

- Gay and lesbian parenting has become more common and accepted, and evidence shows that children raised by gay and lesbian parents are similar on measures of well-being to children raised by heterosexual parents.

- Fifteen percent of women do not have children, although many still face stigma for this choice.

CHAPTER 8

Family Work

In 1989, sociologist Arlie Hochschild published a groundbreaking study that described the "second shift" of housework that married women complete after their first shift of paid employment. She interviewed couples like Nancy and Evan Holt, who experienced ongoing conflict about how to divide the household labor. Should Evan contribute his fair share, as Nancy argued, since they both were employed full time? Or did the responsibility remain with Nancy because it was part of her wifely role? She may have a job, Evan argued, but that doesn't mean she should be able to get out of her household responsibilities. Hochschild called these mismatched expectations about paid and unpaid work a "stalled revolution." Women's entry into the labor market had been revolutionary, but changes in men's behaviors at home had not kept pace.

More than twenty years later, in 2011, another sociologist, Kathleen Gerson, published *The Unfinished Revolution*. In this study, she interviewed more than 100 young men and women about their family experiences growing up and about what they hoped to achieve in their own work and family lives. Most of these young people aspired to have egalitarian relationships with employment and caregiving shared equally between partners. But most also expressed real skepticism that they will be able to achieve this equality. As one man said, "Work situations are not very accepting of people who want to put kids in an equal priority with their job" (Gerson, 2011, p. 120).

The word *revolution* is commonly used to describe the changes in women's employment patterns over the 20th century. The breadwinner–homemaker family peaked in the 1950s, and today, dual-earner couples are the majority. Changes in mother's employment have been especially striking: In 1950, only 11 percent of mothers with children younger than age six were in the labor market (Carter et al., 2006); in 2012, that figure was 65 percent (Bureau of Labor Statistics, 2013a). Most women now expect to work throughout their adult lives, and most men expect that their wives and partners will as well.

Although it is true that most mothers maintain some attachment to the labor market, they also tend to curtail their hours or take several years off when they have young children. Someone in the household needs to shop for groceries, clean house, do laundry, prepare and clean up after meals, and care for children, and that someone still tends to be a woman. Men *are* more involved in household labor and childcare, but their movement into household work has not been as dramatic as women's movement into the labor force. In addition, U.S. social policy offers few supports for families as they balance their family and employment responsibilities. Twenty-five years after Hochschild's (1989) stalled revolution, conflicts between work and family responsibilities remain.

This chapter focuses on family labor—the paid, unpaid, and sometimes paid-for labor that families engage in to maintain their households. It starts with a review of separate spheres and an overview of the complexity and pervasiveness of **care work**. Next, we review historical and empirical patterns in employment, housework, and childcare, and we discuss the implications of these patterns for work–family conflict and social policy. Throughout the chapter, we will keep in mind the theme of change and continuity for as much as some changes have been revolutionary, continuities in how families divide the family labor remain.

Ideology of Separate Spheres

Our contemporary ideas about how families should divide the paid and unpaid labor are strongly influenced by the ideology of separate spheres, which we first discussed in Chapter 1. This ideology emerged in the 19th century as the U.S. economy shifted from an agricultural to an industrial base. In an agricultural economy, work and home were one—men, women, and children worked in and around the farm to produce the goods that households needed. Although tasks were gender segregated, all tasks were valued as economic necessities; without the labor of both men and women, households could not survive. With industrialization, work and home became physically and ideologically separate— the public male sphere and the private female sphere. No longer producing goods at home, men now worked for wages in the public sphere and used these wages to support their families financially. By providing this support, men fulfilled their family obligations. Being a good husband and a good father was defined primarily through economic providership, the so-called *provider role*. As long as men fulfilled this role, contribution to the household in other ways was not expected.

In contrast, women's family obligations in an industrial economy focused on the private sphere. They were expected to keep house, care for children, and manage the day-to-day running of the household. Separate spheres ideology redefined this work as "an act of love rather than a contribution to survival" (Coontz, 2005, p. 155), nurturing rather than labor. This cult of domesticity, as it is called, limited women's opportunities in the public sphere and confined their attentions to the home.

Although this separate spheres ideology was assumed to be universal, it was class and race specific. It was primarily middle- and upper-class White families who had the economic resources to live up to this ideal. Middle-class men earned sufficient wages to support their families; most other men did not. Middle-class White women were deemed worthy of protection from the drudgery of paid work. Women of color and working-class White women, particularly immigrants, were not granted this same protection. Although the ideology of separate spheres was influential throughout society, its reality was more limited in scope.

Even today, when high rates of women's employment make the reality of separate spheres even more tenuous, we can still see how the ideology lives on. Women continue to take on primary responsibility for housework. Mothers spend more time with children than fathers do. Men spend more time in the paid labor force than women do. On the macro level, most workplaces are still organized around the ideal-worker norm, which assumes that workers do not have family responsibilities and that they are free to work whenever and wherever the boss needs them. With limited family leave and long work hours, U.S. family policies also reinforce this norm, much more so than in most other industrialized nations.

Defining Care Work

Employment is the most visible kind of work that families engage in. Work hours are monitored, we get paid for the time we spend working, and "what do you do for a living?" is one of the first questions we ask upon meeting someone new. Families need at least one wage-earner, and more often two, to meet the economic needs of a household. Yet maintaining a household and raising a family also require a tremendous amount of unpaid labor, traditionally done by women; this labor is often referred to as care work. Although some people engage in care work as their paid job, for example, childcare workers and home healthcare aides, most care work is unpaid and in the private sphere. In fact, it is so taken for granted that often it is not considered work at all.

Yet the variety of tasks that are included under the umbrella of care work take considerable time and energy. Caring for children is the most visible type of care work, but care work also includes (Carrington 1999):

> *Feeding work*: planning meals; shopping for groceries; cooking meals; knowing what family members like to eat; learning about food and food preparation; monitoring pantry supplies; keeping a food budget; and cleaning up while cooking and after meals.

Care work is pervasive and often invisible.

Housework: cleaning house;[1] caring for clothing and linen; caring for pets and plants; managing household paperwork and financial work; interacting with service or delivery workers; and making household repairs.

Kin work: maintaining relational ties with friends and family, including visiting, calling, and writing letters, cards, and emails; purchasing gifts for birthdays and holidays; organizing family gatherings; and deciding which relationships to focus on at any given time.

Consumption work: monitoring the marketplace by reading catalogs, magazines, and newspaper ads; learning about products from books, radio, and television; comparison shopping; making phone calls about products; maintaining purchase and service records; monitoring product and service quality; commuting to retail sites; waiting on line to purchase items; and keeping a budget.

This exhaustive—and exhausting—list of tasks highlights the many small activities that family members complete to maintain their households. Invisible and undervalued, these tasks form the latticework around which family life is structured. They are both a consequence of family life, that is, things that must be done to maintain a household, and a means by which family identity is created and reinforced. In the process of engaging in these caring activities for and with each other, families are created. Sharing meals, celebrating holidays together, and making an effort to pick up around the house before one's partner gets home "produces a stronger and more pervasive sense of the relationship(s) as a family, both in the eyes of the participants and in the eyes of others" (Carrington, 1999, p. 6). Care work is a way to do family.

---

1. In itself, this includes "vacuuming, sweeping, scrubbing, mopping and waxing floors; cleaning stovetops, ovens, refrigerators, microwaves, coffee pots, food processors, and other small appliances; cleaning kitchen sinks, cabinets, and counters; washing and drying dishes by hand, loading and unloading dishwashers; setting, cleaning, and wiping tables; dusting, cleaning, and polishing furniture; cleaning windows, mirrors, and window coverings; straightening and arranging furniture, books, magazines, newspapers, and toys; dusting and cleaning walls, baseboards, and ceilings; cleaning bathroom sinks, tubs, showers, and toilets; changing linens and making beds; cleaning and organizing closets, cupboards, storage spaces, and garages; emptying garbage and taking it out for collection; separating recyclables and taking them out for collection; cleaning garbage cans and recycling bins; and cleaning out fireplaces" (Carrington, 1999, p. 71). Whew.

Of course, care work has practical value, as well as symbolic value. It is absolutely essential not only to running a household but also to the U.S. economy: The U.S. gross domestic product (GDP) would be 26 percent higher if it included the value of nonmarket work (Bridgman, Dugan, Lal, Osborne, & Villones, 2012). And if families had to pay someone to do the tasks that women do for free, it would cost each family about $60,000 per year (Marquand, 2014).

Empirical Patterns in Employment, Housework, and Childcare

Women's Employment Before 1950

The development of the wage-based industrial economy in the 19th century completely changed family life. Rather than producing the goods they needed, families purchased them using money that family members earned in paid employment. Although most workers in the early years of industrialization were men, many women also were employed. Certain occupations—domestic service, teaching, and nursing—have long been dominated by women and some groups of women have a long history of labor force participation. As shown in Figure 8.1, for example, single women have had relatively high labor force

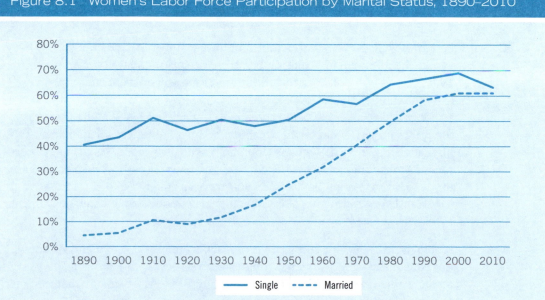

Figure 8.1   Women's Labor Force Participation by Marital Status, 1890–2010

Sources: U.S. Census Bureau, 1975; U.S. Census Bureau, 2011b; U.S. Census Bureau, 2012.

© The Mariners' Museum/CORBIS

African American married women had higher rates of labor force participation than Whites.

participation rates since the late 19th century, with 40 percent to 60 percent of single women working between 1890 and 1960. It was not unusual for young single women to work until marriage or having their first child, although, as we will discuss, women of color often continued their employment even after marriage and motherhood.

What was less common was married women's employment. Until 1930, no more than about 10 percent of married women were in the formal labor market. When we break this down by race, however, the patterns are a bit more complicated. Married White women had the lowest rates of employment, with only 6.5 percent in the labor market in 1920 (Amott & Matthaei, 1996). Those who could afford it would rely on husbands for all of their financial support, whereas others would earn wages at home in the informal market. For example, it was not uncommon for White working-class women to earn money by taking in boarders or doing piecework at home. This kind of labor maintained the image of separate spheres, in that women were doing female-typed jobs and were doing them at home, even though their earnings made essential economic contributions to the family.

Patterns for Black women were different. Black women have had higher employment rates than White women since Reconstruction. For example, in 1920, 32.5 percent of married African American women were employed, a rate five times higher than the rate for White women (Amott & Matthaei, 1996). This can be explained by both economic and ideological factors. Economically, the rural southern economy in which most African Americans lived had a high demand for Black women's labor, both as sharecroppers and as domestic servants. In addition, families relied on the earnings of both women and men to get by. Even after millions of African Americans migrated to cities in the North and West during the Great Migration, economic demands made women's employment a necessity.

Ideological factors also contributed to Black women's employment. Although not considered ideal, women's employment was acceptable in Black communities, free from the stigma that many White women experienced when they were employed. This acceptance went beyond economic necessity as even among the middle and upper-middle classes, Black women had relatively

162   Sociology of Families

high rates of employment. In 1940, almost 40 percent of middle-class Black married women were in the labor market, compared with less than 20 percent of middle-class White married women (Landry, 2000). Bart Landry argues that middle-class Black wives

> pioneered an egalitarian ideology of the family that contrasted sharply with the cult of domesticity so prominent among whites. Instead of following the prevailing segregation of women to the private sphere, with only men allowed entry in the public sphere, black middle-class wives championed a "three-fold commitment" to family, community, and careers. In doing so they offered a different version of "true womanhood," one white women eventually adopted in the 1960s and 1970s. (pp. 5–6)

With their high rates of employment in the early 20th century, middle-class Black wives were on the forefront of family change, committed to supporting their families both financially and domestically. By the late 20th century, middle-class White wives were following in their path.

National-level employment data for Asian American, Latina, and Native American women are not available before the mid-20th century. However, historical records indicate that women in these racial-ethnic groups were also actively involved in financially supporting their families (Amott & Matthaei, 1996). For example, many Latinas in the Southwest worked on farms, in manufacturing, or as domestic servants. Along the West Coast and in the Hawaii territory, Asian American women, which at that time included women mainly of Chinese, Japanese, and Filipino descent, worked on farms, both family-owned and larger plantations, and as domestic servants, whereas others ran family-owned businesses. Native American women were mostly employed in traditional work, including agriculture, fishing, and textile-manufacturing, although women who had been relocated to urban areas also worked in domestic service.

Women's and Men's Employment Since 1950

The second half of the 20th century brought several changes to encourage the employment of married women, as shown in Figure 8.1. Most significantly, the decline in the manufacturing sector in the 1970s and stagnant wages for low-skilled workers since then means that it has become increasingly difficult for men without a college education to support their families. In 2010, the median weekly earnings for men with a high-school diploma was $710. In 1980, those same men would have earned $865 per week (adjusting for inflation), over

20 percent more than they earn today. As well-paid manufacturing jobs have disappeared, due to outsourcing and technological advances, what has taken their place are low-paid, unstable jobs in the service sector, particularly in retail sales.

Other macro-level changes have also encouraged women's employment. The removal of legal barriers to women's employment in traditionally men's jobs, including law, medicine, and business, has created an avenue for women to pursue these rewarding and well-paid professions. A decline in fertility rates after 1964 means that women now spend fewer years caring for young children and are available for employment when their children enter school or move out of the house. Finally, increasing consumer expectations for what it means to live a middle-class life, including high-end electronics, vacations, and a second (or third) family car, means that more families need an additional wage-earner to meet those expectations.

Given these macro-level shifts, it is no surprise that 74 percent of women aged 25 to 54 are in the labor market (Bureau of Labor Statistics, 2014a), as are almost two-thirds of mothers of young children (Bureau of Labor Statistics, 2015). Although women are more attached to the labor force than ever before, we can also see the lingering influences of separate spheres ideology. For example, although most women are in the labor force, many of these women work part time. Among employed women aged 25 to 54, almost 1 in 5 worked part time in 2014; for men, that figure was 1 in 15 (Bureau of Labor Statistics, 2014b). This figure is even higher for women with young children—28 percent (Bureau of Labor Statistics, 2015). In other words, given the numbers of women who work part time and who are not employed, only 56 percent of women aged 25 to 54 are employed full time.

We also see the lingering influence of separate spheres in that most men remain firmly committed to the provider role and both men and women expect men to support their families financially. Unlike women, most men do not consider giving up their jobs or reducing their employment hours to provide care for their families. Although the number of stay-at-home fathers has increased, they remain a distinct minority; only 3.4 percent of stay-at-home parents are fathers, increasing from 1.6 percent in 2001 (Harringon, Van Deusen, & Mazar, 2012).

Stay-at-home fathers often face stigma for making this choice (Doucet, 2004; Rochlen, McKelley, & Whittaker, 2010). Because masculinity and providership are so closely intertwined, men who are not employed are viewed suspiciously as failed men. One father who was the primary caregiver in his family and worked part time stated, "I think there were times when I felt I wasn't being a good man, by not providing more money for the family. And that I wasn't doing something more masculine. And there were times when my wife felt that she wasn't filling her traditional role as a wife and a mother" (Doucet, 2004, p. 288). The power of separate spheres ideology—that so closely links breadwinning with masculinity and caregiving with femininity—continues to shape how contemporary families organize and understand their family lives.

Housework

Another arena of both rapid change and persistent inequality is housework. Take a look at Figure 8.2, which shows the average weekly hours spent on housework for men and women since 1965. Women have significantly reduced the time they spend on household tasks over the past 45 years, from 30 hours per week in 1965 to 16 hours per week in 2009–2010. Men have doubled their housework time over the same period, from 5 hours to 10 hours per week. Yet the gap persists, with women spending about 60 percent more time on household tasks than men do. Several factors affect how much time men and women spend on housework, including number of children, age, social class, whether one rents or owns a home, and marital status. Yet, even when all of these factors are controlled, women spend more time on housework than men.

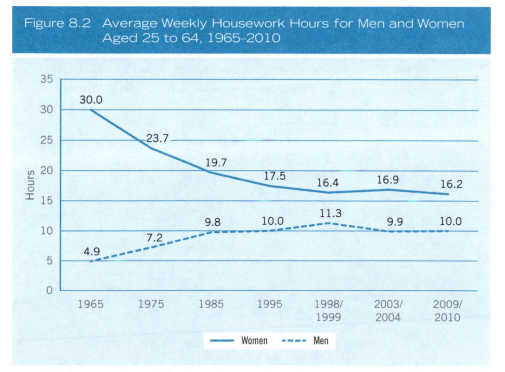

Figure 8.2   Average Weekly Housework Hours for Men and Women Aged 25 to 64, 1965–2010

Source: Bianchi, Sayer, Milkie, & Robinson, 2012.

Men have doubled the time they spend on housework since 1965.

What accounts for this continuing gender gap in housework? Three explanations have been offered: *time availability*, *power dependency*, and *the gender perspective*. The *time availability* model argues that women spend more time than men on housework because they spend less time in the labor market. Not only are women more likely than men to work part time, they also work fewer hours when they are employed full time—an average of 8.5 hours per day for men and 7.9 hours for women (Bureau of Labor Statistics, 2013a). Thus, women have more time available to complete household tasks. Yet, this begs the question as to *why* women spend less time in employment than men. The often unstated assumption in heterosexual families is that women are better suited to domesticity than are men. In addition, persistent wage inequality means that in most families, men earn more than women. When families decide that one partner needs to cut back on employment to take care of domestic responsibilities, that partner tends to be a woman. Thus, differences in employment hours can explain why women spend more time on housework than men, but it doesn't explain why domesticity continues to be defined as women's work and employment as men's work.

The second explanation for the gender gap in housework is derived from social exchange theory and focuses on power and economic dependency. This *power-dependency* model argues that (a) housework is an unpleasant task that individuals would rather not do, (b) earnings are resources that increase power and reduce dependency in a relationship, and (c) the less powerful and more dependent partner in a relationship will do more housework because they cannot leverage their partner to do more. According to this model, women spend more time on housework than men because they earn less; this financial dependency reduces women's power and leaves them responsible for housework. When women's earnings are similar to that of their husbands, they can use this bargaining power to reduce their housework time or to push their husbands to do more. In a more power-balanced relationship, men would be more responsive to those demands.

Evidence for this perspective is strong. For example, several researchers (Bittman, England, Sayer, Folbre, & Matheson, 2003; Brines, 1994; Greenstein, 2000) have found that women decrease the time they spend on housework as their earnings increase relative to their husbands' earnings. In addition, Sanjiv Gupta (2007) found that regardless of husbands' earnings, housework time has an inverse relationship with women's income—the more a woman earns, the less time she spends on housework.

We also see evidence for the power-dependency model among same-sex couples. Christopher Carrington (1999) conducted interviews and home observations with gay and lesbian couples in the San Francisco Bay Area. He found that despite describing their relationships as egalitarian (which is also typical among heterosexual couples), most couples tended to be specialized, with one partner more responsible for economic support and the other partner more responsible for household maintenance. Although the couples often explained this in terms of personality or interests, Carrington found that income was an important part of the story: The higher earning partner contributed less to household tasks than did the lower earning partner.

The power-dependency model shows how access to economic resources influences family life; yet, economic resources alone are not a sufficient explanation for the housework gap. In fact, gender remains the most reliable predictor of housework patterns in heterosexual couples. Regardless of work hours, education, or income, women spend more time on housework than men. To explain this, the *gender perspective* focuses on the pervasive influence of gender on individuals, interactions, and institutions (Risman, 1999). To put it simply, women do more housework than men because they are expected to—by themselves, their partners, and the institutional structures of which they are a part.

Candace West and Don Zimmerman (1987) coined the term "doing gender" to emphasize the ways in which gender is an interactive process that is created by our social behaviors. In other words, gender is not something we *have*; it is something we *do*. By enacting or avoiding particular behaviors, we demonstrate our gender. For example, housework is a way to do gender: women do gender by completing household tasks, which demonstrates their femininity, and men do gender by avoiding them, which demonstrates their masculinity. According to the gender perspective, housework is not only a practical activity necessary to maintain family and home life, but it is also an ideological activity that reinforces appropriate masculinity and femininity.

We see evidence of the gender perspective when we observe what happens when men and women move in and out of various living arrangements. Gupta (1999) found that when moving from living alone into heterosexual cohabitation or marriage, men reduce their housework hours by 29 percent and women increase theirs by 17 percent. Similarly, when moving from cohabitation or marriage into living alone, men increase their housework time by 61 percent and women decrease theirs by 16 percent. The gendered context of cohabitation and marriage is structured so as to expect women to take care of housework. When men live alone, they take care of these tasks themselves. But as soon as a woman enters the picture, the responsibility becomes hers. The gendered context of heterosexual co-residence, with or without marriage, puts housework squarely on women's shoulders.

This is not to say that same-sex couples are immune to gendered expectations. Carrington (1999) found that in gay male couples, partners tend to downplay the time and energy either partner spends on domesticity and that lesbian couples tend to emphasize it. To protect their gender identity, men were depicted as economic providers even when they spent much of their time in domestic labor. Similarly, women were depicted as nurturers and caregivers even when they spent little time on domestic tasks. Carrington's research demonstrates how cultural expectations about gender, providership, and housework maintain their ideological power even among same-sex couples.

The gender perspective also demonstrates a major limitation of the power-dependency model. As discussed, there is a negative linear relationship between income and housework for women—the more she earns, the less time she spends on housework. Yet for men, the picture is a bit different. Men increase their housework hours as their wives' income becomes more similar to theirs, which is consistent with the power-dependency argument. However, once women start earning more than their husbands, and particularly when the husband is completely economically dependent on his wife, his time on housework declines. In an attempt to neutralize the stigma he faces as a man who is economically dependent on a woman, he compensates by limiting the time he spends on nonmasculine tasks like housework.

Finally, the persistence of gendered expectations about housework can be observed in that few people, neither men nor women, report housework inequality as unfair. This goes back to the provider role. Even though women are employed, they are often not seen as providers or breadwinners, nor do they see themselves in this way (Potuchek, 1997). Their earnings may make important contributions to the financial maintenance of the family, but their identities as wives and mothers remain firmly attached to caregiving, just as men's identities as husbands and fathers continue to be associated with breadwinning. The symbolic meaning of employment is gendered in such a way as to reinforce women's responsibility for domestic tasks. Because housework continues to be defined as a woman's responsibility, even when she is employed, it is not considered inequitable if she does more.

Macro-Level Perspectives on Housework Although most of the research on housework focuses on the micro level—how much time individuals spend on housework in various circumstances—more recent research uses a macro-level lens to understand housework patterns. These researchers compare the division of labor across countries, taking into account policy regimes and overall levels of gender inequality. This research finds that structural and cultural contexts matter for how men and women divide the housework: "[C]ouples in more gender egalitarian societies divide housework more equally than those in less gender egalitarian societies, even when holding constant individual characteristics" (Lachance-Grzela & Bouchard, 2010, p. 774).

Jennifer Hook (2010) found that both married *and* single men do more housework in countries where women's employment is more common, suggesting that a high level of women's employment contributes to a cultural shift in gender expectations that influences all members of society, even men who are not living with women. In other research, Hook (2006) found that when governments encourage paternity leave, thereby challenging separate spheres ideology, men spend more time on housework even if they have never taken paternity leave. These macro-level patterns emphasize how closely housework is tied to gender inequality in the larger society. The more a society encourages and values gender equality, the more these values are enacted in the private sphere.

Childcare

Chapter 7 described how changing ideas about children and parents have influenced how mothers and fathers spend time with their children. In this chapter, we discuss childcare as it relates to the other kinds of labor that families engage in. Let's start by looking at Figure 8.3, which shows a surprising trend. One would expect that as women's labor force participation rates increased,

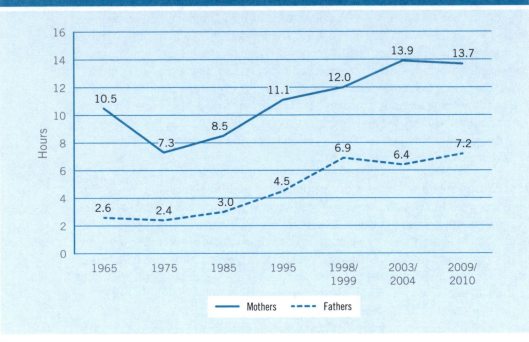

Figure 8.3 Average Weekly Hours Married Parents Spend on Childcare, 1965–2010

Source: Bianchi et al., 2012.

the time they spent with their children would have decreased. Yet, Figure 8.3 shows just the opposite. After a dip in mother's time with children in the 1970s and 1980s, it is now almost 40 percent higher than it was in 1965 despite the increases in women's labor force participation since then. Men's childcare time has been increasing since the 1960s and is at a peak. What happened? As you learned in the previous chapter, expectations about good parenting have intensified, and both mothers and fathers spend more time interacting with and caring for their children in a variety of contexts. They sacrifice other ways of spending their time—housework time, leisure time, and time alone—to spend more time with their children.

One primary concern about a mother's employment is the question of who will care for the children when she is at work. With more than 60 percent of mothers of young children employed at least part time, paid childcare providers are in high demand. Figure 8.4 shows the percentage of children younger than age 5 who are in various kinds of care arrangements. The most common arrangements are relatives (27 percent of young children), organized facilities (25 percent), and

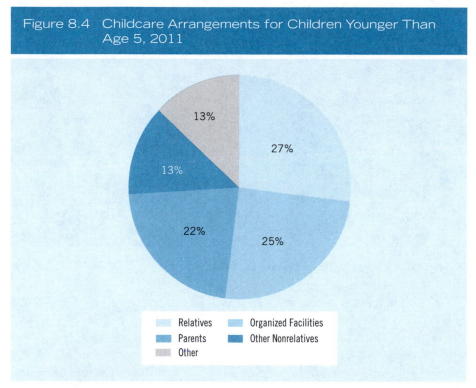

Figure 8.4   Childcare Arrangements for Children Younger Than Age 5, 2011

13%
27%
13%
22%
25%

Relatives   Organized Facilities
Parents   Other Nonrelatives
Other

Source: Laughlin, 2013.

parents, either the father providing care while the mother works or the mother watching the child while she works (22 percent).

Because the childcare system in the United States is market based, the type and quality of care varies widely by family income:

> The affluent have multiple market options that are flagged, like products on a supermarket shelf, by a nuanced array of labels—nannies, babysitters, housekeepers, au pairs, preschools, day care—and for school-aged children, fee-based after-school programs, lessons, and other specialized activities focused on sports, music, drama, dance, computers, and science. . . . At the other end of the class spectrum, parents from lower (and even middle) incomes lack the means to purchase quality paid care. Even if they qualify for government subsidies, they often confront long waiting lists. Low-income solo mothers and their children who are without kin or friends able to lend a daily hand lead especially pressed lives. (Thorne, 2004, p. 166)

One quarter of young children are cared for in organized care centers.

The growth in the "24/7 economy" (Presser, 2003) means that about 20 percent of U.S. workers work evenings and nights, work a rotating schedule, or work varying hours (Bianchi, 2011a). In addition, about one in three American workers work on the weekend. For married parents, this nonstandard schedule decreases the time they spend with each other, but it increases the time fathers spend caring for children while the mother works. Single parents are in a much more difficult position as finding childcare outside of regular daytime hours can be challenging if not impossible. For example, in the California Childhoods Project, Thorne (2004) tells the story of Betty Jones:

> a low-income solo African American mother who worked the late afternoon and evening shift as a custodian in an Oakland hospital. Her car had broken down months before and she couldn't afford repairs, so her 11-year old son Tyrone took responsibility for bringing himself and his 6-year-old sister to school on a city bus. After school, Tyrone picked up his younger sister and they walked to a bus stop to begin an hour-long daily ride, including a transfer, from Oakland to San Leandro where their grandmother lived. The grandmother took them with her to her evening job as a custodian in an office building. After she got off work at 10 or 11 p.m., she drove the kids back to their apartment. (p. 168)

This situation is far from ideal as the children have to travel long distances and accompany their grandmother to work until late in the evening, which is a far cry from the enrichment activities that a better-off family would be able to purchase. But if Betty did not have her mother nearby to help, the situation would be even more precarious.

Childcare is a major expense for families with children. Adjusted for inflation, average childcare costs have increased 70 percent since 1985. In 2011, the average weekly cost of care for children younger than age 5 was $179 per week or $716 per month (Laughlin, 2013). Many families calculate the costs of childcare through the lens of women's earnings. Does she earn enough to outweigh the cost of childcare? If most of her earnings will go to childcare, many families decide that it is not worth it for her to work. Notice how this decision-making process assumes that childcare is the women's responsibility. She either has to earn enough to pay for it or to forgo employment all together. Childcare is not conceptualized as a family expense but as a direct cost of women's, but not men's, employment.

Even with these high costs, childcare workers often make poverty-level wages and receive no benefits. In 2011, childcare workers, 96 percent of whom are women, earned $383 per week on average, about half as much as women workers in general (Bureau of Labor Statistics, 2013b). Childcare workers, many of whom are mothers themselves, take care of other people's children for poverty-level wages and often struggle to care for their own. About one third of childcare workers are women of color, which is well above their percentage in the overall labor market (Tuominen, 2003).

Work–Family Conflict and Social Policy

Given all the work that is necessary to take care of one's family—earning wages, caring for children, and maintaining the house—it is not surprising that many parents feel overwhelmed. Meeting responsibilities at work, getting children to and from school or childcare on time, putting meals on the table, and keeping the house at least somewhat presentable are major demands on time and energy that are often in conflict.

The nature of the work–family conflict that families experience depends on their place in the class system. Suzanne Bianchi (2011a) differentiates families with "too much work" from those with "too little work." For high-income professional families, the problem is "too much work"—expectations for long hours at work and an unwavering commitment to job and career leaves limited time for home and family. For lower income families, the problem is often "too little work"— too few hours working at jobs with inadequate pay, which leaves families economically vulnerable and can negatively affect well-being for family members, especially children. In addition, middle-income families face "work [that] offers little flexibility, requires mandatory overtime on short notice, or offers wages that can support a family only if both parents in two-parent families work full time or if single parents hold multiple jobs" (Bianchi, 2011a, p. 24). Although most public conversation about work–family balance focuses on the challenges faced by the most privileged families, families across the income distribution face unique challenges that deserve public attention and remedy.

U.S. family policies are notorious for lagging behind those of other countries. Our individualistic culture tends to focus on individual rather than on collective solutions to the problem of work–family conflict. For example, employed parents, particularly women, often receive the message that their problem is simply a matter of time management. Popular magazines, books, and websites suggest that harried working mothers can find balance by following a few simple pieces of advice, like keeping a regular laundry schedule and planning the week's meals on the weekend. As useful as advice like this might be for a specific individual, it locates the problem—and the solution—in the individual, rather than in social arrangements. It turns a public issue into a private trouble, and in so doing, it lets us off the hook for our collective responsibility to support families.

The United States is the only developed country, and one of only four countries in the world, that does not offer paid maternity leave; the others are Tonga, Suriname, and Papua New Guinea (World Bank Group, 2015). Most developed nations also offer paid paternity leave and generous supports for childcare. U.S. policy is much more limited. The U.S. Family and Medical Leave Act (FMLA), which was passed in 1993, entitles employees to 12 weeks of unpaid leave to care for an infant or for their own or a family member's medical needs. Not only is this leave unpaid, meaning that many workers cannot afford to take it, it also applies only to employers who have 50 or more employees, which leaves out a significant portion of the labor force.

Figure 8.5 shows how the United States compares with the other developed countries in the OECD (World Bank Group, 2015). It shows the days of guaranteed paid maternal, paternal, and parental (which can be taken by mothers or fathers) leave. The final column shows guaranteed unpaid leave for mothers and fathers, which in all countries except the United States is *in addition* to the paid leave. These data show clearly that the United States is an outlier among market-based democracies. We are the only nation not to offer paid leave, and even our unpaid leave is minimal compared with what other countries require of employers. For example, Sweden offers parents 16 months (480) days of paid leave plus another 109 days of unpaid leave (most of which are designated for mothers only). Germany offers more than three months of paid maternity leave; a year of paid parental leave that can be divided between mothers and fathers; and an additional 679 days of unpaid parental leave.

Figure 8.5 Days of Government-Mandated Maternity, Paternity, and Parental Leave in OECD Countries

Figure 8.5 Days of Government-Mandated Maternity, Paternity, and Parental Leave in OECD Countries

	Days of Paid Maternity Leave	Days of Paid Paternity Leave	Days of Paid Parental Leave (can be taken by mothers or fathers)	Days of Additional Unpaid Leave (includes maternity, paternity, and parental leave)
Australia	0	0	126	239
Austria	112	0	0	647
Belguim	105	10	120	0
Canada	105	0	245	28
Chile	126	5	84	0
Czech Republic	196	0	1095	0
Denmark	126	14	224	0
Estonia	140	10	435	590
Finland	147	24	215	0
France	112	11	0	1025
Germany	98	0	360	679
Greece	119	2	0	120
Hungary	168	5	590	0
Iceland	90	90	90	0
Ireland	182	0	0	238
Israel	98	0	0	368
Italy	150	1	300	0
Japan	98	0	309	0
Korea	90	3	0	2
Luxembourg	112	2	180	0
Netherlands	112	2	0	0
New Zealand	112	0	0	308
Norway	0	0	343	0

(Continued)

Figure 8.5 (Continued)

	Days of Paid Maternity Leave	Days of Paid Paternity Leave	Days of Paid Parental Leave (can be taken by mothers or fathers)	Days of Additional Unpaid Leave (includes maternity, paternity, and parental leave)
Poland	182	14	182	898
Portugal	0	0	120	0
Slovak Republic	238	0	899	0
Slovenia	105	30	130	0
Spain	112	13	0	1095
Sweden	0	0	480	109
Switzerland	98	0	0	14
United Kingdom	14	14	259	91
United States	0	0	0	84

Source: World Bank Group, 2015.

Although some private corporations in the United States offer generous leave policies, especially for their higher level employees, the government does not mandate that they do so. In addition, having policies on the books does not mean that employees feel comfortable taking them. Corporate culture tends to expect that workers prioritize their jobs over anything else in their lives (Fried, 1998). Long hours, mandatory overtime, and being available 24–7 have become standard expectations in many professions. Although corporate policy might technically allow a worker to take time off after the birth of a child or to work flex-time to facilitate taking care of family responsibilities, many workers fear that doing so will lead to wage and career stagnation.

The **motherhood penalty**—the fact that women with children earn significantly less than those without children—is well documented. Differing work hours, levels of human capital, and occupational choices can explain only part of this penalty. What is left is discrimination. In an experiment that asked participants to evaluate job applicants who shared all the same characteristics except for their parental status, Shelley Correll, Stephen Benard, and In Paik (2007) found that mothers were judged to be less competent, less committed, less worthy of promotion, and less likely to be hired than women without children; if they were hired, they were offered a lower salary than other women. In contrast, fathers experience a **fatherhood bonus**—fathers are judged to be more committed, more promotable, and more worthy of being hired, and at a higher wage, than nonfathers.

Policies can be effective tools to support women's employment, encourage men's participation in family caregiving, and minimize gender inequality at work and at home. Ironically, policies that provide generous family leaves for women can reinforce, rather than reduce, gender specialization in market and nonmarket work if men are not offered similar benefits. If employers expect that women, but not men, will be on leave for an extended period after the birth of a child, they are less likely to hire or promote them. But if fathers are also encouraged to take leave, it not only increases men's involvement with their children but it also improves women's wages and career prospects. In Sweden, for example, where strong incentives exist for fathers to take at least two months of paid leave, men have increased the time they spend with their children and women have maintained stronger connections to the labor force.

Recent research in the United States has identified important ways that institutional constraints impact family–work attitudes and decisions. David Pedulla and Sarah Thébaud (2015), for example, found that when men and women had access to supportive policies like subsidized childcare, paid family leave, and flexible scheduling, they preferred egalitarian relationships, where financial support and caregiving were shared equally between partners. When these policies were not in place, however, they fell back into preferences for traditional breadwinner–caregiver gender arrangements or preferred to forgo children and family all together. Even the most privileged women are not immune to these institutional constraints. Pamela Stone (2008) found that the highly educated and accomplished lawyers, physicians, and managers whom she interviewed were pushed out of their high-demand professions because they were incompatible with the responsibilities of parenting. This pattern of highly educated women choosing to be stay-at-home mothers is often called *opting out*, but Stone's research emphasizes that their experiences are less about *choosing* family over work and more about the ways that workplaces and policies have not responded to the needs of today's families. Certainly, these privileged women have more options than women who do not have a high-earning spouse to depend on. But the focus on individual choice obscures how social structure—institutions, policies, and gender arrangements—create the context for that choice. Many mothers—and fathers—would choose to do things differently if their structural circumstances allowed it.

Change, Continuity, and Diversity in Family Work

In taking a closer look at family work—employment, housework, and childcare—patterns of change and continuity are clear. On the side of change, we see increases in women's labor force participation, particularly for mothers of young children, and increases in the time men spend on housework and childcare. These changes have not completely undermined traditional ideas about the division of labor in families, however, as we also see gendered continuities in family labor: Women are less attached to the labor market than are men, men are still expected to be the economic providers for their families, and women are still expected to take on responsibility for housework. The lack of social policies to support families as they balance employment and care responsibilities also reinforces the ideal worker norm, a norm that has little relevance for most contemporary families. This discussion of family labor also emphasizes the importance of family diversity and inequality. In particular, we see how gender and class shape the patterns and challenges of family labor, and we see how even same-sex couples are influenced by gendered expectations about providership and care work.

MAIN IDEAS

- The ideology of separate spheres has changed, and it continues to influence contemporary families.

- Much care work is invisible and devalued, although it is absolutely necessary for maintaining households and families.

- Unmarried women have a long history of labor force participation as do married women of color. White married women increased their labor force participation over the 20th century.

- Men have not shifted their time and energy to care work to the same extent that women have done so for employment.

- Gender inequalities in housework persist and can be explained by time availability, power-dependency, and gender theories. Housework inequalities manifest on both the micro and macro levels.

- Both mothers and fathers are spending more time with their children today than they did in the past even though more mothers are employed.

- Families face unequal access to quality childcare.

- U.S. family policy lags significantly behind other countries.

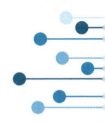

CHAPTER

9

Family Lives of Older Adults

Dana is a 48-year-old grandmother. She describes herself as a "play gramma": "Basically [the grandkids] come here and we play games and that kind of thing. . . . I never take them to doctor's appointments or anything. I'm pretty much a play gramma; we just do the fun stuff. We watch a lot of cartoons" (Harrington Meyer, 2014, pp. 41–42). Marta, age 54, describes herself similarly, "I just play with them: I'm a leisure grandma. I just play and have fun with them" (p. 41). Other grandparents, like 57-year-old Deanne, play a more instrumental role in her children's and grandchildren's lives. She describes being a grandmother as "the best job in the world" (p. 1), but she also says, "I sometimes just want a day off. Yesterday I would have loved a nap but I had to take care of the granddaughters and do the dishes" (p. 9). Deanne receives "constant" requests for help from her daughter, which she usually obliges. She loves her grandchildren and values being able to help her daughter, but she is also tired and could use a break. Similar ambiguity is expressed by adult children and grandchildren who are caring for aging parents. They love their parents and value being able to care for them, but this care comes with significant costs, including depression, financial strain, and time constraints (Silverstein & Giarrusso, 2010).

Popular images of older people living in the United States tend to vacillate between the doting grandmother and the isolated invalid. Although these extremes do exist, the reality for most is somewhere in between. Many older Americans do have close relationships with adult children and grandchildren, but intergenerational tensions, conflicts, and estrangements are also common. And although most unmarried older men and women live alone, they prefer it that way. As Dee, an 80-year-old woman in New York, put it, "I love my daughter. I know she loves me. But I don't get along with [her and her husband] that well. They both drive me kinda crazy" (Klinenberg, 2012). American norms of individualism are such that U.S.-born older people want to maintain independence as long as possible, so as to avoid becoming what they perceive as a burden on one's family.

This chapter explores the family experiences of older adults. Older people are living longer and healthier, and their family lives are increasingly complex. Economic vulnerability in younger generations means that they rely on the support of their parents and grandparents and that children and grandchildren reciprocate by providing billions of dollars' worth of care to aging relatives. Because life expectancies are longer than they have ever been, change, more than continuity, characterizes the contemporary family experiences of older Americans.

Defining Old Age

Like the transition to adulthood, the transition to old age is an ambiguous one, marked by both chronological and behavioral indicators. One can join AARP (known formerly as the American Association of Retired Persons) at age 50, start qualifying for senior discounts at 55, and receive full Social Security benefits between 65 and 67, depending on year of birth. Retirement is often used as a behavioral marker of old age, but what about the one in five Americans aged 65 and older who are in the labor force, including 11 percent of 74- to 79-year-olds? Are they not yet "old?" Grandparenthood is another common marker of older age, but the average age for becoming a first time grandparent in the United States is 49 for women and 52 for men (Leopold & Skopek, 2015), which is far younger than what most people would consider old age.

The Pew Research Center (2009) asked a nationally representative sample of Americans about their perceptions of, and experiences with, aging. According to the respondents, the average person becomes old at age 68. But things get more complicated when we break that perception down by age: Respondents younger than 30 believe that old age begins at 60, whereas the middle-aged put the threshold at 70 and those over 65 say that old age begins at 74. Pew also asked respondents about behavioral markers of old age (Figure 9.1). Most respondents report that a person is old when he or she can't live independently or can't drive a car. About half say a person is old when he or she forgets familiar names or is in failing health. A significant minority say that old age is marked by bladder control problems, lack of sexual activity, or retirement. Far fewer report that having grandchildren or having gray hair makes a person old.

Most commonly, researchers use age 65 as the threshold for defining older Americans. Yet, the experiences of a 65-year-old are often quite different from that of an 85-year-old even though we tend to include them in the same category. Some researchers have tried to deal with this by dividing aging people into three groups: the young old (aged 65 to 74), the old old (aged 75 to 84), and the oldest old (aged 85 and older). Almost all of the experiences of old age, from health status to retirement status to living arrangements, are experienced differently by people in each of these three age groups. For example, the young old are most likely to be in the labor force, and the oldest old are more likely to

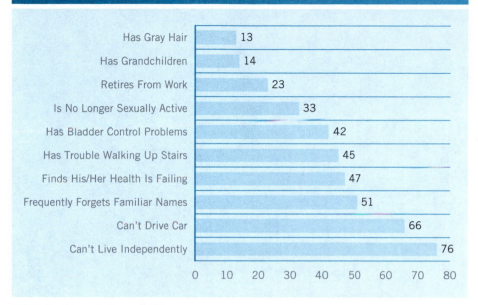

Figure 9.1   Percentage Saying a Person Is Old If . . .

Has Gray Hair	13
Has Grandchildren	14
Retires From Work	23
Is No Longer Sexually Active	33
Has Bladder Control Problems	42
Has Trouble Walking Up Stairs	45
Finds His/Her Health Is Failing	47
Frequently Forgets Familiar Names	51
Can't Drive Car	66
Can't Live Independently	76

Source: Pew Research Center, 2009.

be in frail health. To talk about all three age categories as a single, homogenous group is problematic. No matter how you slice it, though, one thing is clear: Old age is for other people (Pew Research Center, 2009). Most people older than age 65 say they do not feel old. Even among those 75 and older, only one third report that they feel old. Clearly, age is in the eye of the beholder.

Demographic Context

To understand the family experiences of older Americans, let's start with a macro-level view of the older population in the United States. Figure 9.2 is showing the age and sex structure of the U.S. population, what is called a **population pyramid**. And in the left side of the figure, showing data for 1900, you can see why it is called this: The distribution is shaped like a pyramid, with a wide base made up of large numbers of people at younger ages and a narrower peak, reflecting much smaller population sizes at the oldest ages. Under conditions of high mortality and high fertility, as was the case in the United States in 1900, each age group is smaller than the one below it. The U.S. population structure in 2010 (on the right side of the figure) looks much different. Until the oldest ages, the distribution looks more like a rectangle than a pyramid, reflecting the drastic decline in mortality over the 20th century.

Figure 9.2   Age and Sex Structure of the U.S. Population

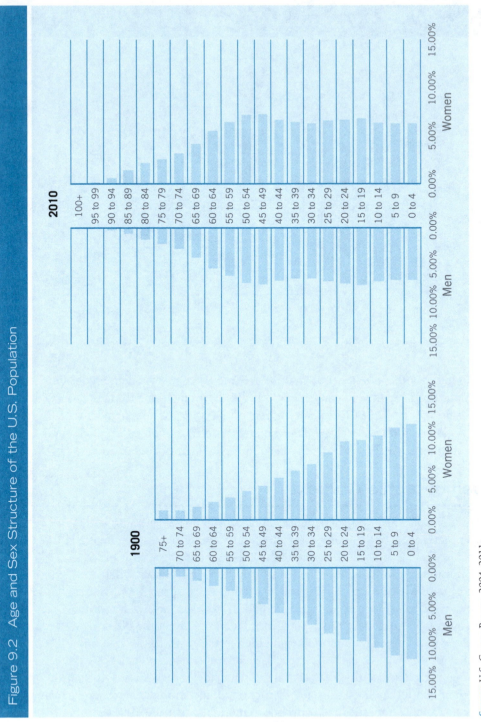

Source: U.S. Census Bureau, 2004, 2011a.

Most Americans live into their 60s, 70s, and 80s, and more than 60,000 are centenarians, meaning they are at least 100 years old.

As you can see in the population pyramids, the size of the older population has been increasing over time. In 2013, greater than 44.7 million people aged 65 years or older lived in the United States. This represents 14 percent of the population, more than triple the percentage in 1900. It is estimated that in 2040, 82 million Americans—over one in five—will be aged 65 or older (Administration on Aging, 2014). On average, an American who celebrates his or her 65th birthday can expect to live another 18 to 20 years. Women tend to live longer than men, and as a consequence, there are more women than men in every age group older than age 65.

Most older adults are living alone or with a spouse (Figure 9.3). In 2014, 72 percent of men aged 65 and older were living with a spouse, and this has not changed much since 1960. What has changed is that men are now more likely to be living alone (19 percent) than to be in some other living arrangement (9 percent), such as living with other relatives. Women's living arrangements are more varied. In 2014, almost half (46 percent) lived with a spouse, 35 percent lived alone, and the remaining 19 percent lived in some other arrangement.

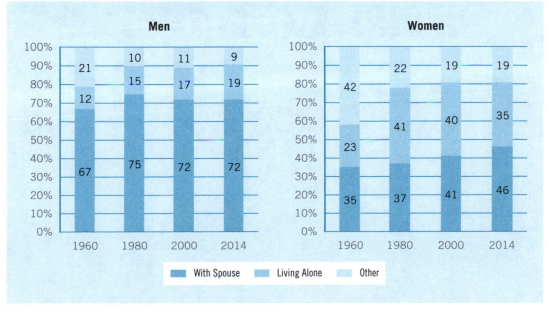

Figure 9.3 Living Arrangements of Americans Aged 65 or Older, 1960–2014

Sources: Administration on Aging, 2014; Bianchi & Casper, 2000.

In 1960, these percentages were 35 percent, 23 percent, and 42 percent, respectively. These changes for men and women reflect longer life expectancies and advances in health that allow Americans to remain independent at older ages. In 2010, only 3.5 percent of people aged 75 to 84 lived in an institutional setting like a nursing home or residential care facility, although this rose to 13 percent for those aged 85 and older (Congressional Budget Office, 2013).

Another reason why more older Americans are living alone is because they can afford to. The poverty rate for people aged 65 and older is 9.5 percent, which is 30 percent lower than the rate for 18- to 64-year-olds and more than 50 percent lower than the rate for children. This wasn't always the case. In 1959, older Americans had the *highest* poverty rates with more than one third falling below the poverty line. Changes in the Social Security program that tied benefits to inflation and the creation of Medicare in the 1960s helped to reduce poverty among the oldest Americans. There is some evidence, however, that these patterns may not continue beyond the current generation. Fewer of today's workers are covered by employer or union pensions; declining wages means saving for retirement is more challenging; and Social Security payments may not be able to keep up with the growing demand.

Even though older Americans today, as a group, are better off than they were 50 years ago, not all have benefitted equally. Just like in the younger population, hierarchies of gender and race shape access to financial resources for aging people.

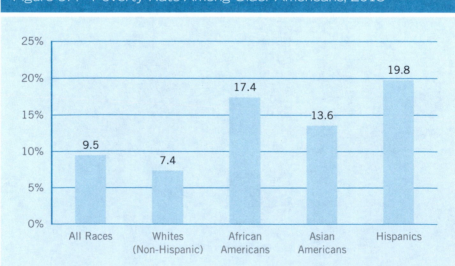

Figure 9.4 Poverty Rate Among Older Americans, 2013

Source: DeNavas-Walt & Proctor, 2014.

For example, older women are 70 percent more likely than older men to be poor (11.6 percent compared with 6.8 percent). Older people of color also have higher poverty rates than Whites (Figure 9.4): 7 percent of Whites older than age 65 have incomes below the poverty line compared with 17 percent of African Americans, 14 percent of Asian Americans, and 20 percent of Hispanics. Alternative measures of poverty also paint a more complex picture (Cubanski, Casillas, & Damino, 2015). Poverty measures that take into account increased medical expenses associated with older age and geographic differences in the cost of living increase the poverty rate for older Americans to 15 percent, which is a 50 percent increase over the official measure. In addition, 24 percent of older people can be considered **near poor**, in that their incomes are close to, but not below, the poverty line; this is in addition to the 9.5 percent who are officially defined as poor.

Changing immigration patterns are also shaping the racial-ethnic makeup of the older population. In 2010, 12 percent of U.S. adults ages 65 and older were foreign born (Population Reference Bureau, 2013); the size of the older foreign-born population is expected to quadruple to more than 16 million by 2050. Thirty-eight percent of the older foreign-born population is from Latin America, 29 percent from Asia, and 28 percent from Europe. A majority entered the United States before 1970, and only 10 percent have been in the country fewer than 10 years. Foreign-born older adults are more likely to live in multigenerational households, especially those who migrated after age 60, and they are more likely than their U.S.-born peers to face poverty and economic disadvantage. Despite this, they also display a health advantage relative to U.S.-born older people.

Consider what this changing demographic context for aging Americans—people living longer, healthier, more independently, and with unequal access to resources—means for family life: Lifelong marriages now last 60 years instead of 30; parents who spend 20 years rearing their children have at least 20 more relating with them as adults; grandparents watch their grandchildren grow well into adulthood; and financial resources are shared across generations. As we discussed in Chapter 2, intergenerational family ties are central parts of family life. Lower fertility means fewer siblings, and lower mortality means that vertical generational ties—ties among children, parents, and grandparents—are more prominent. These bean pole families structure family life throughout the life course and shape the family experiences of older adults.

Romantic Relationships Among Older Adults

"The current generation of older Americans faces more complex family and marital histories than any prior generation. . . . Researchers are uncovering greater heterogeneity and complexity in the family life of older Americans, [which] is likely to have important consequences for individual health and well-being as well as policy ramifications for the changing types of institutional support older adults require" (Manning & Brown, 2011, p. 193). As shown in Figure 9.5, 72 percent of men and 46 percent of women aged 65 and older are married. (The rate for men is higher because women are more likely to be widowed.) About one in four older Americans who are married are in a second or higher order marriage, and the rest are in first marriages. About one in seven older women and one in eight older men are divorced, and 4 percent of men and women older than age 65 have never been married. In addition, aging Whites are more likely than aging Hispanics and African Americans to be married and less likely to be divorced (Manning & Brown, 2011).

Although marriage is the most common relationship type for older Americans, cohabitation among this age group has also been growing, with the rate doubling between 2000 and 2010. Fifteen percent of cohabiting men and 12 percent of cohabiting women are aged 55 and older (U.S. Census Bureau, 2013b). Currently, about 8 percent of unmarried people in their 50s and 4 percent in their 60s are cohabiting; this drops to 1 percent for those aged 70 and older (Figure 9.6).

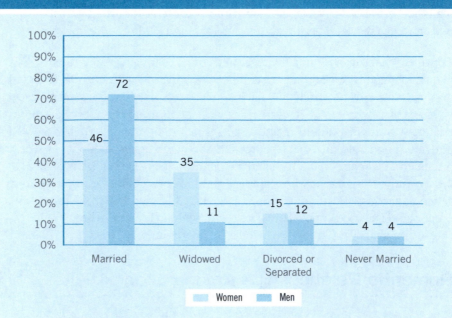

Figure 9.5   Marital Status of Older Adults (65+)

Source: Administration on Aging, 2014.

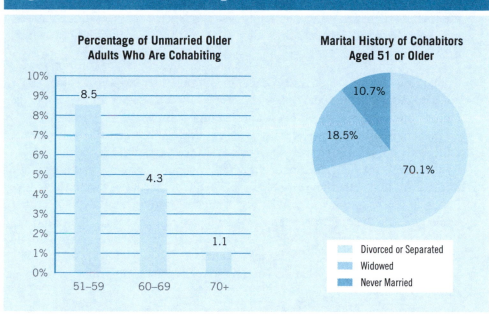

Figure 9.6   Cohabitation Among Older Adults

Percentage of Unmarried Older Adults Who Are Cohabiting

- 51–59: 8.5
- 60–69: 4.3
- 70+: 1.1

Marital History of Cohabitors Aged 51 or Older

- 70.1%
- 18.5%
- 10.7%

Legend:
- Divorced or Separated
- Widowed
- Never Married

Source: Brown et al., 2006.

Seventy percent of these cohabitors are divorced, 18 percent are widowed, and 11 percent have never been married (Brown, Lee, & Bulanda, 2006).

Why are more older adults living together? First, more people entering this age group are unmarried, either divorced or having never been married, meaning that they are available to form a new cohabiting union. Second, unlike earlier generations of older people who had little direct experience with cohabitation and often disapproved of it, today's older people, especially those in their 50s and 60s, are more likely to have cohabited at some point in their adult lives. They bring this experience with, and approval of, cohabitation into the older ages, increasing the likelihood of cohabitation.

Older people cohabit for different reasons than their younger counterparts. Cohabitation after age 50 is rarely a precursor to marriage and instead is a long-term alternative to it (Brown, Bulanda, & Lee, 2012; King & Scott, 2005). Although both younger and older cohabitors benefit from shared living expenses, financial motivations for cohabitation differ for these two groups. Young people are often motivated to cohabit because they lack the financial resources to marry; aging people cohabit to protect their existing financial resources. People who are widowed or divorced would become ineligible for their former spouse's Social Security or pension benefits if they remarried; cohabitation allows them to continue receiving these funds. For the financially better-off, cohabitation also ensures that assets will be passed on to children and grandchildren after their death, rather than inherited by a new spouse.

Cohabiting relationships are also common among older gay and lesbian couples. According to federal data, 11 percent of same-sex couple households include one member age 65 or older (Manning & Brown, 2011) and 71 percent of older same-sex couples have lived together for at least five years. Older gay and lesbian couples have been a visible part of the movement to legalize same-sex marriage. One of the first four same-sex couples in the world to marry in the Netherlands in 2001 had been together 36 years. In the United States, an 84-year-old woman who was denied the federal estate tax exemption when her wife died in 2009 sued the federal government for recognition of their New York marriage. She won her case in 2013 when the Supreme Court struck down the Defense of Marriage Act; this set the stage for the 2015 Supreme Court decision that declared all state-level bans on same-sex marriage unconstitutional.

AP Photo/Peter DeJong

Ton Jansen and Louis Rogmans, center, were among the first four same-sex couples in the world to get married in the Netherlands in 2001.

Another romantic arrangement among aging adults that has received more attention in recent years is *living apart together* (LAT). LAT relationships refer to couples who are in committed, long-term relationships but who choose not to share a household. This offers people the companionship and emotional support of a romantic relationship without the responsibilities of shared living (Benson & Coleman, 2016). Older women, in particular, who have spent their lives taking care of partners and children, appreciate the autonomy that living alone allows. Living apart from a new partner allows them to maintain this autonomy, while experiencing the intimacy of a romantic union. Because most family research in the United States uses household-based definitions, we don't know how many older Americans are in LAT relationships. In Europe, however, evidence suggests that older people are more likely than those who are younger to live apart together (Manning & Brown, 2011).

Grandparenting

Although grandparenthood certainly isn't new, grandparenthood in its current form is. Grandparenthood has become a distinct phase in the life course, an intergenerational role that one occupies for a significant proportion of one's life (Leopold & Skopek, 2015). When life expectancy was shorter, one was a grandparent for fewer years, and when fertility was higher, those years overlapped with active parenting. Parents would still be raising their youngest children when their oldest children start having children of their own. Today, most people become grandparents only after they are done rearing their children, and adults who become grandparents in their 50s can expect 35 years of grandparenting ahead of them (Leopold & Skopek, 2015).

In one of the first explorations of the grandparent role, Andrew Cherlin and Frank Furstenberg (1986) found that grandparents fell into one of three role types—remote (29 percent of the sample), companionate (55 percent), or involved (16 percent). More recent research found similar results by using a slightly different typology (Mueller, Wilhelm, & Elder, 2002). This suggests that the dominant grandparenthood role in the United States is characterized by companionship—someone who shares time with grandchildren, offers guidance and advice, and generally avoids much of the discipline and financial responsibility associated with parenting. The grandparent role is not static, however; it varies over the life course and can be enacted differently with each grandchild. For example, grandparents tend to interact more frequently with younger grandchildren than with older grandchildren (Silverstein & Marenco, 2001) and with grandchildren who live closer.

Monkeybusinessimages/iStock

With more longevity and better health, grandparents are playing a more active role in grandchildren's lives.

Grandparent–grandchild relationships are, in many ways, contingent on parents, as the parents act as a bridge between the older and younger generations. When parents and grandparents have conflicted relationships, the relationship between grandparents and grandchildren is more distant. Parent relationship status also affects grandparent–grandchild relationships. In cases of nonmarital childbearing or a parental divorce, relationships with paternal grandparents are often weakened, whereas maternal grandparent relationships are strengthened. As a result, there is a matrifocal tilt in grandparent relationships (Mueller et al., 2002) in the United States, with closer ties between grandchildren and grandparents from the mother's side of the family.

Grandparents as Caregivers

Grandparents are an important safety net for families who need help caring for children. Whether as occasional babysitters, regular childcare providers, or full-time guardians, grandparents make important contributions to child and family well-being. About 10 percent of grandparents live with at least one grandchild (Ellis & Simmons, 2014), and another 25 percent provide regular babysitting or childcare (Luo, LaPierre, Hughes, & Waite, 2012). Thus, grandparents are frequent caregivers for families, and this is especially true for grandmothers.

Grandparent care can be divided into two types. The first type includes grandparents who provide childcare for, but do not live with, grandchildren. Among grandparents who live within 50 miles of grandchildren, almost half are regular babysitters, and one in three provide care while parents are working (Guzman, 2004). Parents often prefer grandparent care because they perceive it to be more trustworthy and nurturing than formal childcare settings. Plus, many families cannot afford the high cost of childcare, so they rely on grandparents to fill that gap. Four of five families with young children who use grandparent care do not pay for it, and those who do pay much less than market rates (Guzman, 2004). Scott Bass and Francis Caro (1996) estimated that grandparent care saves parents in the United States $17 to $29 billion a year, which amounts to $25 to $43 billion in 2015 dollars.

Most grandparents view their caregiving role for grandchildren positively (Harrington Meyer, 2014). It allows them to be an active part of their grandchildren's lives, and they are glad to be able to support their adult children in their parenting responsibilities. However, grandparents also express reservations about providing this care. Many grandparents who care for grandchildren are still employed, so they face similar challenges of balancing employment and caregiving responsibilities as do parents. Grandparents report adjusting work schedules, reducing leisure activities, and helping their children financially instead of saving for their retirement (Harrington Meyer, 2014). Many are providing childcare more frequently than they had anticipated and more frequently than they find ideal. As Madonna Harrington Meyer (2012) described it:

> [Grandmothers] are happy to spend time with their grandchildren, help raise them and provide high-quality care for them. They sparkle when they talk about their grandkids. Grandchildren are a source of great joy. They love them. And they love just how much the grandkids love them. But they are also grateful when their day's duties come to a close. (p. 76)

This ambivalence is also reflected in research on how caring for grandchildren affects grandparents' well-being (Silverstein & Giarrusso, 2010). Studies show that caring for grandchildren is positively related to physical health, mental health, feelings of usefulness, and social capital, but it can also lead to financial worries and feelings of stress and overload.

The second type of grandparent care is co-residential, meaning that grandparents are living in the same household as their grandchildren. Since 1970, the percentage of children living with grandparents has doubled from 3 to more

Six percent of children live with a grandparent acting as a primary caregiver.

than 6 percent (Ellis & Simmons, 2014). Most of these households are multigenerational, meaning that three generations—grandparents, parents, and grandchildren—are living together, most often in the grandparents' household. Others are in **skipped generation households**, where grandparents and grandchildren live together without a parent, and grandparents are the primary caregivers. This occurs when parents cannot care for children, usually as a result of incarceration, substance abuse, mental and physical health problems, or death. Thus, grandparents who provide full-time care tend to do so under difficult circumstances, which can have a negative effect on their health and well-being (Hughes, Waite, LaPierre, & Luo, 2007). In addition, 57 percent of grandparents who are caregivers are employed (Ellis & Simmons, 2014), so they are also faced with balancing work and care responsibilities.

Figure 9.7 shows the percentage of children across multigenerational and skipped generational households by race-ethnicity. Skipped generation households, where the child and grandparent are living without a parent present, are most common for White children (24 percent) and Black children (28 percent), whereas only 3 percent of Asian children and 12 percent of Hispanic children who live with grandparents do so without their parents present in the household. Most Asian children living with grandparents are also living with both parents, whereas the largest proportion of Black and Hispanic children are living with a grandparent and their mothers.

Grandparent care is also common in Native American families; Native American grandparents are about three times as likely as grandparents in the overall population to be caring for a grandchild (Mutchler, Baker, & Lee, 2007). This reflects both cultural preference and need. Native American grandparents are valued for the linkages to tribal tradition, language, and culture that they can provide for young people. Weibel-Orlando (2009) refers to grandparents in this role as "cultural conservators." They care for their grandchildren to help them connect to their cultural history. In addition to this cultural role, high rates of poverty, single parenthood, and substance abuse in Native American communities also increase the need for grandparents to provide care for children when parents cannot.

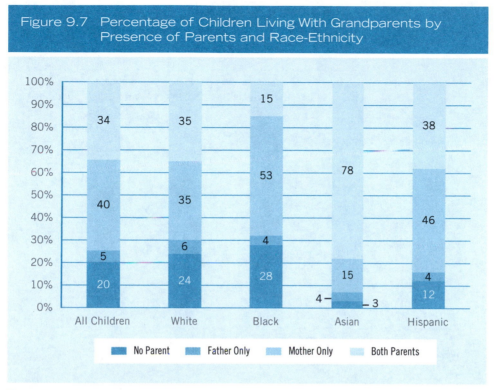

Figure 9.7   Percentage of Children Living With Grandparents by Presence of Parents and Race-Ethnicity

Source: Ellis & Simmons, 2014.

Intergenerational Solidarity and Ambivalence

Much of the research on the families of older Americans has focused on intergenerational relationships, particularly relationships with their adult children. Two concepts—**intergenerational solidarity** and **intergenerational ambivalence**—are central to understanding these relationships. *Solidarity* refers to the sense of cohesion among family members. *Ambivalence* refers to the combination of positive and negative feelings that characterize many intergenerational relationships. We may feel close to our families, but this does not erase the tensions and conflicts that can also be present.

Solidarity between adult children and their parents is high. Eighty percent of adults report that they feel close to their parents (Lawton, Silverstein, & Bengtson, 1994), and about the same percentage of parents reports that they feel close to their adult children (Swartz, 2009). In addition, 80 percent of parents speak with an adult child at least weekly; among adult children, more than two thirds speak to their mother and more than half speak to their father at least

Figure 9.8 Typology of Solidarity in Intergenerational Relationships

	Tight-Knit	Sociable	Obligatory	Intimate but Distant	Detached
Geographic proximity	X	X	X	—	—
Frequency of contact	X	X	X	—	—
Emotional closeness	X	X	—	X	—
Shared values	X	X	—	X	—
Instrumental exchanges	X	—	/	—	—
Prevalence:					
Relationship with mother	31%	28%	16%	19%	7%
Relationship with father	20%	23%	16%	14%	27%

Source: Silverstein & Bengston, 1997.

once per week (Swartz, 2009). One in five adults speaks to their mothers daily. Face-to-face contact is also frequent; 40 percent of adult children see a parent at least once per week, and more than half live within a one hour's drive (Lawton et al., 1994). According to a recent analysis by *The New York Times*, the median distance adults live from their mothers is 18 miles (Bui & Miller, 2015).

On average, intergenerational solidarity is high. But these averages can hide significant variation. Working with several dimensions of solidarity—geographic proximity, contact, emotional closeness, shared values, and exchanges of instrumental and financial support—Merril Silverstein and Vern Bengston (1997) developed a typology of intergenerational relations, as depicted in Figure 9.8, that captures this complexity. Analyzing nationally representative survey data, they found that their respondents, all of whom had at least one living parent, fell into one of five categories:

1. *Tight-knit* relations, where adult children report high levels of solidarity on all dimensions.

2. *Sociable* relations, where adult children live close to parents, are in frequent contact with parents, feel emotionally close to parents, and

share similar opinions and values with parents, but they are not involved in functional exchanges.

3. *Obligatory* relations, where adult children live close to and are in frequent contact with parents and are slightly more likely to provide and receive functional assistance, but they do not have value consensus with parents nor do they feel emotionally close to parents.

4. *Intimate but distant* relations, where adult children feel emotionally close to and express value consensus with parents, but they do not live near parents, experience frequent contact with parents, or exchange assistance with parents.

5. *Detached* relations, where adult children do not engage with parents on any of the dimensions.

This typology captures the solidarity and ambivalence that characterize intergenerational relationships. In relationships with both mothers and fathers, most adult respondents were in the middle three categories—neither tight-knit nor detached. For example, 16 percent of relationships were obligatory, where children lived near parents and were in frequent contact with them, and often gave or received practical support, yet they did not feel emotionally close to them nor have a strong sense of shared values. Geographic proximity, frequent contact, and even exchange of instrumental and financial help does not eliminate the potential for intergenerational family conflict. In fact, these characteristics might actually increase tension and difficulty (Kalmijn, 2014). In addition, the extent of relationship solidarity may depend on who is asked; parents are more likely to say that they are emotionally close to their adult children than adult children are to say they are emotionally close to their parents (Swartz, 2009).

Other research has shown how patterns of solidarity vary by gender, race-ethnicity, and social class. The closest intergenerational relationships can be found between mothers and daughters and among African Americans and those with lower incomes (Silverstein & Bengston, 1997). Natalia Sarkisian and Naomi Gerstel (2012) found similar patterns: African Americans and Latinos were more likely than Whites to live near or with kin, to be in frequent contact with kin, and to give and receive help with transportation, household tasks, and childcare. However, they also found that Whites were more likely than African Americans and Latinos to exchange financial assistance. This is mainly a result of social class. Whites are more likely to give and receive financial assistance because they have more resources available to share; in addition, when children receive financial gifts or loans from their parents, Whites tend to receive higher amounts than others (Swartz, 2009).

Intergenerational Exchanges

Of the various dimensions of intergenerational solidarity, the exchange of instrumental help and financial support across the generations—often referred to as **functional solidarity**—is among the most frequently studied. Instrumental exchanges include help with things like childcare, errands, housework, household repairs, and personal care. Financial support refers mostly to occasional loans or gifts (e.g., parents helping a child with the down payment to purchase a home) but can also include ongoing support (e.g., monthly contributions to one's food budget), although this kind of support is relatively rare outside of early adulthood. Although functional exchanges occur less frequently than socioemotional exchanges, they are not uncommon: Parents provide functional support to adult children on average a few times a year (Fingerman, Miller, Birditt, & Zarit, 2009), and most older persons in need of help get it from family members. The Pew Research Center (2009) found that 58 percent of adults with parents older than age 65 helped their parents with tasks like errands, housework, or home repairs.

Parents Helping Adult Children

A common assumption about intergenerational exchanges is that adult children are doing most of the giving and parents are doing most of the receiving. However, research has shown again and again that most instrumental and financial help flows *down* the generations, from parents to adult children, rather than up. It is only when parents reach the oldest ages and are in failing health that the flow reverses (Seltzer & Bianchi, 2013). The kind of help parents provide their adult children depends on children's needs, and parents don't provide equal help to all of their children (Fingerman et al., 2009). Children receive more help when they are young, unmarried, or experiencing physical or mental health problems. When adult children have children of their own, parents help with childcare and household tasks. Instrumental help is more common among those with lower levels of income, whereas financial help is more common among the financially better-off—the more resources parents have, the more they can share those resources with their children (Fingerman et al., 2015).

Adult Children Helping Parents

One challenge of an aging population structure is the question of who will take care of the increasing numbers of older people. This is true on the macro-level when one considers the costs of government programs to support older adults like Social Security and Medicare, as well as on the micro-level with interpersonal caregiving. Caregiving to older adults includes "providing personal care, doing household chores, preparing meals, shopping, taking care of finances, providing companionship, checking up regularly, arranging and supervising activities and outside services, and coordinating medical care" (Silverstein & Giarrusso, 2010, p. 1047). Although 80 percent of older people who are married receive this help from a spouse (Lima, Allen, Goldscheider, & Intrator, 2008), they make up only about half of the older population in need of help. Those without a spouse rely most frequently on adult children to provide this care. According to the Pew Research Center, 23 percent of middle-aged adults are caring for an older parent, family member, or friend (Stepler, 2015).

Women are more likely than men to be both intergenerational care recipients and caregivers; mothers receive more care than fathers, and daughters provide more care than sons (Suitor, Sechrist, Gilligan, & Pillemer, 2011). There are two reasons for this. One, women live longer than men and usually outlive their husbands; husbands tend to receive needed care from their spouses, whereas widows rely on their children. Second, mothers tend to be closer to their children than are fathers. This is especially the case when parents are not married. Unmarried and divorced fathers have less close relationships with their adult children and, as we will discuss in more detail, are especially vulnerable to not having a family caregiver.

The context for caring for aging parents has changed in the last few decades. Americans are living longer, but they are also remaining healthier into older ages, experiencing fewer limitations in their ability to care for themselves. According to the U.S. Census Bureau, only 7 percent of those aged 65 and older need help with basic personal care tasks like bathing and grooming, and only 15 percent need help with other tasks like housework and shopping (Brault, 2012). This need is highest among the oldest old—those aged 85 and older.

Because adults are older when they start needing help with personal care and daily tasks, this means their children are also older when they start providing this help. The **sandwich generation** includes middle-aged adults who are caring for both children and older family members. Although this term was originally coined to describe parents who are sandwiched between the care needs of young children and aging parents, the term is now understood more broadly. Some adult children are in their 50s and 60s by the time their parents need care, so they are beyond the years of caring for young children. However, as the transition to adulthood lengthens (as we discussed in Chapter 4), more middle-aged adults are caring for aging parents while assisting young adult children. And other adults are sandwiched between caring for grandchildren and an aging parent. If we assume 25-year generations, a 55-year-old could be helping to care for an 80-year-old parent and a 5-year-old child of their 30-year-old son or daughter. And let's not forget about the 5 million adult grandchildren who are caregivers for their grandparents; it is these grandchildren who are more likely to be sandwiched between care for their older relatives and care for their young children.

Ambivalence, Individualism, and Intergenerational Support

The challenges of sandwich caregiving are not unique to the United States, but they are exacerbated here because we offer few public supports for caregiving. Without subsidized childcare, adequate minimum wages, guaranteed parental leave, adequate pensions, and guaranteed health care, including residential care for the oldest Americans, we are left cobbling together individual solutions to collective problems. This puts more responsibility on all generations to care for each other. Although most are willing to accept this responsibility, it is not without costs as it puts additional financial, time, interpersonal, and emotional burdens on individuals and families.

Most Americans believe that they have an obligation to care for family members who need help while at the same time valuing independence and individualism. Surveys show that almost three fourths of Americans agree that adult children should provide financial assistance to parents if they need it, and about half agree that parents should provide financial assistance to their adult children (Lye, 1996). This help does not come without ambivalence, however. As Diane Lye (1996) puts it:

> On the one hand, norms of obligation mandate that adult children and parents should assist and care for each other over the life course. On the other hand, norms of independence mandate that adults should assume responsibility for their own well-being, that nuclear families should maintain themselves independently of wider kin networks, and that outsiders, including kin, should respect the privacy of nuclear families. Relations between adult children and their parents represent a delicate balancing of these two norms. (p. 95)

Many families achieve this balancing act by offering or accepting support when needed but by forming an individualistic narrative that downplays that support. In his study of the wealth gap between Whites and African Americans, for example, Thomas Shapiro (2004) found that White respondents who had received significant help from their parents, such as a down payment to purchase a home or tuition for a grandchild's private school, nonetheless reported that their financial well-being resulted primarily from their own hard work and thrift. One couple had received cash gifts of more than $10,000 from their parents over the years, as well as gifts of family vacations. When asked how they acquired their savings, they responded, "we worked for it" (Shapiro, 2004, p. 78). No doubt they did work hard for it, but they also benefitted from the financial help provided by their parents, help that gave them and their children opportunities for wealth accumulation and educational success that they otherwise would not have had. American norms of individualism render much of this intergenerational help invisible.

Family Complexity and Aging Families

As family structure has become more complex, intergenerational relationships have as well. Divorce, remarriage, and nonmarital childbearing all shape how parents and adult children experience their relationships with each other. For example, consider stepfamilies. Because stepfamilies are incompletely institutionalized, which we discussed in Chapter 6, the responsibilities between stepparents and stepchildren in later adulthood are less clearly defined than relationships between biological parents and children. Are stepchildren obligated to care for a stepparent in old age? Should a stepparent care for a stepchild's children? Generally, the answers to these questions depend on the quality of the relationship: The closer the relationship and the longer the stepparent has been a part of the family, the more intergenerational obligation exists, especially when the biological parent is still living. In other words, the more that stepkin view themselves as family, the more intergenerational assistance is exchanged.

Because the increase in nonmarital fertility is relatively new, we don't have much research on intergenerational relationships for these most recent cohorts of children, parents, and grandchildren. However, the research on divorced families is clear: On average, divorce reduces intergenerational support between adult children and their parents. As Teresa Swartz (2009) summarizes:

> Divorced parents report less contact and lower quality relationships with their adult children and live further away from them. . . . Divorced parents give less financial and instrumental support to their adult children than continuously married parents, with divorced fathers providing 25% less of

these types of aid to their adult children than do continuously married fathers, and divorced mothers providing 15% less than do continuously married mothers. . . . Divorce also weakens beliefs about family intergenerational responsibility. (p. 202)

Some of these differences, such as differences in financial support, can be explained, in part, by divorced parents' lower financial resources compared with married parents, but other differences emerge because of the average lower quality relationships between divorced parents and adult children.

The effects of divorce on intergenerational relationships in adulthood are especially salient for fathers. Although both mothers and fathers who are divorced report lower levels of contact and exchange with their adult children, the effects for fathers, especially noncustodial fathers, are much stronger (Swartz, 2009). For example, I-Fen Lin (2008) found that adult children are less likely to support divorced fathers in old age than to support divorced mothers. However, fathers who are close to their noncustodial children when they are young tend to remain close to them in adulthood (Aquilino, 2006). This suggests that strained intergenerational relationships are not an automatic outcome of divorce, but they are a reflection of the tensions that exist in conflicted families. Families that can minimize this conflict before, during, and after a divorce are more likely to have closer relationships in adulthood. Similar patterns are likely to hold for children born to unmarried parents whose relationships dissolve.

Change, Continuity, and Diversity in the Family Lives of Older Adults

Focusing on the family lives of today's older Americans is a discussion about change more than about continuity. Although some continuities are evident, such as women's role as caregivers and the vulnerability of poor older adults, they are far outweighed by the changes. The main reason for this is longer life expectancies—unlike other stages of life, this one simply didn't exist for large numbers of earlier generations. They died too soon. But today, most Americans live into their 70s and 80s, bringing the family complexities of their earlier years, and that of their children and grandchildren, with them. The older population is increasingly diverse, not only in terms of race but also in terms of relationship status and family roles. More older adults are cohabiting; more are caring for grandchildren as occasional, regular, and custodial caregivers; and immigration is increasing the racial-ethnic diversity of the older population.

MAIN IDEAS

- The size of the older adult population is larger than it has ever been, and older people are staying healthier into older ages. Today's generation also has more financial resources than earlier generations.

- Most older Americans are married or widowed, but increasing numbers of them are divorced and cohabiting.

- Grandparenting is taking up a larger proportion of the life course, and grandparents provide a significant amount of care for grandchildren in both shared and separate households.

- Intergenerational relationships are characterized by solidarity and ambivalence as norms to provide care conflict with American norms of individualism.

- Most intergenerational assistance moves down the generations until the oldest ages when children and grandchildren provide care for aging parents.

- Family complexity in younger years shapes the familial resources available in the older years.

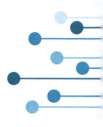

CHAPTER
10

Social Policy and the Future of Families

By now, you are well familiar with the sociological perspective on families. We've outlined the different approaches to defining family, the changes that families in the United States have gone through over the past 300 years, the ways that today's family patterns are rooted in the past, and the diversity in family structures and opportunities. In this final chapter, we will delve more deeply into the book's primary themes, exploring their implications for social policy and the future of families in the United States.

Defining Family

In Chapter 2, we examined four ways that sociologists define family: structurally, household based, role based, and interactionally. In learning more about various dimensions of family life—the transition to adulthood, relationship formation and dissolution, childrearing, family labor, and the family lives of older Americans—you had opportunity to see the implications of these different definitions on families.

Structurally, for example, we looked at data showing the percentage of births to unmarried mothers; the marital status of the older population; and changes in the divorce rate over time. All of these reflect structural definitions of family, people to whom one is related by blood or marriage. The many formal and informal benefits that accrue to families that are legally defined as such reinforces this structural understanding. For example, cohabiting couples are less likely than married couples to be considered family because they lack a formal legal tie (Powell, Bolzendahl, Geist, & Steelman, 2010); a boyfriend or girlfriend just does not have the same status as a spouse in the eyes of many. Public policy also tends to use structural definitions. Social Security survivors benefits, for example, are provided to spouses but not to unmarried partners. Priority for immigrant visas is given to spouses, parents, and children of U.S. residents and citizens. Blood relatives are given priority over nonrelatives to care for foster children in most cases. By prioritizing blood and legal ties over other kinds of relationships, these policies reinforce a structural definition of family.

A second approach to defining family focuses on households. Standard North American Family (SNAF) ideology (remember this from Chapter 1?) tends to conflate families and households by assuming that all members of a family live together and that households include only members of a nuclear family. The discomfort that Americans feel about young adults who live with their parents reflects this ideology—rather than living with their parents, they should be in their own household forming their own nuclear family. The reluctance of many U.S.-born older adults to move in with their adult children also reinforces this ideal as doing so would diminish their standing as head of their own household. Immigrant families, however, often see things differently. They are more likely to express an extended family ideal than a nuclear family one, making multigenerational households more acceptable. The growing frequency of shared custody among divorced families is also challenging this household-based definition as many children are a part of families in two different households.

A third way to define families is to focus on roles and the scripts associated with those roles. For example, we explored how father, mother, and child roles have changed over time. Fathers went from moral overseers to breadwinners, mothers from producers to caregivers, and children from workers to innocents. We discussed how these roles continue to change as more fathers incorporate caregiving into their breadwinning identity and more mothers incorporate employment into their caregiver identity. For some groups of mothers, particularly women of color, this interweaving of employment and caregiving is nothing new as it has been part of their mothering practices for generations (Collins, 2000). This emphasizes the variability in the ways that roles are enacted even when dominant scripts are more narrowly defined. Dominant scripts do not change overnight. Even today, narrow expectations about mothers' caregiving and fathers' breadwinning influences women's and men's decisions about employment and careers. Some young women intentionally choose a career path that will allow a primary focus on childrearing; similarly, some young men choose a career path to maximize earnings so as to be able to support a family.

Even as some roles change, other roles, such as stepparenthood, remain undefined, "incompletely institutionalized" to use Andrew Cherlin's (1978) phrase. Some stepparents act as primary parents, and others have a more distant relationship. Although this is true for biological and adoptive parents as well, the expectations for the parenting role are clearer than they are for stepparents. Parents may behave counter to role expectations, but the expectations are there nonetheless. For stepparents, the expectations are less clearly defined, and the role varies depending on external factors like child's age, caregiving experience, preferences of the child's biological parents, and interest in being a caregiver.

In the absence of clear expectations, stepparents have more latitude to opt out of parenting. That the law has no way to recognize the stepparenting role also reinforces its ambiguity.

Finally, families can be defined through interaction and through the sense of collective identity that emerges through shared activity. It is by acting like a family that a group becomes a family. To advocate for marriage equality, same-sex couples demonstrated their similarity to heterosexual married couples—raising children, paying a mortgage, and caring for each other in old age. These images were successful in convincing most Americans that same-sex families were, in fact, *real* families, doing the things that families do, and deserved the same legal protections as all other families. This political strategy was successful because it drew on the growing relevance of interactionist definitions of family.

Family Change

As you have seen throughout the book, the family is a dynamic institution, adapting to changes going on in the social context around it. Examples of this are endless. The breadwinner–homemaker ideal emerged in the 19th century in response to the growing wage economy. Young adults today are more dependent on their parents than they were in the 20th century because the expansion of higher education, higher housing costs, and an uncertain labor market mean it takes longer to achieve financial independence. White married women entered the labor force in large numbers in the 1970s because their husbands could no longer earn enough to support their families on a single income. The availability of reliable forms of birth control, which emerged from both medical advances and the removal of legal proscriptions against them, gave heterosexual couples more control over how many children to have, when to have them, and whether to have them at all.

One of the biggest changes we have seen in recent decades is the changing role of marriage in family life. For most of American history, marriage was necessary to form an independent household, live with a romantic partner, or have children. Today, one can do these things without being married. And many of us do. Americans are delaying marriage until they reach their late 20s, or even older, and 40 percent of children are born to unmarried mothers. In some communities, such as among African Americans and those experiencing economic disadvantage, the rate is even higher. Rather than a requirement for living an adult life, marriage has become optional.

This shift is so profound that demographers have referred to it as the **second demographic transition**. The first demographic transition refers to the decline in mortality and fertility that took place in industrialized countries over the course of the 19th century; one result of this transition was dramatic improvements in child well-being—infant mortality declined, parents invested more in each child, and public education became more widely available, creating opportunities for children across the class structure. The second demographic transition, which started in the late 20th century throughout much of the industrialized world, includes "delays in fertility and marriage; increases in cohabitation, divorce, and nonmarital childbearing; and increases in maternal employment" (McLanahan, 2004, p. 607), which are essentially all of the recent family changes we've discussed throughout this book.

Sara McLanahan (2004) argues that, unlike the first demographic transition, which improved family outcomes across all social strata, the second demographic transition is experienced differently by families in different social locations. Even though maternal employment is high for families across the class structure, other features of the transition differ. As you have learned, more educated Americans marry later, have more stable marriages, have children within marriage, and invest increasing amounts of time, money, and energy into childrearing. Less educated Americans are more likely to cohabit than marry, to have children outside of marriage, and to experience relationship instability. They also have fewer resources to invest in children. It seems fair to say that privileged families have benefitted from the family changes brought about by the second demographic transition, whereas less privileged families have not. As you will see in the subsequent discussion, the struggles of less privileged families have been made worse by the absence of public policies to support families in these demographic shifts.

Family Continuity

As much as families have changed, today's family patterns and inequalities are also rooted in the practices and ideologies of the past. Take the separate spheres ideology. The idea that the public sphere is for men and the private sphere is for women is pretty outdated. Women make up half of the labor force. Most mothers are employed, and men have doubled the time they spend on housework and childcare. The breadwinning husband and homemaking wife is an ideal that describes few families in reality.

But this separate spheres ideology lives on, most significantly in the ideal worker norm, the expectation that workers put work before everything else, including family responsibilities. Professional occupations, for example, are steeped in a culture of overwork, with professionals in law, medicine, higher education, finance, and technology expected to put in 50 to 60 hours per week. Workers on the other side of the occupational hierarchy are also held to the ideal worker norm. For them, the norm manifests in the expectation that they be available for any shift, including last-minute and variable shifts, with no recognition that this might interfere with caregiving responsibilities. How is one supposed to find childcare at the last minute? Sixty-hour workweeks and last-minute shifts might work if you have a stay-at-home spouse, but few of us do. The ideal worker norm does not take this into account.

One major consequence of the lingering effects of separate spheres ideology is the lack of a comprehensive family policy to help families balance their employment and caregiving responsibilities. As discussed in Chapter 8, the United States is one of only four nations in the world that has no guaranteed paid family leave to care for newborns. The United States is also an outlier in childcare policies, one of the few developed nations that does not offer federal support for childcare and early childhood education. Basically, U.S. family policy continues to assume a breadwinner–homemaker family model. This assumption has real and consequential implications for families—what kind of work people do, what kind of care children receive, and ultimately, what kind of opportunities children will have throughout their lives.

Consider childcare policy. Although the United States has a patchwork of tax policies that provide some relief for the costs of childcare for some families, we lack any comprehensive universal policy to provide affordable, high-quality childcare and preschool for young children. Increasingly, researchers are recognizing the central role of early childhood education on children's cognitive development. The kinds of interactions children have with caregivers—how many words they hear, what kinds of play they engage in, how caregivers respond to children's cues—shape children's language development and cognitive capacities. The lack of consistent standards for childcare providers and preschools, along with their high cost, means that some children receive high-quality care and some don't, reinforcing and recreating inequality in children's opportunities and outcomes.

Americans are so accustomed to trying to find individual solutions to structural challenges that we often fail to recognize that there are alternatives. Most industrialized countries offer more support for childcare and early childhood education than we do. It didn't have to be this way. In 1971, Congress passed the bipartisan Comprehensive Child Development Act, which would have guaranteed universal access to high-quality care for all children, regardless of a family's income. The act was vetoed by President Richard Nixon, citing concerns about "the potential 'family weakening' role of the law" (Palley & Shdaimah, 2014, p. 51)

Unlike other developed countries, the United States lacks universal childcare programs.

and its supposed communist implications. Imagine how different today's family lives would be without the daily worries about the availability, cost, and quality of childcare. President Nixon's decision to veto the legislation over 40 years ago reverberates for families today.

As Elizabeth Palley and Corey Shdaimah (2014) describe it, U.S. policy assumes that a family's need for childcare is an "unusual, unexpected, or temporary condition" and that "only in aberrant situations [does] one's family care responsibilities interfere with one's ability to work. In 'normal' situations, families are expected to provide care for each other, and this cannot be an obstacle to workplace performance" (p. 118). In other words, U.S. family policy assumes that "normal" families continue to follow the breadwinner–homemaker model.

Family Diversity, Inequality, and Social Policy

Family diversity is more visible today than it was in the past, but it wasn't all that uncommon even then. If a "traditional" family pathway is defined as an enduring first marriage with children and excludes divorce, childlessness, and nonmarital fertility, then almost one third of White women born between 1914 and 1924 followed an "untraditional" family path. Two thirds of Black women and 40 percent of Hispanic women did the same (Wu & Li, 2005). Families in the 1950s and early 1960s were more stable than families today, but they were also more stable than families that came before. The mid-20th century was an unusual time period—growing middle class, lower economic inequality, and earlier family formation. When we use this time period as our comparison, today's family patterns seem especially complex. But a longer view tells a different story, as you have seen throughout the text.

Family diversity—the variety of family structures and processes that exist—is closely tied to inequality. A family's location in race and class hierarchies creates opportunities for some and limits opportunities for others. For example, most of the differences in marriage and childbearing patterns across racial-ethnic groups can be explained by social class. African Americans have lower rates of marriage and higher rates of nonmarital childbearing because a higher proportion of African Americans than other racial-ethnic groups is poor or working class and lacks access to educational and economic opportunities available to other groups. Similarly, middle-class children have access to high-quality childcare and preschool, and they enter kindergarten already educationally ahead of their peers from working-class and poor families. This structural inequality, reinforced by social policies, creates the context for family inequality and diversity. Below, I describe two sets of policies that are especially relevant for diversity and inequality between families: housing policies and welfare policies.

Housing Policy and Family Inequality

Housing is more than a roof over one's head. As Janet Giele (2013) states:

> The quality of individual family housing varies with family size, income, minority status, region of the country, and rural or urban location. Just as families vary in income and wealth or poverty status, they also vary in size and quality of their dwelling, the amount of income they have to pay for rent or a mortgage, the quality of the neighborhood, and access to public services, community connections, and safe surroundings.

> The price and quality of a family's housing has consequences for its integration into the larger neighborhood and community. Adult family members' job opportunities and commuting time are influenced by the distance of their homes from their jobs. Children's success in school and their

ability to stay out of trouble, delay marriage, continue their education, and find good jobs is shaped by the quality of the neighborhood schools and the safety of its streets. (p. 190)

This is not simply a matter of families choosing where they would like to live. Structural inequalities give families differential access to housing options, and housing policies create opportunities for some families while diminishing them for others.

Consider home ownership. According to the Congressional Budget Office (2015), the federal government spends $130 billion annually to support home ownership through tax deductions for mortgage interest and property taxes; this benefit helps mostly middle- and upper-class families and can be claimed by every eligible homeowner. In contrast, housing supports for low-income families, including public housing and rent vouchers, cost the federal government about $50 billion per year, and only a quarter of eligible recipients receive benefits. Essentially, taxpayers are subsidizing home ownership for the middle class, whereas those with the lowest incomes face waiting lists, dilapidated buildings, and inadequate supply of affordable housing, particularly in urban areas.

Home ownership is the primary means for middle-class families to build wealth, and wealth creates opportunities. For example, families can use home equity to pay for children's college education. This allows some young adults to graduate from college with little or no debt and to begin their adult life on a more stable economic footing. Housing wealth also accounts for most inheritances, so that advantages of home ownership are passed on to future generations. Throughout U.S. history, African Americans have been denied access to land and home ownership, limiting their ability to build wealth and creating inequalities between Black and White families. The effects of that historical discrimination, coupled with new forms of discrimination, continue to reverberate today.

Melvin Oliver and Thomas Shapiro (2006) identify three policy mechanisms that have limited the opportunities for African Americans to own property and, as a consequence, to build wealth. First is the failure of policies during post–Civil War Reconstruction to provide any material support to former slaves. The calls from Black leaders for "40 acres and a mule," which would have distributed former Confederate land to freedmen and freedwomen, went unheeded. Instead, most former slaves had little choice but to continue working land owned by Whites, building White wealth instead of their own.

A second policy mechanism that created structural inequalities is related to suburbanization. Suburbanization, or the movement of homes and businesses to areas just outside of cities, "was principally financed and encouraged by actions of the federal government, which supported suburban growth from the 1930s through the 1960s by way of taxation, transportation, and housing policy" (Oliver & Shapiro, 2006, p. 16). Most significantly, the federal government established the Federal Housing Authority (FHA), whose lending rules favored investment in new White suburbs over mixed-race and Black neighborhoods in cities. FHA rules also increased segregation, based on the fear that integrating neighborhoods would cause property values to decline. "While these governmental policies [to expand home ownership] collectively enabled over thirty-five million families between 1933 and 1978 to participate in homeowner equity accumulation, they also had the adverse effect of constraining black Americans' residential opportunities to central-city ghettos of major U.S. metropolitan communities and denying them access to one of the most successful generators of wealth in American history—the suburban tract home" (Oliver & Shapiro, 2006, p. 16).

The third mechanism that created and reinforced structural inequalities in housing and wealth for families continues today: inequities in access to

© Bettmann/CORBIS

Opportunities for homeownership during post–World War II suburbanization were closed to most African American families.

mortgages (Pager & Shepard, 2008). African Americans and Latinos continue to be denied mortgages more frequently than Whites and to be charged higher interest rates even after controlling for income and credit history. As a result of predatory lending practices, people of color were also disproportionately hit by the 2007 housing crisis, in which property values plummeted and millions of families owed more on their homes than the homes were worth. In addition, people of color continue to be steered by real estate professionals to purchase homes in a limited number of neighborhoods, neighborhoods where property values grow more slowly and school quality is lower than in White neighborhoods. Even middle-class Blacks and Latinos have a harder time getting mortgages and moving into the neighborhood of their choice compared with lower-class Whites (Pager & Shepard, 2008).

These three policy mechanisms have created the inequities in housing and wealth that families experience today. That yesterday's Black families were denied these opportunities is a major reason why today's Black families have 13 times less wealth than White families (Kochhar & Fry, 2014). Even today's college-educated African Americans have less wealth than Whites because they have not inherited wealth from previous generations. Housing segregation, particularly between Whites and Blacks, remains high, and as a result, school segregation is as high today as it was in the 1970s. Black and Latino children live in neighborhoods with lower quality schools, less safe conditions, and fewer community resources than their White and Asian peers. These housing and neighborhood conditions, created and reinforced by social policy, create barriers to upward mobility and reinforce existing inequalities between families.

State Welfare Policy and Family Inequality

The **welfare state** includes government benefit programs that support the welfare of its citizens. Although the term "welfare" is often used to refer to cash payments for poor families, the term welfare state is used more broadly to apply to any social program that provides benefits to promote the well-being of participants. Compared with other developed nations, the U.S. welfare state is weak. We offer fewer programs and lower benefit levels. In the United States, families and individuals are expected to take care of themselves, rather than to pay higher taxes in exchange for a stronger government safety net.

Questions about how best to support poor families have long existed. As far back as the Colonial era, communities differentiated between the deserving and the undeserving poor. The former includes widows, children, aging adults, and people with disabilities, people who are judged to be poor as a result of no fault of their own. In contrast, the undeserving poor are seen as lazy, immoral, and responsible for their own poverty. This differentiation is built into our welfare programs; some people are seen as deserving of community help, and others are not.

The federal welfare state in the United States was created in 1935 with the Social Security Act. As we discussed, the wage economy grew dramatically in the early 20th century. Wages were volatile, and people who were too ill or too old to work were unable to support themselves or their families (Martin & Weaver, 2005). By the time the unemployment rate reached 34 percent in 1932 during the Great Depression, the political will to do something to protect workers and families was strong. The Social Security Act created three major social welfare programs that still exist in some form today: unemployment insurance, old age and disability insurance, and cash support for poor children. Three years later in 1938, the Fair Labor Standards Act established a minimum wage for some workers. In the years after these policies were implemented, old age and disability insurance, unemployment insurance, and the minimum wage were expanded so that more citizens were eligible to receive the benefit.

Unlike these other programs, cash support for poor families became more restrictive. The original goal of what came to be called Aid to Families with Dependent Children (AFDC) "was to provide aid to all children whose mothers lacked the support of a breadwinner, no matter how they got to that position" (Gordon & Batlan, 2011). However, provisions in the law and the law's implementation over its initial years restricted assistance to children in "suitable homes" as judged by local authorities. This often meant that children of unmarried mothers (as opposed to children of widows) and children of color were deemed ineligible. By the 1960s, however, welfare rights activists started organizing against these restrictions and their demeaning enforcement (such as man raids, when a caseworker would show up at an unmarried recipient's home in the middle of the night to see whether a man was sleeping there). By the 1970s, most recipients of cash benefits were children and their never married mothers rather than the "deserving" widows that the program was intended for in 1935.

The next major expansion of the U.S. welfare state came in the 1960s when programs such as Medicare (government health insurance for the older population), Medicaid (government health insurance for poor families), and food stamps were enacted. This is also the era when Social Security benefits for retirees and people with disabilities were tied to inflation, meaning that benefit levels automatically increase as the cost of living increases. This is the only welfare program that includes this provision at the federal level, which can be seen as an indicator of the perceived deservedness of its recipients.

At the same time that policy makers were tying Social Security benefits to inflation, the relative benefits provided to poor families through AFDC contracted. In 1970, average AFDC benefits brought families to 70 percent of the poverty threshold. By the time AFDC was abolished in 1996, benefits were so low that families received funds that amounted to only 38 percent of the threshold (Wexler & Engel, 1999). Between 1960 and 1970, the number of welfare recipients more than doubled, raising concerns both about program costs and whether the government was encouraging poor women to have children outside of marriage. As Sandra Wexler and Rafael Engel (1999) put it, "By the 1980s, the AFDC program itself, and the dependency it was said to produce among its recipients, had come to be seen as the 'problem'" (p. 41). In other words, poverty was no longer the problem—welfare was.

Political and public pressure against welfare continued to mount, and in 1996, the Personal Responsibility and Work Opportunity Reconciliation Act (PRWORA) was passed. This act abolished AFDC and replaced it with

AP Photo/Cameron Craig

Activists protest against the provisions of PRWORA in 1996.

Temporary Assistance to Needy Families (TANF). It includes four main provisions. First, federal funding is given in block grants to the states, so that each state has more control over how the policy is enacted and who is eligible to be served by it. Second, unlike AFDC, TANF is not an entitlement. This means that one can be eligible for assistance but not receive it if the state runs out of funding. Third, TANF includes time limits, so that recipients can receive benefits for no more than five years over their lifetime. Finally, TANF is a work first policy, meaning that it prioritizes getting adult participants into the labor force. Recipients are required to engage in work activities, including full-time or part-time employment, on-the-job training, or vocational education for up to 12 months.

The creation of TANF resulted in a dramatic reduction in the number of families receiving cash benefits, from a peak of 14.2 million individuals in 1994 to 3.8 million in 2013 (Danziger, 2010). Seventy-six percent of recipients are children. The movement of families off of public assistance, however, did not necessarily move them out of poverty or improve their well-being. Most former welfare recipients who moved into the labor force are working low-wage, unstable jobs that do not pay enough to lift a family out of poverty. Even if they are taking home more income than they would have received from TANF (which isn't hard to do since the average TANF benefit for a family of three is $378 per month), they also have increased costs, including for transportation and childcare. Although PRWORA included a significant expansion of funds for childcare subsidies for poor families, it isn't enough: Only one in five eligible families receive this benefit (Danziger, 2010). Many TANF recipients who cannot find work have health problems, or children with health problems, that create an additional barrier to stable employment.

As TANF receipt has been limited, the food stamp program, now called the Supplemental Nutrition Assistance Program (SNAP), has grown. Unlike TANF, SNAP is an entitlement, so all who are eligible can receive benefits. Because it is an entitlement, SNAP is more responsive than TANF to economic cycles, with the number of recipients declining during good economic times and rising when times are tough. In 2015, almost 46 million Americans received SNAP benefits, 12 times more than the number receiving TANF. The average SNAP benefit level for an individual is $127 per month. Even when TANF and SNAP benefits are combined, in no state do these programs come close to raising families out of poverty (Floyd & Schott, 2015). The highest average benefit level is in Alaska, where combined TANF and SNAP benefits bring family income to almost 80 percent of the poverty threshold. In 16 states, combined benefits are lower than half of what a family would need to be considered nonpoor.

Income-based programs (or "means-tested" programs, to use policy lingo) like TANF and SNAP make up a small proportion of government spending on social programs. Most social spending goes to Social Security and Medicare, which are universal entitlement programs for aging adults. As discussed in Chapter 9, these programs have been largely responsible for lifting older persons out of poverty since the 1960s. Less than 10 percent of Americans older than age 65 are poor, which is the lowest proportion for any age group. This case demonstrates the power of social policy to shape family opportunity and well-being. Policy has been used to improve the well-being of some families, as it has for people over age 65, and at the same time, it has been indifferent to (or, some would argue, hostile toward) the well-being of other families.

Future of American Families

The sociological perspective emphasizes the ways that families are rooted in social context. For example, sociologists look at the lengthening transition to adulthood as a response to economic uncertainty and expansion of higher education, not a measure of immaturity or laziness. We analyze family patterns as public issues, not private troubles (Mills, 1959), drawing attention to the social system and how it shapes family functions, structures, and opportunities. As I reflect on where families in the United States have been and where they might be going, I see three trends that will continue to shape this social context and have strong implications for families.

Economic Inequality and the Growing Class Divide in Families

No matter what area of family life one focuses on—fertility, childrearing, extended family relationships, work–family balance, marriage, cohabitation, divorce, or the transition to adulthood—social class is a central part of the story. We have examined innumerable examples throughout this book. Class matters for family structure and family opportunity.

For the last four decades, income and wealth inequality in the United States has been rising, returning to rates not seen since the early 20th century (McCall & Percheski, 2010). U.S. economic growth has primarily benefited top earners rather than being spread across the labor force, and this trend has accelerated since the 1970s. Since 1973, for example, the wages of workers at the 80th percentile, who earn more than 80 percent of workers, grew 21 percent, whereas the wages of a worker at the median grew a negligible 3.3 percent (Gordon, 2016). Since 2007, wages have declined for all but the top 20 percent of workers. Thus, growing income inequality in the United States is being driven primarily by increases at the top of the distribution (McCall & Percheski, 2010). The long erosion of the value of the minimum wage and declining labor union representation have contributed to wage stagnation for the rest of the work force. Wealth inequality is even more pronounced than income inequality, with the wealthiest 10 percent of households holding 76 percent of the wealth, compared with 28 percent of the income (Beddoes, 2012). In addition, economic inequality in the United States is higher than it is in other advanced economies.

At the same time that economic inequality is growing, the links between economic opportunity and marriage and fertility patterns have also strengthened. Marriage used to be something that almost everyone did—Black or White, rich or poor, educated or uneducated. It wasn't considered optional; it was an expected feature of adult life for most Americans. Economic inequality started growing in the late 20th century just as other cultural changes, like individualism, access to reliable contraception, and women's economic opportunities, were growing as well. Together, these conditions changed the family landscape, with more economically disadvantaged families of all races increasingly opting out of marriage. However, because African Americans, Latinos, and Native Americans continue to earn lower incomes and have less wealth than Whites and Asian Americans, racial gaps in family patterns have also grown, demonstrating the intersections between race and class in U.S. social structures.

The declining fortunes of the working class since the mid-20th century not only shape marriage and fertility patterns, but they also shape caregiving—the ability of family members to take care of each other. Highly educated workers not only have more economic resources, but they also have more access to paid sick time, vacation time, and paid family leave; more control over their work; and more flexibility in how and when work gets done. Less privileged workers couldn't be in a more different situation. Their work schedules can change week to week, or even day to day, with little or no notice; they have little control over their work; and they can be fired for staying at home with a sick child (Clawson & Gerstel, 2014).

To the extent that economic inequality continues to grow, it is likely that class differences in family patterns will expand as well. Policies on the local and state levels, such as requiring employers to offer paid sick leave and raising the minimum wage above the federal level, may help stabilize families in those communities. It may also be the case, however, that a tipping point has been reached, and even if economic prospects improve, low marriage rates for certain segments of the population will continue.

Immigration, Race-Ethnicity, and Family Ties

The future of families in the United States will also depend on trends in immigration patterns and policies. The increasing racial diversity of the United States is, in large part, a result of the Immigration and Nationality Act of 1965, which removed national origin quotas for immigration and prioritized family reunification. Since 1965, 76 percent of immigrants to the United States have been from Asia and Latin America, completely changing the racial-ethnic makeup of the U.S. population; the Asian population grew from 1 to 6 percent and the Latino population from 4 to 18 percent (Pew Research Center, 2015). The Census Bureau projects that the United States will become a majority–minority nation in 2044, meaning that no racial-ethnic group will make up more than half of the population. Four states—California, Hawaii, New Mexico, and Texas—are already majority–minority (and Hawaii is the only state that has never had a White majority).

The countries of origin for today's immigrants matter for their family patterns. Although they are from a diversity of countries, cultures, and religions, they tend to share norms of **familism**, "a strong commitment and obligation to family over that of the individual" (Pyke, 2014, p. 254), a contrast with the individualistic norms that have typically characterized U.S. culture. This collective orientation leads to family patterns like higher rates of marriage, lower rates of divorce and nonmarital childbearing, and more multigenerational households. For example, the marriage gap by race and immigration status is shown in Figure 10.1, illustrating two trends during the span of 2008 to 2010. First, immigrants of all races marry at higher rates than the U.S. born, and second, the racial gap in marriage is smaller among immigrants.

Although immigrant family structures tend to look different than those of the U.S. born, these differences typically fade by the third generation. The example of Latinos is illustrative. Although Latinos experience levels of economic disadvantage similar to that of Blacks, in terms of income, education, and wealth, their marriage patterns are more similar to that of Whites. This Latino paradox is usually explained by generational status and assimilation; first- and second-generation Latinos are forming families based on the norms of their home countries, which place a high premium on marriage. Yet, "in the third generation and beyond, Hispanic women's family patterns increasingly resemble those of black Americans. Exposure to economic disadvantage in the United States, then, combined with the widespread individualistic ethos here, eventually trumps whatever pro-marriage disposition Hispanics might have had" (Raley, Sweeney, & Wondra, 2015, p. 102).

To the extent that today's immigrants assimilate to U.S. family norms at the same rates that they have in the past, we would expect their family patterns to continue

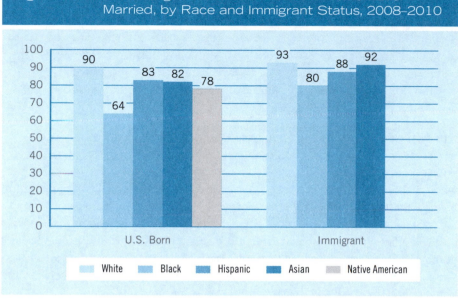

Figure 10.1   Percentage of 40- to 44-Year-Old Women Ever Married, by Race and Immigrant Status, 2008–2010

U.S. Born:
- White: 90
- Black: 64
- Hispanic: 83
- Asian: 82
- Native American: 78

Immigrant:
- White: 93
- Hispanic: 80
- Asian: 88
- Native American: 92

Legend: White, Black, Hispanic, Asian, Native American

Source: Qian, 2014.

to resemble those of their U.S.-born peers. However, if patterns of assimilation shift or slow down, then family patterns may continue to be influenced by norms of familism from countries of origin. For example, continued influx of immigrants from home countries can help to keep that country's culture alive in the U.S. context. Culture is never static so it will inevitably adapt to some degree, but if third- and fourth-generation immigrants continue to live in ethnic enclaves, practice traditional religion, and marry co-ethnics, familistic norms may be kept alive. This also may be facilitated by the relative ease of travel to, and communication with, countries of origin relative to earlier waves of migration.

Immigration will also continue to shape patterns of racial-ethnic intermarriage. In 2010, 15 percent of new marriages were interracial (Pew Research Center, 2012). Nine percent of Whites and a quarter of Latinos married someone of a different racial-ethnic group with no differences by gender. For African Americans and Asian Americans, however, rates of intermarriage vary widely by gender: 24 percent of Black men and 9 percent of Black women intermarried, as did 36 percent of Asian American women and 17 percent of Asian American men. Native Americans also intermarry at very high rates, 58 percent in 2013 (Wang, 2015).

To the extent that racial-ethnic diversity increases, racial-ethnic intermarriage also becomes more common. Jennifer Lee and Frank Bean (2010) found that more racially diverse cities have higher rates of intermarriage and more people identifying as multiracial, suggesting that diversity can lower racial boundaries. However, not all racial groups experience this integration. Cities with a high proportion of African Americans, for example, have lower rates of intermarriage, as do cities that are new destinations for Latino immigrants. Thus, growing rates of intermarriage among Whites, Asians, and Latinos may contribute to ongoing isolation for African Americans, who face stronger racial boundaries than other racial-ethnic groups (Lee & Bean, 2010).

Finally, the ties among immigration, race-ethnicity, and family inequality will be shaped by what kind of immigration reform, if any, is enacted. Immigration policies that determine who is allowed to live and work in the country legally and who must remain hidden in the shadows to avoid deportation will shape the future of U.S. families. Immigration policies that privilege more educated workers, as today's policies do, will mean more growth in populations that tend to have more stable families. Proposed immigration reforms that would allow undocumented immigrants to gain legal residency or citizenship would be life-changing for these Americans, opening doors for higher education, employment, and civic participation that are likely to have positive outcomes for families.

Unfinished Revolution in Gender and Sexuality

The last five decades have been characterized by revolutionary changes in gender and sexuality in families. We've witnessed high rates of maternal employment, fathers increasing the time they spend with their children, legalization of same-sex marriage, and young men's and women's aspirations to form egalitarian partnerships. However, evidence also points to areas where inequality remains firmly entrenched. Children continue to be socialized in highly gendered ways; occupational gender desegregation has stalled since the early 1990s, leaving most women concentrated in lower-wage, feminized occupations; and institutions continue to resist structural change that would better support families in their caregiving and wage earning, such as paid leave, flexible scheduling, and wage increases.

Entrenched ideas about gender and sexuality are illustrated by Emily Kane's (2012) book *The Gender Trap*. This title captures how difficult it is to disentangle ourselves from unequal gender structures. Interactional and institutional constraints trap us in conventional gender expectations, only some of which individuals are aware of or find problematic. Kane interviewed parents about how they navigate gender in their parenting. Her research highlights the many subtle and explicit ways that children are steered toward gender conformity by parents, peers, and the wider society, and how this conformity is understood primarily through the lens of individual choice. Parents were ensnared in gender traps that discouraged boys from displaying any traits judged to be too feminine, like sensitivity; encouraged girls to be feminine, but not too feminine; and assumed that children will grow up into heterosexual adults in neo-traditional partnerships, where the woman combines employment and caregiving and the man focuses on breadwinning. Kane's research shows how contemporary parenting practices continue to privilege heterosexual masculinity and to devalue femininity, suggesting that the gender trap will continue for future generations.

The gender and sexual revolution is ongoing, and change is uneven. Women have been more welcomed into formerly male spheres than the other way around. A complicating dimension is that most Americans do not want a complete revolution in gender and sexual arrangements. Some gendered practices, like wives taking their husbands' last names are rarely questioned and are not viewed by most as a gendered question at all. Americans are comfortable with a certain amount of gender inequality. We want women to have equal opportunity in the workforce, but we aren't entirely comfortable with a male preschool teacher or stay-at-home dad. We embrace a rhetoric of equality and individual choice at the same time that beliefs in gender essentialism—the idea that women and men are fundamentally different—persist (England, 2010; Kane, 2012).

Transfamilies, too, offer a unique case to illustrate the complexities of gender and sexual change in families. Transfamilies refer to families where one member of a romantic couple has changed, or is in the process of changing, sexes (sometimes the term is used more broadly to include any family that has a transgendered member). On the one hand, transfamilies, and transgendered people more generally, can be seen as challenging traditional assumptions that gender is natural and that one's gender identity always corresponds with one's genetic makeup. But sociological research with transfamilies suggests that pressures toward gender and sexual conformity are strong. For example, many transfamilies pass as unremarkable heterosexual couples, making them invisible as a distinct family form and minimizing the extent to which they can challenge gender and sexual assumptions in everyday interactions. Carla A. Pfeffer (2010) also found that women partners of transgender men tended to do more housework and emotion work than their partners. They, like women in other kinds of heterosexual relationships, provided individualistic explanations for this inequality that minimized the gendered dimensions of their experiences. Thus, even in families where gender is actively being challenged and (literally) recreated in some ways, traditional gender ideas are reinforced in other ways.

Although many scholars have written about the stalled gender and sexual revolution, others say, "Be patient! Revolution takes time." Expecting significant change overnight is unrealistic. Oriel Sullivan (2015), for example, argues that changes in men's commitment to caregiving have been substantial. Although parity with women has not been achieved, the magnitude of the change should not be discounted. That more men are fighting for access to paternity leave (Scheiber, 2015), and highly visible fathers like Mark Zuckerberg of Facebook are taking it, also reflects, and reinforces, this change.

We also see evidence of change in Kristen Myers and Ilana Demantas's (2015) research with heterosexual married men who lost their jobs during the recent recession. In the past, working-class men who lost their jobs and became economically dependent on their wives resisted doing work around the house because it would further diminish their status as failed breadwinners (Rubin, 1994). Yet, the men that Myers and Demantas (2015) interviewed willingly took on those tasks as they felt it was the fair thing to do since their wives were shouldering the burden of financial support for the family. They felt some of the same loss of masculinity for being out of work that men have felt in the past, but they also felt a responsibility to do more around the house. They changed their behavior not out of an ideological commitment to gender equality or to feminism but because it was the fair thing to do in their relationships. In adjusting to their circumstances, these men demonstrated the gender flexibility that Kathleen Gerson (2011) argues is essential for a family's ability to navigate the complex gendered domains of work and caregiving.

We are in the midst of an ongoing gender and sexual revolution. Negotiations in gender and sexual structures are underway, and the potential for significant and lasting change exists. However, the transformative possibilities in these negotiations are not automatic. They must be enacted. For example, Katrina Kimport (2014) argues that same-sex couples' "practice of marriage may hold the possibility of exposing the institution's heteronormative underpinning—but only when we look for it" (p. 129). Same-sex marriage may remove gender as a central organizing feature of family life, or it may do nothing more than reinforce marital privilege and further marginalize families of other kinds. Similarly, men's involvement in caregiving and women's commitment to paid labor have the potential to disrupt gender inequalities in families, but that potential has yet to be fully enacted.

Change, Continuity, and Diversity in American Families

The ongoing gender and sexual revolution, growing racial-ethnic diversity, and growth in economic inequality create the social context in which contemporary families live. We have seen much change in family life, but some conditions, including the ways that gender, race, and class hierarchies create inequalities in families, continue. As social actors, our choices and opportunities as individuals are constrained by the social context around us as we are held accountable to structural and institutional expectations. Yet, structures and institutions also change. Collectively, we have the power to influence the direction of these changes or, at the very least, their consequences. In the past few years, we have heard more political conversation about economic inequality, immigration reform, and the need for universal policies to support families. As individuals and as members of communities, we can advocate for structural conditions that will foster the well-being of American families. There will be disagreement on what those conditions should be. But the debate is necessary so that families in all their diversity can flourish.

MAIN IDEAS

- Each of the four ways of defining family—structurally, household based, role based, and interactionally—has implications for families.

- Families have changed in innumerable ways throughout history. The changes in the latter part of the 20th century have been called the second demographic transition.

- Today's family patterns also have continuities with the past. For example, the ideology of separate spheres continues to influence U.S. family policy.

- Historical and contemporary housing policies have created racial wealth inequality that continue to influence todays' families.

- U.S. welfare policy has prioritized support for aging families over support for poor families.

- U.S. families will continue to be influenced by economic inequality, immigration patterns and policies, and the unfinished revolution in gender and sexuality.

GLOSSARY

beanpole family: extended family structure consisting primarily of vertical kinship ties and few horizontal kinship ties.

calling: type of courtship in which mothers and daughters invited young men to visit them in the family home.

care work: work necessary to maintain a household and care for family members, including feeding work, housework, consumption work, kin work, and childcare.

cohabitation: co-residential romantic unions where the partners are unmarried.

cohort (generational) replacement: social change that occurs when older generations die and are replaced in the population by younger generations.

coming out: when a person shares that they are gay, lesbian, bisexual, or transgendered (GLBT) with friends and family.

companionate marriage: ideal type of marriage that arose over the 19th century, characterized by the romantic ties between husband and wife and the fulfillment of gender-distinct roles.

conflict theory: theoretical framework that emphasizes unequal power relationships and competition for scarce resources.

covenant marriage: type of legal marriage available in a few states that requires couples to undergo premarital counseling and allows divorce only if adultery, abuse, or other serious offenses can be proven.

coverture: legal principle in which a wife's legal identity was subsumed under that of her husband.

culture of individualism: cultural model that celebrates independence, autonomy, self-reliance, and being true to oneself.

culture of marriage: cultural model that valorizes marriage as ideal, sees divorce as a last resort, and thinks marriage is best for everyone.

deductive reasoning: moves from the abstract to the specific, for example, from theory to hypotheses to data collection and analysis.

empirical: observable by the senses.

extended family: family members other than spouses and children. Includes lineal, collateral, in-law, and fictive kinship.

familism: cultural norm that privileges commitment and obligation to family over the individual.

family continuities: ideological and behavioral threads that link the family patterns of today to those in the past.

family diversity: variation in family patterns and structures that result from inequality in access to social resources.

family wage: earnings that are high enough to support a family.

fatherhood bonus: empirical finding that fathers earn more than men without children.

feminist theory: theoretical framework that analyzes gender inequalities and how to eliminate them.

functional solidarity: exchange of instrumental help and financial support across generations.

gender: socially constructed system of stratification that divides people into groups based on biological sex and identity.

generational dissonance: cultural tensions between immigrant parents and U.S.-born children.

GLBT: gay, lesbian, bisexual, and transgendered; umbrella term to describe sexual and gender minorities.

homogamy: partnering with others who have characteristics, such as race, education level, and religion, similar to ourselves.

hooking up: sexual encounter that takes place outside of a committed relationship; the term encompasses a range of sexual behaviors.

household: residential unit in which members share resources.

household-based definition of family: family members are those who share a household.

hypothesis (plural: hypotheses): specific, testable statement derived from theory.

ideal type: analytical framework developed by theorist Max Weber to describe the typical characteristics of a construct or phenomenon.

immigrant family: family where at least one member is foreign born.

incomplete institution: term coined by sociologist Andrew Cherlin to describe institutions, such as stepfamilies, that do not have clear behavioral norms.

individualized marriage: ideal type of marriage that developed in the late 20th century that is built on self-fulfillment and personal growth.

inductive reasoning: moves from the specific to the abstract, for example, from data to theory.

institution: see **social institution**.

institutional marriage: ideal type of marriage that characterized American families before industrialization, built on economic necessity, familial and community obligation, and social regulations.

intensive mothering: ideology of mothering that says that children are best cared for by mothers; that mothers should invest large amounts of time and energy into childrearing; and that mothering requires sacrifice.

interactionist definition of family: families are created through shared activities and relationships.

intergenerational ambivalence: combination of positive and negative feelings that characterize most intergenerational relationships.

intergenerational solidarity: sense of cohesion among family members.

intersectional: theoretical concept that considers how gender, race, social class, sexual identity, and other hierarchies intersect and interact to shape experiences and opportunities.

kinkeeping (or kin work): work done by family members, usually women, to maintain ties with extended family.

life course theory: theoretical framework that considers how the passage of time, both aging and historical context, shapes experiences.

living apart together (LAT): committed romantic couples who have chosen not to share a household.

longitudinal research: research that studies a phenomenon over time.

macro-level research: research where the cases being studied are larger social entities, such as nations.

marriage market: structural patterns that shape our romantic options.

marriage squeeze: when the pool of available romantic partners is limited.

micro-level research: research where the cases being studied are individuals.

mixed methods: research that includes the analysis of both quantitative and qualitative data.

mixed-status family: family in which family members differ in their immigration status, for example, where one member is undocumented and another is a U.S. citizen.

mother worry: mental labor that mothers do to manage the high expectations for being a good mother.

motherhood penalty: empirical finding that mothers earn less than women without children.

multigenerational household: three or more generations living together in a single household.

multipartner fertility: having biological children with more than one partner.

near poor: characteristic of individuals and households whose incomes are slightly above the official poverty line.

norms: social expectations that guide behavior.

nuclear family: adult couple and their minor children.

population pyramid: figure to depict the age structure of a population.

provider role: idea that men fulfill their family duties by acting as the primary breadwinner.

qualitative data: data that are expressed in words or images. Useful for revealing commonalities, processes, and meaning.

quantitative data: data that are expressed in numbers. Useful for describing frequencies of a phenomenon and determining causal relationships between variables.

race (race-ethnicity): socially constructed system of stratification that divides people into groups based on phenotype and/or ancestry.

rating and dating complex: term coined by Willard Waller in 1937 to describe the intense peer competition for dating popularity on college campuses of that era.

replacement level fertility: level of fertility required to maintain the size of the population.

role: set of behavioral and ideological expectations attached to a social position, such as mother, spouse, or grandparent.

role-based definition of family: focuses on families as a set of interdependent roles and scripts.

sandwich generation: adults who are caring for both children and older family members.

scientific method: careful collection and analysis of data to make theoretical and empirical generalizations.

second demographic transition: profound shift in family life in industrialized countries in the late 20th century, including changes in fertility, marriage, divorce, cohabitation, nonmarital childbearing, and maternal employment.

separate spheres ideology: ideology that separated the masculine public sphere of work from the feminine private sphere of home. It developed in the 19th century in response to industrialization and urbanization.

serial cohabitation: when people cohabit with a series of partners in relatively short-term and unstable unions.

sexual debut: first sexual experience.

sexual identity: socially constructed system of stratification that divides people into groups based on the gender(s) of those to whom one is sexually attracted.

skipped generation household: when nonconsecutive generations share a household, such as a grandchild living with a grandparent without a parent present.

social class: socially constructed system of stratification that divides people into groups based on access to material resources, such as income and wealth.

social exchange theory: theoretical framework that explores how relationships are built, maintained, and dissolved through the exchange of material and symbolic resources.

social institution: cluster of patterned behaviors governed by social norms and enacted by individuals occupying social roles.

social location: term used to describe one's place in social hierarchies and social systems.

social patterns: phenomena that transcend an individual and exist in social structure.

sociological imagination: term coined by C. Wright Mills in 1959 to describe a focus on social patterns, what he called "public issues," instead of "personal troubles."

sociology: scientific study of institutions.

Standard North American Family (SNAF): ideological code describing a married heterosexual couple with children, where the man is a breadwinner and the wife focuses on caregiving.

structural definition of family: family are those to whom one is related by marriage, blood, or adoption.

structural-functionalism: theoretical framework that sees society as an organism, made up of different parts that work together to support its functioning.

symbolic interactionism: theoretical framework that sees social life as a system of meanings created through interaction.

theory: set of propositions that explains a phenomenon.

transfamily: family in which one member of a romantic couple has changed, or is in the process of changing, sex or gender identity. Sometimes also includes any family that has a transgendered family member.

transnational family: when members of a nuclear family live in two (or more) countries.

uncoupling: term coined by sociologist Diane Vaughan in 1986 to describe the process of breaking up.

welfare state: government benefit programs that support the welfare of its citizens, including Social Security, Medicare and Medicaid, and cash assistance to poor families.

REFERENCES

Acosta, K. L. (2013). *Amigas y amantes: Sexually nonconforming Latinas negotiate family*. New Brunswick, NJ: Rutgers University Press.

Administration on Aging. (2014). *A profile of older Americans: 2014*. Retrieved July 23, 2015, from http://www.aoa.acl.gov/Aging_Statistics/Profile/index.aspx

Alba, J. C., & G. M. Martinez. (2006). Childlessness among older women in the United States: Trends and profiles. *Journal of Marriage and Family, 68*(4), 1045–1056.

Amato, P. R. (1994). Life-span adjustment of children to their parents' divorce. *The Future of Children, 4*(1), 143–164.

Amato, P. R. (2005). The impact of family formation change on the cognitive, social, and emotional well-being of the next generation. *The Future of Children, 15*(2), 75–96.

Amato, P. R. (2010). Research on divorce: Continuing trends and new developments. *Journal of Marriage and Family, 72*(3), 650–666.

Amato, P. R., & C. J. Anthony. (2014). Estimating the effects of parental divorce and death with fixed effects models. *Journal of Marriage and Family, 76*(2), 370–386.

Amato, P. R., & S. Irving. (2006). Historical trends in divorce in the United States. In M. A. Fine & J. H. Harvey (Eds.), *Handbook of divorce and relationship dissolution* (pp. 41–57). Mahwah, NJ: Lawrence Erlbaum.

Amato, P. R., C. E. Meyers, & R. E. Emery. (2009). Changes in nonresident father-child contact from 1976 to 2002. *Family Relations, 58*(1), 41–53.

Amott, T., & J. Matthaei. (1996). *Race, gender, and work: A multi-cultural economic history of women in the United States*. Boston, MA: South End Press.

Aquilino, W. S. (2006). The noncustodial father–child relationship from adolescence into young adulthood. *Journal of Marriage and Family, 68*(4), 929–946.

Arias, E. (2002). *United States life tables, 2000* [National Vital Statistics Reports, 51(3)]. Hyattsville, MD: National Center for Health Statistics.

Armstrong, E. A., P. England, & A. C. K. Fogarty. (2012). Accounting for women's orgasm and sexual enjoyment in college hookups and relationships. *American Sociological Review, 77*(3), 435–462.

Averett, K. H. (2016). The gender buffet: LGBTQ parents resisting heteronormativity. *Gender & Society, 30*, 189–212.

Axinn, W. G., & A. Thornton. (1992). The relationship between cohabitation and divorce: Selectivity or causal influence. *Demography, 29*(3), 357–374.

Bailey, B. L. (1988). *From front porch to back seat: Courtship in twentieth-century America*. Baltimore, MD: The Johns Hopkins University Press.

Barber, B. L., & D. H. Demo. (2006). The kids are alright (at least, most of them): Links between divorce and dissolution and child well-being. In M. A. Fine & J. H. Harvey (Eds.), *Handbook of divorce and relationship dissolution* (pp. 289–311). Mahwah, NJ: Lawrence Erlbaum.

Bass, S. A., & F. G. Caro. (1996). The economic value of grandparent assistance. *Generations, 20*(1), 29–33.

Beddoes, Z. M. (2012, October 13). For richer, for poorer. *The Economist*. Retrieved January 28, 2016, from http://www.economist.com/node/21564414

Behnke, A. O., B. A. Taylor, & J. R. Parra-Cardona. (2008). "I hardly understand English, but . . .": Mexican origin fathers describe their commitment as fathers despite the challenges of immigration. *Journal of Comparative Family Studies, 39*, 187–205.

Bengston, V. L. (2001). Beyond the nuclear family:

The increasing importance of multigenerational bonds. *Journal of Marriage and Family, 63*(1), 1–16.

Benson, J. J., & M. Coleman. (2016). Older adults developing a preference for living apart together. *Journal of Marriage and Family*. doi:10.1111/jomf.12292

Berger, P., & H. Kellner. (1964). Marriage and the construction of reality: An exercise in the microsociology of knowledge. *Diogenes, 12*(46), 1–24.

Bernard, J. (1972). *The future of marriage*. New Haven, CT: Yale University Press.

Bianchi, S. M. (2011a). Changing families, changing workplaces. *Future of Children, 21*(2), 15–36.

Bianchi, S. M. (2011b). Family change and time allocation in American families. *The ANNALS of the American Association of Political and Social Science, 638*, 21–44.

Bianchi, S. M., & L. M. Casper. (2000). American families. *Population Bulletin, 55*, 4.

Bianchi, S. M., L. C. Sayer, M. A. Milkie, & J. P. Robinson. (2012). Housework: Who did, does or will do it, and how much does it matter? *Social Forces, 91*(1), 55–63.

Biblarz, T. J., & E. Savci. (2010). Lesbian, gay, bisexual, and transgender families. *Journal of Marriage and Family, 72*(3), 480–497.

Biblarz, T. J., & J. Stacey. (2010). How does the gender of parents matter? *Journal of Marriage and Family, 72*, 3–22.

Bittman, M., P. England, L. Sayer, N. Folbre, & G. Matheson. (2003). When does gender trump money? Bargaining and time in household work. *American Journal of Sociology, 109*(1), 186–214.

Blackstone, A. (2014). Childless . . . or childfree? *Contexts, 13*(4), 68–70.

Blackstone, W. (1979). *Commentaries on the laws of England* (Vol. 1). Chicago, IL: University of Chicago Press. (Original work published 1765)

Blumer, H. (1969). *Symbolic interactionism: Perspective and method*. Englewood Cliffs, NJ: Prentice-Hall.

Bogle, K. A. (2008). *Hooking up: Sex, dating, and relationships on campus*. New York, NY: New York University Press.

Bohra-Mishra, P., & D. S. Massey. (2015). Intermarriage among new immigrants in the USA. *Racial and Ethnic Studies, 38*(5), 734–758.

Bosman, J. (2015, January 24). One couple's unanticipated journey to center of landmark gay rights case. *The New York Times*. Retrieved February 5, 2015, from http://nyti .ms/1z4suwQ

Bramlett, M. D., & W. D. Mosher. (2002). Cohabitation, marriage, divorce, and remarriage in the United States. *Vital Health Statistics, 23*(22), 1–93.

Brault, M. W. (2012). *Americans with disabilities: 2010* (Current Population Reports P70–131). Washington, DC: U.S. Census Bureau.

Braver, S. L., & M. E. Lamb. (2013). Marital dissolution. In G. W. Peterson & K. R. Bush (Eds.), *Handbook of marriage and the family* (3rd ed., pp. 487–516). New York: Springer.

Bridgman, B., A. Dugan, M. Lal, M. Osborne, & S. Villones. (2012). Accounting for household production in the national accounts, 1965–2010. *Survey of Current Business, 92*(5), 23–36.

Brines, J. (1994). Economic dependency, gender, and the division of labor at home. *American Journal of Sociology, 100*(3), 652–688.

Brodzinsky, D. M. (2012). Adoption by lesbians and gay men: A national survey of adoption agency policies and practices. In D. M. Brodzinsky & A. Pertman (Eds.), *Adoption by lesbians and gay men: A new dimension in family diversity* (pp. 62–84). New York, NY: Oxford University Press.

Brown, S. L. (2004). Family structure and child well-being: The significance of parental cohabitation. *Journal of Marriage and Family, 66*(2), 351–367.

Brown, S. L., J. R. Bulanda, & G. R. Lee. (2012). Transitions into and out of cohabitation in later life. *Journal of Marriage and Family, 74*(4), 774–793.

Brown, S. L., G. R. Lee, & J. R. Bulanda. (2006). Cohabitation among older adults: A national portrait. *Journal of Gerontology: Social Sciences, 61B*(2), S71–S79.

Bui, Q., & C. C. Miller. (2015, December 23). The typical American lives only 18 miles from mom. *The New York Times.* Retrieved December 23, 2015, from http://nyti.ms/1V7Y6J4

Bumpass, L. L., & R. K. Raley. (1995). Redefining single-parent families: Cohabitation and changing family reality. *Demography, 32*(1), 97–109.

Bureau of Labor Statistics. (2013a). *American Time Use Survey – 2012 results.* Washington, DC: Author. Retrieved January 11, 2015, from http://www.bls.gov/news.release/archives/atus_06202013.pdf

Bureau of Labor Statistics. (2013b). *Women in the labor force: A databook* (BLS Reports, Report 1040). Washington, DC: Author.

Bureau of Labor Statistics. (2014a). *3. Employment status of the civilian noninstitutional population by age, sex, and race.* Washington, DC: Author.

Retrieved January 11, 2015, from http://www.bls.gov/cps/cpsaat03.htm

Bureau of Labor Statistics. (2014b). *8. Employed and unemployed full- and part-time workers by age, sex, race, and Hispanic or Latino ethnicity.* Washington, DC: Author. Retrieved January 11, 2015, from http://www.bls.gov/cps/cpsaat08.htm

Bureau of Labor Statistics. (2015). *Employment characteristics of families – 2014.* Washington, DC: Author. Retrieved January 7, 2016, from http://www.bls.gov/news.release/pdf/famee.pdf

Burgess, E. W., & H. J. Locke. (1945). *The family: From institution to companionship.* New York, NY: American Book Company.

Burr, J. A., & J. E. Mutchler. (1999). Race and ethnic variation in norms of filial responsibility among older persons. *Journal of Marriage and Family, 61*(3), 674–687.

Cancian, F. (1987). *Love in America: Gender and self-development.* Cambridge, England: Cambridge University Press.

Cancian, M., D. R. Meyer, P. R. Brown, & S. T. Cook. (2014). Who gets custody now? Dramatic changes in children's living arrangements after divorce. *Demography, 51*(4), 1381–1396.

Caplow, T., L. Hicks, & B. J. Wattenberg. (2000). *The first measured century: An illustrated guide to trends in America, 1900 – 2000.* Washington, DC: American Enterprise Institute Press.

Carlson, M. J., S. S. McLanahan, & J. Brooks-Gunn. (2008). Coparenting and nonresident fathers' involvement with youth children after a nonmarital birth. *Demography, 45*(2), 461–488.

Carlson, M., S. McLanahan, & P. England. (2004). Union formation in fragile families. *Demography, 41*(2), 237–261.

Carnevale, A. P., S. J. Rose, & B. Cheah. (2014). *The college payoff: Education, occupations, lifetime earnings.* Washington, DC: Georgetown University Center on Education and the Workforce.

Carr, P. J., & M. J. Kefalas. (2011). Straight from the heartland: Coming of age in Ellis, Iowa. In M. C. Waters, P. J. Carr, M. J. Kefalas, & J. Holdaway (Eds.), *Coming of age in America: The transition to adulthood in the twenty-first century* (pp. 28–58). Berkeley: University of California Press.

Carrington, C. (1999). *No place like home: Relationships and family life among lesbians and gay men.* Chicago, IL: University of Chicago Press.

Carter, S. B., S. S. Gartner, M. R. Haines, A. L. Olmstead, R. Sutch, & G. Wright. (2006). *The historical statistics of the*

United States millennial edition. New York, NY: Cambridge University Press.

Carver, K., K. Joyner, & J. R. Udry. (2003). National estimates of adolescent romantic relationships. In P. Florsheim (Ed.), *Adolescent romantic relations and sexual behavior: Theory, research, and practical implications* (pp. 23–56). Mahwah, NJ: Lawrence Erlbaum.

Centers for Disease Control and Prevention. (2015). *National marriage and divorce rate trends.* Retrieved March 21, 2016, from http://www.cdc.gov/nchs/nvss/marriage_divorce_tables.htm

Cheadle, J. E., P. R. Amato, & V. King. (2010). Patterns of nonresident father contact. *Demography, 47*(1), 205–225.

Cherlin, A. J. (1978). Remarriage as an incomplete institution. *American Journal of Sociology, 84*(3), 634–650.

Cherlin, A. J. (1978). Remarriage as an incomplete institution. *American Journal of Sociology, 84*(3), 634–650.

Cherlin, A. J. (2004). The deinstitutionalization of American marriage. *Journal of Marriage and Family, 66*(4), 848–861.

Cherlin, A. J. (2009). *The marriage-go-round: The state of marriage and the family in America today.* New York, NY: Knopf.

Cherlin, A. J., & F. F. Furstenberg, Jr. (1986). *The new American grandparent: A place in the family, a life apart.* New York, NY: Basic Books.

Chishti, M., & F. Hipsman. (2014). Unaccompanied minors crisis has receded from headlines but major issues remain. Migration Policy Institute. Retrieved January 26, 2015, from http://www.migrationpolicy.org/article/unaccompanied-minors-crisis-has-receded-headlines-major-issues-remain

Clawson, D., & N. Gerstel. (2014). *Unequal time: Gender, class, and family in employment schedules.* New York, NY: Russell Sage Foundation.

Cohany, S. R., & E. Sok. (2007). Trends in labor force participation of married mothers of infants. *Monthly Labor Review, 130*(2), 1–16.

Collins, P. H. (1994). Shifting the center: Race, class, and feminist theorizing about motherhood. In E. N. Glenn, G. Chang, & L. R. Forcey (Eds.), *Mothering: Ideology, experience, and agency* (pp. 45–65). New York, NY: Routledge.

Collins, P. H. (2000). *Black feminist thought: Knowledge, consciousness, and the politics of empowerment* (2nd ed.). New York, NY: Routledge.

Collins, W. A., D. P. Welsh, & W. Furman. (2009). Adolescent romantic relationships. *Annual Review of Psychology, 60,* 631–652.

Coltrane, S. (1996). *Family man: Fatherhood, housework, and gender equity.* New York, NY: Oxford University Press.

Coltrane, S. (1998). *Gender and families.* Thousand Oaks, CA: Pine Forge Press.

Comprehensive Child Development Act of 1971, Pub.L. 93-202, enacted 1972.

Congressional Budget Office. (2013). Rising demand for long-term services and supports for elderly people. Retrieved January 11, 2016, from https://www.cbo.gov/publication/44363

Congressional Budget Office. (2015). Federal housing assistance for low-income households. Retrieved January 20, 2016, from https://www.cbo.gov/publication/50782

Coontz, S. (1992). *The way we never were: American families and the nostalgia trap.* New York, NY: Basic Books.

Coontz, S. (2005). *Marriage, a history: How love conquered marriage.* New York, NY: Penguin Books.

Coontz, S. (2010). The evolution of American families. In B. J. Risman (Ed.), *Families as they really are* (pp. 30–47). New York, NY: W.W. Norton.

Copen, C. E., K. Daniels, J. Vespa, & W. D. Mosher. (2012). *First marriages in the United States: Data from the 2006 – 2010 National Survey of Family Growth* (National Health

Statistics Reports, number 49). Washington, DC: National Center for Health Statistics.

Correll, S. J., S. Benard, & I. Paik. (2007). Getting a job: Is there a motherhood penalty? *American Journal of Sociology, 12*(5), 1297–1339.

Cubanski, J., G. Casillas, & A. Damino. (2015). *Poverty among seniors: An updated analysis of national and state level poverty rates under the official and supplemental poverty measures.* Menlo Park, CA: Henry J. Kaiser Family Foundation.

D'Emilio, J., & E. B. Freedman. (1988). *Intimate matters: A history of sexuality in America.* New York, NY: Harper & Row.

Danziger, S. K. (2010). The decline of cash welfare and the implications for social policy and poverty. *Annual Review of Sociology, 36,* 523–545.

Day, J. C., with A. Jamieson. (2003). *School enrollment: 2000* (Census 2000 Brief, C2KBR-26). Washington, DC: U.S. Department of Commerce.

Defense of Marriage Act of 1996, Pub.L. 104–199, 110 Stat. 2419, enacted September 21, 1996, 1 U.S.C. § 7 and 28 U.S.C. § 1738C.

Demo, D. H., & M. A. Fine. (2010). *Beyond the average divorce.* Thousand Oaks, CA: Sage.

Demos, J. (1982). The changing faces of fatherhood:

A new exploration in American family history. In S. H. Cath, A. R. Gurwitt, & J. M. Ross (Eds.), *Father and child: Developmental and clinical perspectives* (pp. 425–450). Boston, MA: Little, Brown.

DeNavas-Walt, C., & B. D. Proctor. (2014). *Income and poverty in the United States: 2013.* Washington, DC: U.S. Government Printing Office.

DeVault, M. L. (1991). *Feeding the family: The social organization of caring as gendered work.* Chicago, IL: University of Chicago Press.

Doucet, A. (2004). "It's almost like I have a job, but I don't get paid": Fathers at home reconfiguring work, care, and masculinity. *Fathering, 2*(3), 277–303.

Dow, D. M. (2016). Integrated motherhood: Beyond hegemonic ideologies of motherhood. *Journal of Marriage and Family, 78,* 180–196.

Dreby, J. (2010). *Divided by borders: Mexican migrants and their children.* Berkeley: University of California Press.

Durso, L. E., & G. J. Gates. (2012). *Serving our youth: Findings from a national survey of service providers working with lesbian, gay, bisexual, and transgender youth who are homeless or at risk of becoming homeless.* Los Angeles, CA: The Williams Institute with True Colors Fund and The Palette Fund.

Edin, K. (2000). What do low-income single mothers say about marriage? *Social Problems, 47*(1), 112–133.

Edin, K., & L. Lein. (1997). *Making ends meet: How single mothers survive welfare and low-wage work.* New York, NY: Russell Sage Foundation.

Edin, K., & T. J. Nelson. (2013). *Doing the best I can: Fatherhood in the inner city.* Berkeley: University of California Press.

Elder, G. H., Jr. (1985). Perspectives on the life course. In G. H. Elder, Jr. (Ed.), *Life course dynamics: Trajectories and transitions, 1968–1980* (pp. 23–49). Ithaca, NY: Cornell University Press.

Elder, G. H., Jr. (1994). Time, human agency, and social change: Perspectives on the life course. *Social Psychology Quarterly, 57*(1), 4–15.

Elder, G. H., Jr., M. K. Johnson, & R. Crosnoe. (2003). The emergence and development of life course theory. In J. R. Mortimer & M. J. Shanahan (Eds.), *Handbook of the life course* (pp. 3–19). New York, NY: Kluwer Academic/Plenum.

Ellis, R. R., & T. Simmons. (2014). *Coresident grandparents and their grandchildren: 2012.* Washington, DC: U.S. Census Bureau.

England, P. (2010). The gender revolution: Uneven and

stalled. *Gender & Society, 24*(2), 149–166.

England, P., E. F. Shafer, & L. L. Wu. (2012). Premarital conceptions, postconception ("shotgun") marriages, and premarital first births: Education gradients in U.S. cohorts of White and Black women born 1925-1959. *Demographic Research, 27*(6), 153–166.

Fair Labor Standards Act of 1938, Pub.L. 75-718 (52 Stat. 1060), enacted June 25, 1938.

Farrell, B. G. (1999). *Family: The making of an idea, an institution, and a controversy in American culture.* Boulder, CO: Westview Press.

Fass, P. S., & M. A. Mason. (2000). *Childhood in America.* New York, NY: New York University Press.

Felkey, A. (2011). Will you covenant marry me? A preliminary look at a new type of marriage. *Eastern Economic Journal, 37*(3), 367–389.

Finer, L. B., & J. M. Philbin. (2014). Trends in ages at key reproductive transitions in the United States, 1951–2010. *Women's Health Issues, 24*(3), e271–e279.

Fingerman, K. L., Y.-P. Cheng, L. Tighe, K. S. Birditt, & S. Zarit. (2012). Relationships between young adults and their parents. In A. Booth, S. L. Brown, N. S. Landale, W. D. Manning, &

S. M. McHale (Eds.), *Early adulthood in family context* (pp. 59–85). New York, NY: Springer.

Fingerman, K. L., K. Kim, E. M. Davis, F. F. Furstenberg, Jr., K. S. Birditt, & S. H. Zarit. (2015). "I'll give you the world": Socioeconomic differences in parental support of adult children. *Journal of Marriage and Family, 77*(4), 844–865.

Fingerman, K., L. Miller, K. Birditt, & S. Zarit. (2009). Giving to the good and the needy: Parental support of grown children. *Journal of Marriage and Family, 71*(5), 1220–1233.

Floyd, I., & L. Schott. (2015). *TANF cash benefits have fallen by more than 20 percent in most states and continue to erode.* Center on Budget and Policy Priorities. Retrieved January 23, 2016, from http://www .cbpp.org/sites/default/files/ atoms/files/10-30-14tanf.pdf

Foner, N., & J. Dreby. (2011). Relations between the generations in immigrant families. *Annual Review of Sociology, 37*, 545–564.

Ford, J., P. England, & J. Bearak. (2015). The American college hookup scene: Findings from the Online College Social Life Survey [PowerPoint presentation]. In *TRAILS: Teaching resources and innovations library for sociology.* Washington, DC: American Sociological Association.

Retrieved from http://trails .asanet.org

Forrest, W. (2014). Cohabitation, relationship quality, and desistance from crime. *Journal of Marriage and Family, 76*(3), 539–556.

Fried, M. (1998). *Taking time: Parental leave policy and corporate culture.* Philadelphia, PA: Temple University Press.

Furstenberg, F. F. (2014). Fifty years of family change: From consensus to complexity. *The ANNALS of the American Academy of Political and Social Science, 654*, 12–30.

Furstenberg, F. F., & A. J. Cherlin. (1991). *Divided families: What happens to children when parents part.* Cambridge, MA: Harvard University Press.

Furstenberg, F. F., Jr. (2010). On a new schedule: Transitions to adulthood and family change. *The Future of Children, 20*(1), 67–87.

Fussell, E., & F. F. Furstenberg, Jr. (2005). The transition to adulthood during the twentieth century: Race, nativity, and gender. In R. A. Settersten, Jr., F. F. Furstenberg, & R. G. Rumbaut (Eds.), *On the frontier of adulthood: Theory, research, and public policy* (pp. 29–75). Chicago, IL: University of Chicago Press.

Gates, G. J., M.V. L. Badgett, J. E. Macomber, & K.

Chambers. (2007). *Adoption and foster care by gay and lesbian parents in the United States*. Los Angeles, CA: The Williams Institute, UCLA School of Law. Retrieved January 8, 2015, from http://williamsinstitute.law.ucla.edu/wp-content/uploads/Gates-Badgett-Macomber-Chambers-Final-Adoption-Report-Mar-2007.pdf

General Accounting Office. (2004). *Defense of Marriage Act: Update to prior report*. Retrieved January 18, 2015, from http://www.gao.gov/products/GAO-04-353R

George, T. (2010). *Residential time summary reports filed in Washington from July 2009 to June 2010*. Olympia: Washington State Center for Court Research. Retrieved January 13, 2015, from http://www.courts.wa.gov/wsccr/docs/ResidentialTimeSummaryReport2010.pdf

Gerson, K. (2011). *The unfinished revolution: Coming of age in a new era of gender, work, and family*. New York, NY: Oxford University Press.

Gibson, C., & E. Lennon. (2011). *Table 1: Nativity of the population and place of birth of the Native population: 1850 to 1990*. Washington, DC: U.S. Census Bureau, Population Division. Retrieved January 7, 2015, from https://www.census.gov/population/www/documentation/twps0029/tab01.html

Gibson-Davis, C. (2014). Magic moment? Maternal marriage for children born out of wedlock. *Demography, 51*(4), 1345–1356.

Giele, J. Z. (2013). *Family policy and the American safety net*. Thousand Oaks, CA: Sage.

Giordano, P. C., W. D. Manning, & M. A. Longmore. (2006). Adolescent romantic relationships: An emerging portrait of their nature and developmental significance. In A. C. Crouter & A. Booth (Eds.), *Romance and sex in adolescence and emerging adulthood: Risks and opportunities* (pp. 127–149). New York, NY: Psychology Press.

Goldberg, A. E. (2010). *Lesbian and gay parents and their children: Research on the family life cycle*. Washington, DC: American Psychological Association.

Gooding, G. E., & R. M. Kreider. (2009). Women's marital naming choices in a nationally representative sample. *Journal of Family Issues, 31*(5), 681–701.

Goodwin, P. Y., W. D. Mosher, & A. Chandra. (2010). *Marriage and cohabitation in the United States: A statistical portrait based on Cycle 6 (2002) of the National Survey of Family Growth* [Vital Health Stat 23(28)]. Atlanta, GA: National Center for Health Statistics.

Gordon, C. (2016). *Growing apart: A political history of American inequality*. Institute for Policy Studies. Retrieved January 28, 2016, from http://scalar.usc.edu/works/growing-apart-a-political-history-of-american-inequality/index

Gordon, L. (1979). The struggle for reproductive freedom: Three stages of feminism. In Z. R. Eisenstein (Ed.), *Capitalist patriarchy and the case for socialist feminism* (pp. 107–136). New York, NY: Monthly Review Press.

Gordon, L., & F. Batlan. (2011). The legal history of the aid to dependent children program. The Social Welfare History Project. Retrieved January 23, 2016, from http://www.socialwelfarehistory.com/programs/aid-to-dependent-children-the-legal-history/

Gordon, M. M. (1964). *Assimilation in American life: The role of race, religion, and national origins*. New York, NY: Oxford University Press.

Grall, T. (2013). *Custodial mothers and fathers and their child support: 2011* (Current Population Reports, P60–246). Retrieved January 13, 2015, from https://www.census.gov/prod/2013pubs/p60–246.pdf

Greenstein, T. N. (2000). Economic dependence, gender, and the division of labor in the home: A replication and extension. *Journal of Marriage and Family, 62*(2), 322–335.

Gregson, J., & M. L. Ceynar. (2009). Finding "me" again: Women's postdivorce identity shifts. *Journal of Divorce & Remarriage, 50*(8), 564–582.

Greif, G. L., & K. H. Deal. (2012). The impact of divorce on friendships with couples and individuals. *Journal of Divorce and Remarriage, 53*(6), 421–435.

Grieco, E. M., Y. D. Acosta, G. P. de la Cruz, C. Gambino, T. Gryn, L. J. Larsen, E. N. Trevelyan, & N. P. Walters. (2012). *The foreign-born population in the United States: 2010* (American Community Survey Reports, ACS-19). Washington, DC: U.S. Census Bureau.

Gubrium, J. F., & J. A. Holstein. (1990). *What is family?* Mountain View, CA: Mayfield.

Gupta, S. (1999). The effects of transitions in marital status on men's performance of housework. *Journal of Marriage and Family, 61*(3), 700–711.

Gupta, S. (2007). Autonomy, dependence, or display? The relationship between married women's earnings and housework. *Journal of Marriage and Family, 69*(2), 399–417.

Guttmacher Institute. (2014). *Fact sheet: American teens' sexual and reproductive health.*

Guzman, L. (2004). Grandma and grandpa taking care of the kids: Patterns of involvement. *Child Trends Research Brief #2004–17.*

Guzzo, K. B., & F. F. Furstenberg, Jr. (2007). Multipartnered fertility among American men. *Demography, 44*(3), 583–601.

Hamilton, L., & E. A. Armstrong. (2009). Gendered sexuality in young adulthood: Double binds and flawed options. *Gender & Society, 23*(5), 589–616.

Hans, J. D., M. Gillen, & K. Akande. (2010). Sex redefined: The reclassification of oral-genital contact. *Perspectives on Sexual and Reproductive Health, 42*(2), 74–78.

Hansen, K. V. (2005). *Not-so-nuclear families: Class, gender, and networks of care.* New Brunswick, NJ: Rutgers University Press.

Harknett, K., & A. Kuperberg. (2011). Education, labor markets and the retreat from marriage. *Social Forces, 90*(1), 41–64.

Harrington, B., F. Van Deusen, & I. Mazar. (2012). *The new dad: Right at home.* Boston, MA: Center for Work & Family, Boston College Carroll School of Management. Retrieved January 11, 2015, from http://www.bc.edu/content/dam/files/centers/cwf/pdf/The%20New%20Dad%20Right%20at%20Home%20BCCWF%202012.pdf

Harrington Meyer, M. (2012). Grandmothers juggling work and grandchildren in the United States. In S. Arber & V. Timonen (Eds.), *Contemporary grandparenting: Changing family relationships in global contexts*
(pp. 71–89). Bristol, England: The Policy Press.

Harrington Meyer, M. (2014). *Grandmothers at work: Juggling families and jobs.* New York, NY: New York University Press.

Hays, S. (1996). *The cultural contradictions of motherhood.* New Haven, CT: Yale University Press.

Heaton, T. B., C. K. Jacobson, & K. Holland. (1999). Persistence and change in decisions to remain childless. *Journal of Marriage and Family, 61*(2), 531–539.

Hetherington, E. M., & J. Kelly. (2002). *For better or for worse: Divorce reconsidered.* New York, NY: W. W. Norton.

Hitsch, G. J., A. Hortaçsu, & D. Ariely. (2010). Matching and sorting in online dating. *The American Economic Review, 100*(1), 130–163.

Hochschild, A. R., with A. Machung. (1989). *The second shift.* New York, NY: Avon Books.

Holdaway, J. (2011). If you can make it there . . . : The transition to adulthood in New York City. In M. C. Waters, P. J. Carr, M. J. Kefalas, & J. Holdaway (Eds.), *Coming of age in America: The transition to adulthood in the twenty-first century* (pp. 106–132). Berkeley: University of California Press.

Hook, J.L. (2006). Care in context: Men's unpaid work in 20 countries, 1965–2003.

American Sociological Review 71(4), 639–660.

Hook, J. L. (2010). Gender inequality in the welfare state: Sex segregation in housework, 1965–2003. *American Journal of Sociology, 115*(5), 1480–1523.

Huang, C.-C., & K.-Q. Han (2012). Child support enforcement in the United States: Has policy made a difference? *Child and Youth Services Review, 34*(4), 622–627.

Huang, P. M., P. J. Smock, W. D. Manning, & C. A. Bergstrom-Lynch. (2011). He says, she says: Gender and cohabitation. *Journal of Family Issues, 32*(7), 876–905.

Hughes, M. E., L. J. Waite, T. A. LaPierre, & Y. Luo. (2007). All in the family: The impact of caring for grandchildren on grandparents' health. *Journal of Gerontology: Social Sciences, 62B*(2), S108–S119.

Immigration and Nationality Act of 1965, H.R. 2580; Pub.L. 89–236 (79 Stat. 911), enacted June 30, 1968.

Johnson, C. L. (2000). Perspectives on American kinship in the later 1990s. *Journal of Marriage and Family, 62*(3), 623–639.

Jones, J. M. (2013). Same-sex marriage support solidifies above 50% in U.S. *Gallup*. Retrieved March 15, 2016, from http://www.gallup.com/poll/162398/sex-marriage-support-solidifies-above.aspx

Jones, L. E., & M. Tertilt. (2006). *An economic history of fertility in the U.S.: 1826 – 1960* (Working Paper 12796). Cambridge, MA: National Bureau of Economic Research. Retrieved January 14, 2015, from http://www.nber.org/papers/w12796.pdf

Kalmijn, M. (2014). Adult intergenerational relationships. In J. Treas, J. Scott, & M. Richards (Eds.), *The Wiley Blackwell companion to the sociology of families* (pp. 385–403). Chichester, West Sussex, England: Wiley Blackwell.

Kalmijn, M. (2015). How childhood circumstances moderate the long-term impact of divorce on father-child relationships. *Journal of Marriage and Family, 77*(4), 921–938.

Kane, E. W. (2012). *The gender trap: Parents and the pitfalls of raising boys and girls*. New York, NY: New York University Press.

Kaufman, G. (2013). *Superdads: How fathers balance work and family in the 21st century*. New York, NY: New York University Press.

Kayser, K., & S. S. Rao. (2006). Process of disaffection in relationship breakdown. In M. A. Fine & J. H. Harvey (Eds.), *Handbook of divorce and relationship dissolution* (pp. 201–221). Mahwah, NJ: Lawrence Erlbaum.

Kelly, J. B. (1994). The determination of child custody.

The Future of Children, 4(1), 121–142.

Kennedy, S., & C. A. Fitch. (2012). Measuring cohabitation and family structure in the United States: Assessing the impact of new data from the current population survey. *Demography, 49*(4), 1479–1498.

Kids Count. (2015). *Children in immigrant families*. Retrieved December 30, 2015, from http://datacenter.kidscount.org/~/media/541/CI_Children_in_Immigrant_Families.xls

Kiernan, K. (2000). European perspectives on union formation. In L. Waite, C. Bachrach, M. Hindin, E. Thomson, & A. Thornton (Eds.), *The ties that bind: Perspectives on marriage and cohabitation* (pp. 40–58). New York, NY: Aldine de Gruyter.

Kimport, K. (2014). *Queering marriage: Challenging family formation in the United States*. New Brunswick, NJ: Rutgers University Press.

King, V., & M. E. Scott. (2005). A comparison of cohabiting relationships among older and younger adults. *Journal of Marriage and Family, 67*(2), 271–285.

Kingsbury, N., & J. Scanzoni. (1993). Structural-functionalism. In P. G. Boss, W. J. Doherty, R. LaRossa, W. R. Schumm, & S. K. Steinmetz (Eds.), *Sourcebook of family theories and methods: A contextual approach* (pp. 195–217). New York, NY: Plenum Press.

Klinenberg, E. (2012). *Going solo: The extraordinary rise and surprising appeal of living alone*. New York, NY: Penguin Press.

Kochhar, R., & R. Fry. (2014). Wealth inequality has widened along racial, ethnic lines since end of great recession. *Fact Tank: News in the Numbers*. Washington, DC: Pew Research Center. Retrieved January 13, 2016, from http://www.pewresearch.org/fact-tank/2014/12/12/racial-wealth-gaps-great-recession/

Koropeckyj-Cox, T., & G. Pendell. (2007). The gender gap in attitudes about childlessness in the United States. *Journal of Marriage and Family, 69*(4), 899–915.

Kreager, D. A., R. B. Felson, C. Warner, & M. R. Wenger. (2013). Women's education, marital violence, and divorce: A social exchange perspective. *Journal of Marriage and Family, 75*(3), 565–581.

Kuperberg, A. (2014). Age at coresidence, premarital cohabitation, and marriage dissolution: 1985–2009. *Journal of Marriage and Family, 76*, 352–369.

Lachance-Grzela, M., & G. Bouchard. (2010). Why do women do the lion's share of housework? A decade of research. *Sex Roles, 63*(11–12), 767–780.

Lamidi, E., & J. Cruz. (2014). *Remarriage rate in the U.S., 2012* (FP-14–10). Bowling Green, OH: National Center for Family & Marriage Research. Retrieved January 13, 2015, from http://www.bgsu.edu/content/dam/BGSU/college-of-arts-and-sciences/NCFMR/documents/ FP/FP-14–10-remarriage-rate-2012.pdf

Landry, B. (2000). *Black working wives: Pioneers of the American family revolution*. Berkeley: University of California Press.

Lareau, A. (2000). *Home advantage: Social class and parental intervention in elementary education* (updated ed.). Lanham, MD: Rowman & Littlefield.

Lareau, A. (2003). *Unequal childhoods: Class, race, and family life*. Berkeley: University of California Press.

Laughlin, L. (2011). *Maternity leave and employment patterns: 2006 – 2008* (Current Population Report, P70–128). Washington, DC: U.S. Census Bureau.

Laughlin, L. (2013). *Who's minding the kids? Child care arrangements: Spring 2011*. Washington, DC: U.S. Census Bureau. Retrieved January 18, 2015, from http://www.census.gov/content/dam/Census/library/publications/2013/demo/p70-135.pdf

Lawrence v. Texas, 539 U.S. 558 (2003).

Lawton, L., M. Silverstein, & V. Bengston. (1994). Affection, social contact, and geographic distance between adult children and their parents. *Journal of Marriage and Family, 56*(1), 57–68.

Lee, J., & F. D. Bean. (2010). *The diversity paradox: Immigration and the color line in 21st century America*. New York, NY: Russell Sage Foundation.

Lehrer, E. L. (2004). Religion as a determinant of economic and demographic behavior in the United States. *Population and Development Review, 30*(4), 707–726.

Leonhardt, D. (2014, May 27). Is college worth it? Clearly, new data say. *The New York Times*. Retrieved August 9, 2015, from http://nyti.ms/1hsxnlG

Leopold, T., & J. Skopek. (2015). The demography of grandparenthood: An international profile. *Social Forces, 94*(2), 801–832.

Lewin, E. (1998). *Recognizing ourselves: Ceremonies of lesbian and gay commitment*. New York, NY: Columbia University Press.

Lichter, D. T., Z. Qian, & L. M. Mellott. (2006). Marriage or dissolution? Union transitions among poor cohabiting women. *Demography, 43*(2), 223–240.

Lichter, D. T., R. N. Turner, & S. Sassler. (2010). National estimates of the rise in serial cohabitation. *Social Science Research, 39*(5), 754–765.

Lima, J. C., S. M. Allen, F. Goldscheider, & O. Intrator.

(2008). Spousal caregiving in late midlife versus older ages: Implications of work and family obligations. *Journal of Gerontology: Social Sciences, 63B*(4), S229–S238.

Lin, I.-F. (2008). Consequences of parental divorce for adult children's support of their frail parents. *Journal of Marriage and Family, 70*(1), 113–128.

Liptak, A. (2013). *To have and uphold: The Supreme Court and the battle for same-sex marriage.* New York, NY: Byliner/*The New York Times.*

Livingstone, G. (2015). *It's no longer a "Leave It to Beaver" world for American families – But it wasn't back then, either.* Washington, DC: Pew Research Center FactTank. Retrieved December 20, 2015, from http://pewrsr.ch/1VpJzIL

Lofquist, D. A. (2012). *Multigenerational households: 2009-2011* (American Community Survey Briefs, 11-03). Washington, DC: U.S. Census Bureau.

Lopez, G. R. (2001). The value of hard work: Lessons on parent involvement from an (im)migrant household. *Harvard Educational Review, 71*(3), 416–437.

Luo, Y., T. A. LaPierre, M. E. Hughes, & L. J. Waite. (2012). Grandparents providing care to grandchildren: A population-based study of continuity and change. *Journal of Family Issues, 33*(9), 1143–1167.

Luscombe, B. (2010, November 18). Who needs marriage? A changing institution. *TIME.* Retrieved January 11, 2015, from http://content.time.com/time/magazine/article/0,9171,2032116,00.html

Lye, D. N. (1996). Adult child-parent relationships. *Annual Review of Sociology, 22,* 79–102.

Manning, W. D. (2013). *Trends in cohabitation: Over twenty years of change, 1987–2010* (FP-13–12). Bowling Green, OH: National Center for Family & Marriage Research. Retrieved January 11, 2015, from http://www.bgsu.edu/content/dam/BGSU/college-of-arts-and-sciences/NCFMR/documents/FP/FP-13–12.pdf

Manning, W. D., & S. L. Brown. (2011). The demography of unions among older Americans, 1980-present: A family change approach. In R. A. Settersten, Jr. & J. L. Angel (Eds.), *Handbook of the sociology of aging* (pp. 193–210). New York, NY: Springer.

Manning, W. D., S. L. Brown, & K. K. Payne. (2014). Two decades of stability and change in age of first union formation. *Journal of Marriage and Family, 76*(2), 247–260.

Manning, W. D., M. N. Fettro, & E. Lamidi. (2014). Child well-being in same-sex parent families: Review of research for American Sociological Association amicus brief.

Population Research and Policy Review, 33(4), 485–502.

Manning, W.D., P.C. Giordano, & M.A. Longmore. (2006). Hooking up: The relationship contexts of "nonrelationship" sex. *Journal of Adolescent Research 21*(5), 459–483.

Manning, W. D., & P. J. Smock. (2005). Measuring and modeling cohabitation: New perspectives from qualitative data. *Journal of Marriage and Family, 67*(4), 989–1002.

Manning, W. D., P. J. Smock, & D. Majumdar. (2004). The relative stability of cohabiting and marital unions for children. *Population Research and Policy Review, 23*(2), 135–159.

Marquand, B. (2014). The Mother's Day Index 2014: Inequality edition. Retrieved January 11, 2015, from http://www.insure.com/life-insurance/the-mothers-day-index.html

Martin, J. A., B. E. Hamilton, M. J. K. Osterman, S. C. Curtin, & T. J. Matthews. (2015). *Births: final data for 2013* [National Vital Statistics Report 64(1)]. Hyattsville, MD: National Center for Health Statistics.

Martin, P. P., & D. A. Weaver. (2005). Social security: A program and policy history. *Social Security Bulletin, 66*(1), 1–15.

Martin, S. P. (2006). Trends in marital dissolution by women's education in the United States. *Demographic Research, 15,* 537–560.

Mathews, T. J., & B. Hamilton. (2009). *Delayed childbearing: More women are having their first child later in life* (National Center for Health Statistics Data Brief, no 21). Hyattsville, MD: National Center for Health Statistics.

McCall, L., & C. Percheski. (2010). Income inequality: New trends and research directions. *Annual Review of Sociology, 36,* 329–347.

McCarthy, J. (2015a). Record-high 60% of Americans support same-sex marriage. *Gallup.* Retrieved March 15, 2016, from http://www.gallup.com/poll/183272/record-high-americans-support-sex-marriage.aspx

McCarthy, J. (2015b). U.S. support for gay marriage stable after high court ruling. *Gallup.* Retrieved March 15, 2016, from http://www.gallup.com/poll/184217/support-gay-marriage-stable-high-court-ruling.aspx

McClintock, E. A. (2014). Beauty and status: The illusion of exchange in partner selection? *American Sociological Review, 79*(4), 575–604.

McLanahan, S. (2004). Diverging destinies: How children are faring under the second demographic transition. *Demography, 41*(4), 607–627.

McLanahan, S. (2011). Family instability and complexity after a nonmarital birth: Outcomes for children in fragile families.

In M. J. Carlson & P. England (Eds.), *Social class and changing families in an unequal America* (pp. 108–133). Stanford, CA: Stanford University Press.

McLanahan, S., & A. N. Beck. (2010). Parental relationships in fragile families. *Future of Children, 20*(2), 17–37.

McLanahan, S., & G. Sandefur. (1997). *Growing up with a single parent: What hurts, what helps.* Cambridge, MA: Harvard University Press.

McManus, P. A., & T. A. DePrete. (2001). Losers and winners: The financial consequences of separation and divorce for men. *American Sociological Review, 66*(2), 246–268.

Mills, C. W. (1959). *The sociological imagination.* New York, NY: Oxford University Press.

Monte, L. M. (2007). Blended but not the Bradys: Navigating unmarried multiple partner fertility. In P. England & K. Edin (Eds.), *Unmarried couples with children* (pp. 183–203). New York, NY: Russell Sage Foundation.

Monte, L. M., & R. R. Ellis. (2013). *Relationship status at first birth for women age 15–50 in the United States.* Paper presented at the annual meeting of the Population Association of America. Retrieved August 9, 2015, from https://www.census.gov/hhes/

fertility/files/cps/Monte_Ellis_PAA_April-11-13-2013.pdf

Monte, L. M., & R. R. Ellis. (2014). *Fertility of women in the United States: 2012.* Washington, DC: U.S. Census Bureau.

Morgan, S. P. (1991). Late nineteenth- and early twentieth-century childlessness. *American Journal of Sociology, 97,* 779–807.

Mueller, M. M., B. Wilhelm, & G. H. Elder, Jr. (2002). Variations in grandparenting. *Research on Aging, 24*(3), 360–388.

Murdock, G. P. (1949). *Social structure.* New York, NY: Free Press.

Musick, K., & K. Michelmore. (2015). Change in the stability of marital and cohabiting unions following the birth of a child. *Demography, 52*(5), 1463–1485.

Mutchler, J. E., L. A. Baker, & S. Lee. (2007). Grandparents responsible for grandchildren in Native-American families. *Social Science Quarterly, 88*(4), 990–1009.

Myers, K., & I. Demantas. (2015). Being "the man" without having a job and/or providing care instead of bread. In B. J. Risman & V. E. Rutter (Eds.), *Families as they really are* (2nd ed., pp. 632–647). New York, NY: W.W. Norton.

National Center for Education Statistics. (2014a). *Table 326.10.*

Graduation rate from first institution attended for first-time, full-time bachelor's degreeseeking students at 4-year postsecondary institutions, by race/ethnicity, time to completion, sex, control of institution, and acceptance rate: Selected cohort entry years, 1996 through 2007. Retrieved August 9, 2015, from http://nces.ed.gov/programs/digest/d14/tables/dt14_326.10.asp

National Center for Education Statistics. (2014b). *Table 501.20. Labor force participation, employment, and unemployment of persons 16 to 24 years old who are not enrolled in school, by age group, sex, race/ethnicity, and educational attainment: 2011, 2012, and 2013*. Retrieved August 9, 2015, from http://nces.ed.gov/programs/digest/d14/tables/dt14_501.20.asp

National Center for Education Statistics. (2015). *Table 104.20. Percentage of persons 25 to 29 years old with selected levels of educational attainment, by race/ethnicity and sex: Selected years, 1920 through 2014*. Retrieved August 9, 2015, from https://nces.ed.gov/programs/digest/d14/tables/dt14_104.20.asp

National Center for Health Statistics. (1973). *100 years of marriage and divorce statistics: United States, 1867-1967*. Vital and Health Statistics Series 21, No. 24. Retrieved March 21, 2016, from http://www.cdc.gov/nchs/data/series/sr_21/sr21_024.pdf

Nesteruk, O., & A. Gramescu. (2012). Dating and mate selection among young adults from immigrant families. *Marriage and Family Review, 48*(1), 40–58.

Newman, K. S. (2012). *The accordion family: Boomerang kids, anxious parents, and the private toll of global competition*. Boston, MA: Beacon Press.

Nock, S. L., L. A. Sanchez, & J. D. Wright. (2008). *Covenant marriage: The movement to reclaim tradition in America*. New Brunswick, NJ: Rutgers University Press.

O'Brien Hallstein, D. L. (2006). Conceiving intensive mothering. *Journal of the Association for Research on Mothering, 8*(1,2), 96–108.

Obergefell v. Hodges, 576 U.S. (2015).

Ochocka, J., & R. Janzen. (2008). Immigrant parenting: A new framework of understanding. *Journal of Immigrant and Refugee Studies, 6*(1), 85–111.

Oliver, M. L., & T. M. Shapiro. (2006). *Black wealth / white wealth: A new perspective on racial inequality*. New York, NY: Routledge.

Ortman, J. M., V. A. Velkoff, & H. Hogan. (2014). *An aging nation: The older population in the United States* (Current Population Reports, P25-1140). Washington, DC: U.S. Census Bureau.

Osborne, C., & S. McLanahan. (2007). Partnership instability and child well-being. *Journal of Marriage and Family, 69*(4), 1065–1083.

Owen, J. J., G. K. Rhoades, S. M. Stanley, & F. D. Fincham. (2010). "Hooking up" among college students: Demographic and psychosocial correlates. *Archives of Sexual Behavior, 39*(3), 653–663.

Pager, D., & H. Shepard. (2008). The sociology of discrimination: Racial discrimination in employment, housing, credit, and consumer markets. *Annual Review of Sociology, 34*, 181–209.

Palley, E., & C. S. Shdaimah. (2014). *In our hands: The struggle for U.S. child care policy*. New York, NY: New York University Press.

Parsons, T., & R. F. Bales. (1955). *Family, socialization, and the interaction process*. Glencoe, IL: Free Press.

Payne, K. K. (2013). *Children's family structure, 2013* (FP-13–19). Bowling Green, OH: National Center for Family & Marriage Research. Retrieved January 11, 2015, from https://www.bgsu.edu/content/dam/BGSU/college-of-arts-and-sciences/NCFMR/documents/FP/FP-13-19.pdf

Payne, K. K., W. D. Manning, & S. L. Brown. (2012). *Unmarried births to cohabiting and single mothers, 2005 – 2010* (FP-12–06). Bowling Green, OH: National Center for Family & Marriage Research. Retrieved

January 11, 2015, from https:// www.bgsu.edu/content/dam/ BGSU/college-of-arts-and-sciences/NCFMR/documents/ FP/FP-12-06.pdf

Pedulla, D. S., & S. Thébaud. (2015). Can we finish the revolution? Gender, work-family ideals, and institutional constraint. *American Sociological Review, 80*(1), 116–139.

Peplau, L. A., & A. W. Fingerhut. (2007). The close relationships of lesbians and gay men. *Annual Review of Psychology, 58*, 405–424.

Perez v. Sharp, 32 Cal.2d 711 (1948).

Personal Responsibility and Work Opportunity Reconciliation Act of 1996, Pub.L. 104-208.

Pettit, B., & J. Hook. (2005). The structure of women's employment in comparative perspective. *Social Forces, 84*(2), 779–801.

Pew Research Center. (2009). *Getting old in America: Expectations vs. reality.* Washington, DC: Author. Retrieved November 3, 2015, from http://www. pewsocialtrends.org/ files/2010/10/Getting-Old-in-America.pdf

Pew Research Center. (2010). *The decline of marriage and rise of new families.* Washington, DC: Author. Retrieved January 11, 2015, from

http://www.pewsocial trends.org/files/2010/11/ pew-social-trends-2010-families.pdf

Pew Research Center. (2011). *A portrait of stepfamilies.* Washington, DC: Author. Retrieved January 7, 2015, from http://www. pewsocialtrends.org/2011/01/13/ a-portrait-of-stepfamilies/

Pew Research Center. (2012). *The rise of intermarriage: Races, characteristics vary by race and gender.* Washington, DC: Author. Retrieved January 11, 2015, from http://www .pewsocialtrends.org/ files/2012/02/SDT-Intermarriage-II.pdf

Pew Research Center. (2013a). *The rise of Asian Americans.* Washington, DC: Author. Retrieved January 11, 2015, from http:// www.pewsocialtrends.org/ files/2013/04/Asian-Americans-new-full-report-04–2013.pdf

Pew Research Center. (2013b). *A survey of LGBT Americans: Attitudes, experiences, and values in changing times.* Washington, DC: Author. Retrieved November 12, 2015, from http://www.pewsocial trends.org/files/2013/ 06/SDT_LGBT-Americans_06-2013.pdf

Pew Research Center. (2014, December 12). Wealth inequality has widened along racial, ethnic lines since the end of the Great Recession. *Fact Tank: News*

in the Numbers. Retrieved June 27, 2015, from http:// www.pewresearch.org/fact-tank/2014/12/12/racial-wealth-gaps-great-recession/

Pew Research Center. (2015). *Modern immigration wave brings 59 million to U.S., driving population growth and change through 2065: Views of immigration's impact on U.S. society mixed.* Washington, DC: Author. Retrieved January 3, 2016, from http:// www.pewhispanic.org/ files/2015/09/2015-09-28_ modern-immigration-wave_ REPORT.pdf

Pfeffer, C. A. (2010). "Women's work"? Women partners of transgender men doing housework and emotion work. *Journal of Marriage and Family, 72*(1), 165–183.

Population Reference Bureau. (2013). *Elderly immigrants in the United States. Today's research on aging: Program and policy implications* (Issue 29). Washington, DC: Author.

Potuchek, J. L. (1997). *Who supports the family: Gender and breadwinning in dual-earner marriages.* Stanford, CA: Stanford University Press.

Powell, B., C. Bolzendahl, C. Geist, & L. C. Steelman. (2010). *Counted out: Same-sex relations and Americans' definitions of family.* New York, NY: Russell Sage Foundation.

Powell, B., C. Bolzendahl, C. Geist, & L. C. Steelman.

(2015). Changing counts, counting change: American's movement toward a more inclusive definition of family. In B. J. Risman & V. E. Rutter (Eds.), *Families as they really are* (2nd ed., pp. 84–95). New York, NY: W.W. Norton.

Presser, H. B. (2003). *Working in a 24/7 economy: Challenges for American families.* New York, NY: Russell Sage Foundation.

Pyke, K. D. (2014). Immigrant families and the shifting color line in the United States. In J. Treas, J. Scott, & M. Richards (Eds.), *The Wiley Blackwell companion to the sociology of families* (pp. 194–213). Malden, MA: Wiley.

Qian, Z. (2014). The divergent paths of American families. In J. Logan (Ed.), *Diversity and disparities: America enters a new century* (pp. 237–269). New York, NY: Russell Sage Foundation.

Qian, Z., & D. T. Lichter. (2011). Changing patterns of interracial marriage in a multiracial society. *Journal of Marriage and Family, 73*(5), 1065–1084.

Raley, R. K., M. M. Sweeney, & D. Wondra. (2015). The growing racial and ethnic divide in U.S. marriage patterns. *Future of Children, 25*(2), 89–109.

Raley, S., & S. Bianchi. (2006). Sons, daughters, and family processes: Does gender of

children matter? *Annual Review of Sociology, 32*, 401–421.

Raley, S., S. M. Bianchi, & W. Wang. (2012). When do fathers care? Mothers' economic contribution and fathers' involvement in child care. *American Journal of Sociology, 117*(5), 1422–1459.

Rands, M. (1988). Changes in social networks following marital separation and divorce. In R. M. Milardo (Ed.), *Families and social networks: New perspectives on family* (pp. 127–146). Newbury Park, CA: Sage.

Rapp, R. (1992). Family and class in contemporary America: Notes toward an understanding of ideology. In B. Thorne & M. Yalom (Eds.), *Rethinking the family: Some feminist questions* (revised ed., pp. 49–70). Boston, MA: Northeastern University Press.

Rapsey, C., & T. Murachver. (2006). Adolescent sexuality. In R. D. McAnulty & M. M. Burnette (Eds.), *Sex and sexuality. Volume 1. Sexuality today: Trends and controversies* (pp. 61–101). Westport, CT: Praeger.

Rawlings, S. W., K. J. Campbell, M. J. Davies, R. O. Grymes, G. K. Mudd, & A. F. Saluter. (1979). *Household and family characteristics: March 1978* (Current Population Reports, P20-340). Washington, DC: U.S. Census Bureau. Retrieved January 18, 2015, from https://www

.census.gov/hhes/families/files/ scanned/P20-340.pdf

Reed, J. (2007). Anatomy of the breakup: How and why do unmarried couples with children break up? In P. England & K. Edin (Eds.), *Unmarried couples with children: The unfolding lives of new unmarried urban parents* (pp. 133–156). New York, NY: Russell Sage Foundation.

Rehel, E. M. (2014). When dad stays home too: Paternity leave, gender, and parenting. *Gender & Society, 28*(1), 110–132.

Risman, B. J. (1999). *Gender vertigo: American families in transition.* New Haven, CT: Yale University Press.

Rochlen, A. B., R. A. McKelley, & T. A. Whittaker. (2010). Stay-at-home fathers' reasons for entering the role and stigma experiences: A preliminary report. *Psychology of Men and Masculinity, 11*(4), 167–175.

Roe v. Wade, 410 U.S. 113 (1973).

Rose-Greenland, F., & P. J. Smock. (2013). Living together unmarried: What do we know about cohabiting families? In G. W. Peterson & K. R. Bush (Eds.), *Handbook of marriage and the family* (3rd ed., pp. 255–273). New York, NY: Springer.

Rosenfeld, M. J. (2007). *The age of independence: Interracial unions, same-sex unions, and the changing American family.*

Cambridge, MA: Harvard University Press.

Rosenfeld, M. J., & R. J. Thomas. (2012). Search for a mate: The rise of the Internet as a social intermediary. *American Sociological Review, 77*(4), 523–547.

Rubin, L. B. (1994). *Families on the fault line: America's working class speaks about the family, the economy, race, and ethnicity.* New York, NY: HarperCollins.

Rutherford, M. B. (2011). *Adult supervision required: Private freedom and public constraints for parents and children.* New Brunswick, NJ: Rutgers University Press.

Saad, L. (2013). Americans divided on outlook for next generation. *USA Today*/Gallup. Retrieved August 9, 2015, from http://www.gallup.com/poll/159737/americans-divided-outlook-next-generation.aspx

Sabatelli, R. M., & C. L. Shehan. (1993). Exchange and resource theories. In P. G. Boss, W. J. Doherty, R. LaRossa, W. R. Schumm, & S. K. Steinmetz (Eds.), *Sourcebook of family theories and methods: A contextual approach* (pp. 385–411). New York, NY: Plenum Press.

Sallie Mae. (2015). *How America pays for college 2015: Sallie Mae's National Study of College Students and Parents.* Retrieved August 8, 2015, from http://news.salliemae.com/files/doc_library/file/HowAmericaPaysforCollege2015FNL.pdf

Sarkisian, N., M. Gerena, & N. Gerstel. (2007). Extended family integration among Euro and Mexican Americans: Ethnicity, gender, and class. *Journal of Marriage and Family, 69*(1), 40–54.

Sarkisian, N., & N. Gerstel. (2004). Kin support among Blacks and Whites: Race and family organization. *American Sociological Review, 69*(6), 812–837.

Sarkisian, N., & N. Gerstel. (2012). *Nuclear family values, extended family lives: The power of race, class, and gender.* New York, NY: Routledge.

Savin-Williams, R. C., & L. M. Diamond. (2000). Sexual identity trajectories among sexual-minority youths: Gender comparisons. *Archives of Sexual Behavior, 29*(6), 607–627.

Sayer, L. C. (2006). Economic aspects of divorce and relationship dissolution. In M. A. Fine & J. H. Harvey (Eds.), *Handbook of divorce and relationship dissolution* (pp. 385–406). Mahwah, NJ: Lawrence Erlbaum.

Scheiber, N. (2015, September 16). Attitudes shift on paid leave: Dads sue, too. *The New York Times.* Retrieved January 15, 2016, from http://nyti.ms/1ifM6Ha

Schoeni, R. F., & K. E. Ross. (2005). Material assistance form families during the transition to adulthood. In R. A. Settersten, Jr., F. F. Furstenberg, Jr., & R. G. Rumbaut (Eds.), *On the frontier of adulthood: Theory, research, and public policy* (pp. 396–416). Chicago, IL: University of Chicago Press.

Schwartz, C. R., & R. D. Mare. (2005). Trends in educational assortative marriage from 1940 to 2003. *Demography, 42*(4), 621–646.

Seltzer, J. A., & S. M. Bianchi. (2013). Demographic change and parent-child relationships in adulthood. *Annual Review of Sociology, 39*, 275–290.

Settersten, R. A., Jr. (2011). Becoming adult: Meanings and markers for young Americans. In M. C. Waters, P. J. Carr, M. J. Kefalas, & J. Holdaway (Eds.), *Coming of age in America: The transition to adulthood in the twenty-first century* (pp. 169–190). Berkeley: University of California Press.

Settersten, R. A., Jr. (2012). The contemporary context of young adulthood in the USA: From demography to development, from private troubles to public issues. In A. Booth, S. L. Brown, N. S. Landale, W. D. Manning, & S. M. McHale (Eds.), *Early adulthood in family context* (pp. 3–26). New York, NY: Springer.

Shapiro, T. M. (2004). *The hidden cost of being African American: How wealth perpetuates inequality*. New York, NY: Oxford University Press.

Shattuck, R. M., & R. M. Kreider. (2013). *Social and economic characteristics of currently unmarried women with a recent birth: 2011* (American Community Survey Reports ACS-21). Washington, DC: U.S. Census Bureau.

Shehan, C. L., F. M. Berardo, E. Owens, & D. H. Berardo. (2002). Alimony: An anomaly in family social science. *Family Relations, 51*(4), 308–316.

Silverstein, M., & V. L. Bengston. (1997). Intergenerational solidarity and the structure of adult child-parent relationships in American families. *American Journal of Sociology, 103*(2), 429–460.

Silverstein, M., & R. Giarrusso. (2010). Aging and family life: A decade review. *Journal of Marriage and Family, 72*(5), 1039–1058.

Silverstein, M., & A. Marenco. (2001). How Americans enact the grandparent role across the family life course. *Journal of Marriage and Family, 22*(4), 493–522.

Singer, A. (2013). Contemporary immigrant gateways in historical perspective. *Dædalus, The Journal of the American Academy of Arts & Sciences, 142*(3), 76–91.

Smith, D. E. (1993). The Standard North American Family: SNAF as an ideological code. *Journal of Family Issues, 14*(1), 50–65.

Smith, S. R., R. R. Hamon, B. B. Ingoldsby, & J. E. Miller. (2009). *Exploring family theories*. New York, NY: Oxford University Press.

Smith, T. W. (1999). *The emerging 21st century American family* (GSS Social Change Report No. 42). Chicago, IL: National Opinion Research Center.

Smith, T. W. (2004). Coming of age in twenty-first century America: Public attitudes towards the importance and timing of transitions to adulthood. *Ageing International, 29*(2), 136–148.

Smith, T. W., P. V. Marsden, & M. Hout. (2015). *General Social Surveys, 1972–2014*. Chicago, IL: National Opinion Research Center.

Smock, P. J. (2000). Cohabitation in the United States: An appraisal of research themes, findings, and implications. *Annual Review of Sociology, 26*, 1–20.

Smock, P. J., W. D. Manning, & M. Porter. (2005). "Everything's there except money": How money shapes decisions to marry among cohabitors. *Journal of Marriage and Family, 67*(3), 680–696.

Snyder, T. D. (1993). *120 years of American education: A statistical portrait*. Washington, DC: National Center for Education Statistics, U.S. Department of Education.

Social Security Act of 1935, Pub.L. 74-271 (49 Stat. 620).

Stack, C. B. (1974). *All our kin: Strategies for survival in a Black community*. New York, NY: Basic Books.

Stepler, R. (2015). *5 facts about family caregivers*. Pew Research Center Fact Tank. Retrieved December 29, 2015, from http://www.pewresearch.org/fact-tank/2015/11/18/5-facts-about-family-caregivers/

Stone, P. (2008). *Opting out: Why women really quit careers and head home*. Berkeley: University of California Press.

Strohschein, L. (2005). Parental divorce and child mental health trajectories. *Journal of Marriage and Family, 67*(5), 1286–1300.

Suitor, J. J., J. Sechrist, M. Gilligan, & K. Pillemer. (2011). Intergenerational relations in later-life families. In R. A. Settersten, Jr. & J. L. Angel (Eds.), *Handbook of the sociology of aging* (pp. 161–178). New York, NY: Springer.

Sullivan, O. (2015). Men's changing contribution to family work. In B. J. Risman & V. E. Rutter (Eds.), *Families as they really are* (2nd ed., pp. 617–628). New York, NY: W.W. Norton.

Swartz, T. T. (2009). Intergenerational family relations in adulthood: Patterns, variations, and implications in the contemporary United States. *Annual Review of Sociology, 35*, 191–212.

Swartz, T. T., D. Hartmann, & J. R. Mortimer. (2011). Transitions to adulthood in the land of Lake Wobegon. In M. C. Waters, P. J. Carr, M. J. Kefalas, & J. Holdaway (Eds.), *Coming of age in America: The transition to adulthood in the twenty-first century* (pp. 59–105). Berkeley: University of California Press.

Sweeney, M. M. (2010). Remarriage and stepfamilies: Strategic sites for family scholarship in the 21st century. *Journal of Marriage and Family,* 72(3), 667–684.

Swift, A. (2014). *Most Americans say same-sex couples entitled to adopt.* Gallup. Retrieved January 29, 2015, from http://www.gallup.com/poll/170801/americans-say-sex-couples-entitled-adopt.aspx

Tach, L. M., & A. Eads. (2015). Trends in the economic consequences of marital and cohabitation dissolution in the United States. *Demography,* 52(2), 401–432.

Tattersall, I., & R. DeSalle. (2011). *Race? Debunking*

a scientific myth. College Station: Texas A&M University Press.

Teachman, J. (2003). Premarital sex, premarital cohabitation, and the risk of subsequent marital dissolution among women. *Journal of Marriage and Family, 65*(2), 444–455.

Teachman, J. (2008). Complex life patterns and the risk of divorce in second marriages. *Journal of Marriage and Family, 70*(2), 294–305.

The National Marriage Project. (2010). *The state of our unions: Marriage in America 2010: When marriage disappears: The new middle America.* Retrieved January 11, 2015, from http://stateofourunions.org/2010/SOOU2010.pdf

The World Bank. (2015). *Fertility rate, total (births per woman).* Retrieved March 21, 2016, from http://data.worldbank.org/indicator/SP.DYN.TFRT.IN/countries?order=wbapi_data_value_2013+wbapi_data_value+wbapi_data_value-last&sort=asc

Thorne, B. (2004). The crisis of care. In A. C. Crouter & A. Booth (Eds.), *Work-family challenges for low-income parents and their children* (pp. 165–178). Mahwah, NJ: Lawrence Erlbaum.

Thornton, A. (1989). Changing attitudes toward family issues in the United States. *Journal of Marriage and Family, 51*(4), 873–893.

Tong, Y. (2013). Acculturation, gender disparity, and the sexual behavior of Asian American youth. *Journal of Sex Research, 50*(6), 560–573.

Townsend, N. W. (2002). *The package deal: Marriage, work, and fatherhood in men's lives.* Philadelphia, PA: Temple University Press.

Tuan, M. (1998). *Forever foreigners or honorary whites? The Asian ethnic experience today.* New Brunswick, NJ: Rutgers University Press.

Tuominen, M. C. (2003). *We are not babysitters: Family child care providers redefine work and care.* New Brunswick, NJ: Rutgers University Press.

Uhlenberg, P. (1996). Mortality decline in the twentieth century and supply of kin over the life course. *The Gerontologist, 36*(5), 681–685.

U.S. Census Bureau. (1909). *Marriage and divorce 1867–1906.* Washington, DC: U.S. Government Printing Office.

U.S. Census Bureau. (1975). *Historical statistics of the United States, colonial times to 1970, bicentennial edition.* Washington, DC: U.S. Government Printing Office.

U.S. Census Bureau. (2003a). *No. HS-30 marital status of women in the civilian labor force: 1900 to 2002.* Retrieved January 7, 2015, from http://www2.census.gov/library/

publications/2004/compendia/ statab/123ed/hist/hs-30.pdf

U.S. Census Bureau. (2003b). *Statistical abstract of the United States*. Washington, DC: U.S. Government Printing Office.

U.S. Census Bureau. (2004). *Resident population—Estimates by age, sex, and race: July 1, 1900*. Retrieved January 7, 2015, from https://www.census.gov/popest/ data/national/asrh/pre-1980/ tables/PE-11-1900.pdf

U.S. Census Bureau. (2010). *Statistical abstract of the United States*. Washington, DC: U.S. Government Printing Office.

U.S. Census Bureau. (2011a). *Age and sex composition: 2010*. Retrieved January 7, 2015, from http://www.census .gov/prod/cen2010/briefs/ c2010br-03.pdf

U.S. Census Bureau. (2011b). *Statistical abstract of the United States*. Washington, DC: U.S. Government Printing Office.

U.S. Census Bureau. (2012). *Statistical abstract of the United States*. Washington, DC: U.S. Government Printing Office.

U.S. Census Bureau. (2013a). *Table 1: Household characteristics of opposite-sex and same-sex couple households: ACS 2013*. Retrieved January 8, 2015, from http://www.census .gov/hhes/samesex/files/ssex-tables-2013.xlsx

U.S. Census Bureau. (2013b). *Table UC3. Opposite sex unmarried couples by presences*

of biological children under 18, and age, earnings, education, and race and Hispanic origin of both partners. Retrieved August 11, 2015, from http://www .census.gov/hhes/families/data/ cps2013UC.html

U.S. Census Bureau. (2014a). *Historical Table 1. Percent childless and births per 1,000 women in the last 12 months: CPS, selected years, 1976–2012*. Retrieved January 9, 2015, from https://www.census .gov/hhes/fertility/files/cps/ historical/H1.xlsx

U.S. Census Bureau. (2014b). *National characteristics: Vintage 2014*. Retrieved January 7, 2015, from http://www.census .gov/popest/data/national/ asrh/2014/index.html

U.S. Census Bureau. (2014c). *Table A1. Marital status of people 15 years and over, by age, sex, personal earnings, race, and Hispanic origin: 2014*. Retrieved August 9, 2015, from https:// www.census.gov/hhes/families/ data/cps2014A.html

U.S. Census Bureau. (2014d). *Table H-2. Share of aggregate income received by each fifth and top 5 percent of households, all races: 1967 to 2013* (Current Population Survey, Annual Social and Economic Supplements). Retrieved January 7, 2015, from https:// www.census.gov/hhes/www/ income/data/historical/ household/index.html

U.S. Census Bureau. (2014e). *Table H-4. Gini ratios for households, by race and Hispanic*

origin of householder: 1967 to 2013 (Current Population Survey, Annual Social and Economic Supplements). Retrieved January 7, 2015, from https://www.census .gov/hhes/www/income/data/ historical/household/index .html

U.S. Census Bureau. (2014f). *Table 3: Poverty status, by age, race, and Hispanic origin: 1959 to 2013*. Retrieved January 7, 2015, from http://www.census .gov/hhes/www/poverty/data/ historical/people.html

U.S. Census Bureau. (2015a). *Living arrangements of children*. Retrieved January 7, 2015, from https://www.census.gov/ hhes/families/data/children .html

U.S. Census Bureau. (2015b). *Table H1. Households by type and tenure of householder for selected characteristics: 2014*. Retrieved January 7, 2015, from https://www.census.gov/ hhes/families/files/cps2014/ tabH1-all.xls

U.S. House of Representatives, Committee on Ways and Means. (2012). *Background material and data on the programs within the jurisdiction of the Committee on Ways and Means (2012 Green Book)*. Washington, DC: U.S. Government Printing Office. Retrieved January 13, 2015, from http://greenbook .waysandmeans.house .gov/2012-green-book

Vaughan, D. (1986). *Uncoupling: Turning points in*

intimate relationships. New York, NY: Oxford University Press.

Vespa, J., J. M. Lewis, & R. M. Kreider. (2013). *America's families and living arrangements: 2012* (Current Population Reports, P20-570). Washington, DC: U.S. Census Bureau. Retrieved January 18, 2015, from http://www.census.gov/prod/2013pubs/p20–570.pdf

Wallace, W. (1971). *The logic of science in sociology*. Chicago, IL: Aldine Atherton.

Waller, W. (1937). The rating and dating complex. *American Sociological Review, 2*(5), 727–734.

Walsh, L. S. (1979). "Till death us do part": Marriage and family in seventeenth-century Maryland. In T. W. Tate & D. Ammerman (Eds.), *The Chesapeake in the seventeenth century: Essays on Anglo-American society* (pp. 126–153). New York, NY: W.W. Norton.

Walzer, S. (1998). *Thinking about the baby: Gender and transitions into parenthood*. Philadelphia, PA: Temple University Press.

Wang, H., & P. R. Amato. (2000). Predictors of divorce adjustment: Stressors, resources, and definitions. *Journal of Marriage and Family, 6*(3), 655–668.

Wang, W. (2015). Interracial marriage: Who is "marrying out"? *Fact Tank: News in the Numbers*. Washington, DC: Pew Research Center. Retrieved January 20, 2016, from http://www.pewresearch.org/fact-tank/2015/06/12/interracial-marriage-who-is-marrying-out/

Waters, M. C., P. J. Carr, & M. J. Kefalas. (2011). Introduction. In M. C. Waters, P. J. Carr, M. J. Kefalas, & J. Holdaway (Eds.), *Coming of age in America: The transition to adulthood in the twenty-first century* (pp. 1–27). Berkeley: University of California Press.

Weibel-Orlando, J. (2009). Grandparenting styles among American Indians. In J. Sokolovsky (Ed.), *The cultural context of aging* (Web book edition). Westport, CT: Praeger.

Weigel, D. J. (2008). The concept of family: An analysis of laypeople's views of family. *Journal of Family Issues, 29*(11), 1426–1447.

Welter, B. (1966). The cult of true womanhood: 1820-1860. *American Quarterly, 18*(2), 151-174.

West, C., & D. H. Zimmerman. (1987). Doing gender. *Gender & Society, 1*(2), 125–151.

Weston, K. (1991). *Families we choose: Lesbians, gays, kinship*.

New York, NY: Columbia University Press.

Wexler, S., & R. J. Engel. (1999). Historical trends in state-level ADC/AFDC benefits: Living on less and less. *Journal of Sociology and Social Welfare, 26*(2), 37–61.

Williams, S. A. (2014). *Family structure and children's economic well-being: Single-parent families in lone parent households and multigenerational households*. Paper presented at the annual meeting of the Population Association of America, Boston, MA. Retrieved January 5, 2016, from http://paa2014.princeton.edu/abstracts/141343

Wilson, W. (1987). *The truly disadvantaged*. Chicago, IL: University of Chicago Press.

World Bank Group. (2015). *Women, business, and the law 2016: Getting to equal*. Washington, DC: Author.

Wu, L. L., & J.-C. A. Li. (2005). Historical roots of family diversity: Marital and childbearing trajectories of American women. In R. A. Settersten, Jr., F. F. Furstenberg, Jr., & R. G. Rumbaut (Eds.), *On the frontier of adulthood: Theory, research, and public policy* (pp. 110–149). Chicago, IL: University of Chicago Press.

Zelizer, V. A. (1985). *Pricing the priceless child: The changing social value of children*. New York, NY: Basic Books.

INDEX

Sexual revolution, 69
Shapiro, Thomas, 47, 199, 210
Shdaimah, Corey, 208
Silverstein, Merril, 194
Skipped generation
    households, 192
Smith, Suzanne, 46
Smock, Pamela, 87, 90
SNAF (Standard North
    American Family), 7
SNAP (Supplemental Nutrition
    Assistance Program), 215
Sociable relations, 194–195
Social class, 3
    extended families and, 33
    parenting ideologies and,
        145–147
Social divorce, 117–119
Social exchange theory, in the
    study of families, 50–52
Social institution, 5
Social locations, 4
Social patterns, 6
Social policy, and the future of
    families, 203–223
    American families, 216–222
    defining family, 203–205
    family change, 205–206
    family continuity, 206–208
    family diversity and
        inequality, 208–216
    work-family conflict,
        173–177
    See also Family/families
Social Security Act, 213
Sociological imagination, 6
Sociological methods and
    theories, in the study of
    families, 37–54
    change, continuity, and
        diversity in, 54
    micro and macro
        approaches, 40
    research methods, 40–43
    scientific method, 37–39

theoretical frameworks,
    43–53
    See also Family/families
Sociological perspective, 5–11.
    See also Family/families
Sociology, 5
Soul mate, 84
Standard North American
    Family (SNAF), 7–11
Stanley, Scott, 74
State welfare policy, and family
    inequality, 212–216
Stepfamilies, 7
Stone, Pamela, 177
Structural, 22
Structural definitions,
    of family, 27
Structural-functionalism, in the
    study of families, 44–45
Structure, family as, 22–23
Sullivan, Oriel, 222
Supplemental Nutrition
    Assistance Program
    (SNAP), 215
Swartz, Teresa, 199
Symbolic interactionism, in the
    study of families, 48–49,
    118–119

TANF (Temporary Assistance
    to Needy Families), 215
Tender years doctrine, 115
Thébaud, Sarah, 177
Theory, 37–38
Tight-knit relations, 194
Tong, Yuying, 72
Townsend, Nicholas, 144
Transfamilies, 221
Transition. See Adulthood,
    transition to
Transitions, and relationship
    dissolution, 127
Transnational families, 24–25
Transnational parenting,
    147–150

Uncoupling, 104, 111–119
    emotional and social
        divorce, 117–119
    financial divorce, 116–117
    legal divorce, 112–114
    parental divorce, 114–116
Uncoupling (Vaughn), 117–118
Undocumented families,
    147–150
Unfinished Revolution,
    The (Gerson), 157
Unmarried parents,
    relationship dissolution
    among, 122–123
U.S. population, demographic
    snapshot of, 13–18

Vaughn, Diane, 103, 111, 117
Voluntary kin, 31

Wallace, Walter, 38
Waller, Willard, 70
Warner, Cody, 51
Weber, Max, 80
Welfare policy (state), and
    family inequality,
    212–216
Welfare state, 212
Welter, Barbara, 136
Wenger, Marin, 51
West, Candace, 167
Wexler, Sandra, 214
Wilde, Oscar, 127
Women, and employmen,
    161–165. See also
    Family work
Work-family conflict, and
    social policy, 173–177
Wright, James, 113

Young adults. See Adulthood,
    transition to

Zimmerman, Don, 167
Zuckerberg, Mark, 222